Accessible Citizenships

ACCESSIBLE CITIZENSHIPS

Disability, Nation, and the Cultural Politics
of Greater Mexico

JULIE AVRIL MINICH

 Temple University Press
PHILADELPHIA

Temple University Press
Philadelphia, Pennsylvania 19122
www.temple.edu/tempress

Published 2014

LIBRARY OF CONGRESS CATALOGING-IN-PUBLICATION DATA

Minich, Julie Avril, 1977–
  Accessible citizenships : disability, nation, and the cultural politics of greater
Mexico / Julie Avril Minich.
    pages cm
  Includes bibliographical references and index.
  ISBN 978-1-4399-1069-6 (cloth : alk. paper)
  ISBN 978-1-4399-1070-2 (pbk. : alk. paper)
  ISBN 978-1-4399-1071-9 (e-book)
  1. American literature—Mexican American authors—History and criticism.
2. People with disabilities in literature. 3. People with disabilities in motion
pictures. 4. Nationalism and literature—United States. 5. Nationalism and
literature—Mexico. 6. Sociology of disability. I. Title.
PS153.M4M56 2014
810.9'86872—dc23

                                                                    2013016597

  ♾ The paper used in this publication meets the requirements of the
American National Standard for Information Sciences—Permanence
of Paper for Printed Library Materials, ANSI Z39.48-1992

Printed in the United States of America

2 4 6 8 9 7 5 3 1

THE
AMERICAN
LITERATURES
INITIATIVE
A book in the American Literatures Initiative (ALI), a
collaborative publishing project of NYU Press, Fordham
University Press, Rutgers University Press, Temple University
Press, and the University of Virginia Press. The Initiative is
supported by The Andrew W. Mellon Foundation. For more
information, please visit www.americanliteratures.org.

For Jaimie Leanne Minich
and Jonah Minich Davis

Contents

PART THREE   Beyond Citizenship

ACKNOWLEDGMENTS

No scholarship is the work of one person alone. I owe intellectual debts to many more people than I can possibly name in these pages, but I am going to attempt to mention as many as I can of the people who nourished and guided this project, and me, along the way.

As with many first scholarly books, this one began with my dissertation research at Stanford University, and I gratefully acknowledge my dissertation committee: Yvonne Yarbro-Bejarano, my chair, and my primary readers Paula M.L. Moya and Paul Julian Smith. All of them went far above and beyond what should ever be asked of one's graduate mentors. Paul agreed to work with me long-distance from the University of Cambridge. Yvonne and Paula have continued their investment in me long after my graduation, providing invaluable support and guidance as I navigate life on the tenure track. They are amazing, and I am truly honored to call them friends. (Paula also clipped the cover photograph from the *San Jose Mercury News* during the 2006 immigration protests, and brought it to give to me at the defense of my dissertation prospectus.) I also wish to acknowledge the following individuals from my time at Stanford who have been crucial to the early formation of this project, and in many cases, to its ongoing development: Ulka Anjaria, Gordon Brotherston, Guadalupe Carrillo, Micaela Díaz-Sánchez, Vida Mia García, Lauren Hall-Lew, Jennifer Harford Vargas, Texcallini Doris Madrigal, Elda María Román, Lúcia Sá, Ramón Saldívar, Carmen Sanjuán-Pastor, and Stephanie Schmidt. Dearest Uncle Leland, thank you for this lasting intellectual community.

I am reminded every day of my good fortune to leave graduate school for a supportive and intellectually exciting tenure-track job. Miami University was a fantastic place to start my career. I am particularly grateful to the following colleagues, dear friends, and interlocutors: Elena Jackson Albarrán, Juan Carlos Leblanc Albarrán, José Amador, Yu-Fang Cho, Mary Jean Corbett, Sheila Croucher, Madelyn Detloff, Stefanie Dunning, Erin Edwards, Carolyn Haynes, Andrew Hebard, Nalin Jayasena, Katie Johnson, Theresa Kulbaga, Cynthia Lewiecki-Wilson, Anita Mannur, LuMing Mao, Mary McDonald, Patrick Murphy, Rebecca Oliver, Roxanne Ornelas, Jason Palmeri, Tory Pearman, Susan Pelle, Gaile Pohlhaus Jr., Martha Schoolman, Damon Scott, Tatiana Seijas, Lisa Weems, Valerie Michelle Wilhite, and Whitney Womack-Smith. In addition, my students have enriched my intellectual life in crucial ways. In particular, I wish to acknowledge the undergraduate students who took the Latina/o literature survey, the Latino Masculinities capstone, and the Queer Theory seminar with me, as well as the following graduate students: Kasey Butcher, Nicole Cannon, Shanti Chu, José de la Garza-Valenzuela, Lynn Hall, Dinidu Karunanayake, Nona Landis, Tory Lowe, Rachel Oriol, Natasha Sharma, and Christine Wieseler.

I complete this book just as I begin a new position at the University of Texas at Austin, and I also wish to thank the following colleagues at that institution, with the awareness that I will soon realize that there are many more names to be added to this list: Samuel Baker, Mia Carter, Evan Carton, Juan José Colomina, James Cox, Liz Cullingford, Alan Friedman, John Morán González, Nicole Guidotti-Hernández, Laura Gutiérrez,

Neville Hoad, Heather Houser, Coleman Hutchison, Martin Kevorkian, Allen MacDuffie, Deborah Paredez, Domino Pérez, Snehal Shingavi, Frank Whigham, and Michael Winship. Their feedback on Chapter Two is particularly appreciated.

Beyond the institutions where I have worked and studied, I am lucky to have the intellectual companionship of outstanding colleagues and friends—in and out of academia—whose insight has influenced this project in various ways. Among these I include Linda Martín Alcoff, Frederick Aldama, Christie Ayotte, Kyle Behen, Deva Devika Bronson, Claire Decoteau, Alex Espinoza, Kelly Gaines, Armando García, Michael Hames-García, Emily Holmes, Brooke Lerner, Sarah Lonberg-Lew, Amanda Lucas, Michal Lumsden, Ernesto Martínez, Liza Mattison, Sophia McClennen, Jeff Middents, Dayo Nicole Mitchell, Kaidra L. Mitchell, Carol Moeller, Denise Nepveux, Tamiko Nimura, Jesse Lumsden Piscitello, Diane Reiten, John "Rio" Riofrio, Richard T. Rodríguez, José David Saldívar, Tobin Siebers, Brittain Skinner, Melissa Spencer, John Su, Lydia Ruth Tietjen, Margarita Urueña, Chris Volk, Caitlin Wood, Cynthia Wu, and Karla Zepeda. Zachary T. Sugawara came into my life during the final stages of this project, bringing love, joy, and nerdy board games (like a Druid's Deliverance, he prevented much combat damage in the final turn).

The following scholarly organizations provided space for me to present my work and the generous feedback of rigorous interlocutors: El Centro Chicano (Stanford University); the Center for Comparative Studies in Race and Ethnicity (Stanford University); the How Do Identities Matter? and Trans-American Working Groups (Stanford University); at least four different incarnations of Yvonne Yarbro-Bejarano's graduate seminar on Race and Sex in Cultural Representations/Queer of Color Critique (Stanford University); the Miami University English Department; the Miami University Latin American, Latina/o and Caribbean Studies Program; the Miami University Women's, Gender and Sexuality Studies Program; the Miami University Asian and Asian American Studies Program; the UT Austin

English Department; the UT Austin Center for Mexican American Studies; the American Cultures Seminar (Miami University); the Possible Futures Working Group (Miami University); the Roundtable on Latina Feminisms (John Carroll University); the Tepoztlán Institute for Transnational History of the Americas; the Latino Space for Enrichment and Research (The Ohio State University); the Society for Disability Studies; and the Future of Minority Studies Research Project. An earlier version of Chapter One originally appeared in the journal *Modern Fiction Studies*; I am also grateful to the anonymous readers at that journal for their feedback.

Janet Francendese was exactly the editor that this book needed. I am grateful to her for believing in this project and for telling me when to let the book go. I am also grateful to Tim Roberts, to the American Literatures Initiative, to Gary Kramer, to the editorial team at Temple University Press, to Gary Von Euer, and to the anonymous readers at the press whose suggestions for revision made this book a better one.

Two early mentors deserve recognition: Nancy Saporta Sternbach, my honors thesis advisor at Smith College, and Barbara Goodman, my high school AP English teacher, who gave so much of her life to the Georgia public education system. Without these incredible women, I never would have started on the path I am on today. As a proud student of public K–12 schools in the states of Georgia, Ohio, and Michigan, I also wish to thank the many unrecognized people who labor so tirelessly and thanklessly to ensure that children may continue to exercise their right to a free and accessible public education. You are my heroes.

Finally, it is often said (tritely) that we don't choose our family, and I am truly lucky that we don't, because if left to my own devices I never would have been capable of finding (let alone convincing them to choose me!) any collection of people as amazing, hilarious, insightful, brilliant, and beautiful (in every sense of the word) as the Minichs of Americus, Georgia. You have all been there for me in so many countless (and undeserved) ways, and to express my deepest appreciation, I just want to say with the finality of the printed word that I love you *MORE:* Donna Minich, David Minich, Jaimie Leanne Minich, Joseph Davis, Jonathan Minich, Joshua Minich, Katie Hall Minich, Justin Minich, Jonah Minich Davis, and Conrad Hall Minich. Aslan and Dark-and-Stormy really ought to receive many more treats and tuna snacks than I give them. This book is dedicated to my "best good friend," my sister Jaimie, and to my godson Jonah. Jaimie and Jonah teach me every day what a marvelous thing it is to live in a world with so much human variation and so many different kinds of bodies. There is no way to repay them for all of the ways in which they have supported and loved me, but offering them the book is a small start.

Accessibility and Nationalism:
An Introduction

In 1984, as the city of Los Angeles prepared to host the Olympic Games, ten local artists were commissioned to paint murals along the city's freeways, among them Judith Francisca Baca. Baca's contribution, titled *Hitting the Wall: Women in the Marathon* and located on the Harbor Freeway (Interstate 110), honors women athletes of color. At its center is a racially ambiguous runner with strong, sinewy muscles, light hair and dark skin, crossing a finish line with arms outstretched. Behind her are two groups of women runners, one led by a woman in a wheelchair. By featuring women of different races and abilities, the mural invites viewers to imagine Los Angeles as a city of racial, gender, and corporeal equality. *Hitting the Wall* is not merely a celebration, however, for it also prompts critical scrutiny of the Los Angeles urban landscape in two ways. First, there is a subtle tension between the mural's content (an athletic triumph) and its title (the phrase *hitting the wall* is used by runners to describe feeling so overcome by fatigue that moving the body forward seems impossible). *Hitting the Wall* thus simultaneously represents the body in the moment of accomplishing an extraordinary feat of strength and at a point of extreme physical limitation. Second, there is a contradiction between the democratic landscape depicted in the mural and the unequal one in which it was created.[1] The image of the athlete in the wheelchair, for instance, reminds viewers how rare it is to see disabled athletes competing alongside nondisabled athletes. Although the image of the disabled athlete is relatively small, then, it is crucial to the mural's political intervention, as it prompts viewers to contemplate the differences between the social world it depicts (one characterized by equality between women) and the unjust social world that, together, we continue to create and inhabit.

Hitting the Wall thus captures the core theoretical concern of *Accessible Citizenships*: the role of disability images in questioning the construction of political communities and scrutinizing the attendant decisions about who will (and who will not) be included within them. More specifically, this book argues that the corporeal images used to depict national belonging have important consequences for how the rights and obligations of citizenship are distributed. Bodily metaphors used to define nations are a subject of theoretical inquiry for disability scholars, certainly, but they are relevant as well for scholars in any field that takes seriously the issue of political belonging, including Chicana/o studies, border studies, and queer studies (to name those that most directly inform this project). For instance, border anthropologist Jonathan Xavier Inda observes that the "body of the 'illegal' immigrant has served as an important terrain of governmental struggle," resulting in efforts "to exclude the immigrant from the body politic" ("Value of Immigrant Life" 135). The image of the nation as a whole, nondisabled body whose health must be protected from external pollutants justifies the political marginalization not only of immigrants but also of citizens, including those with disabilities and diseases (whose bodies challenge the image of the healthy national body) and racialized and sexual minorities (whose claims to social and political rights are seen to imperil national unity). In other words, the representation of the nation as a whole, healthy body that must be safeguarded against pathogens or parasites has helped to create what historian Mae Ngai calls *alien citizens*:

persons who are "citizens by virtue of their birth . . . but who are presumed to be foreign" (*Impossible Subjects* 2).

Where scholars have, to date, focused on the consequences of the healthy, able-bodied images used to represent the political body, *Accessible Citizenships* examines instead cultural representations that conceptualize political community through images of disability. Such representations, I suggest, have the potential to reconfigure how we perceive the body politic and to transform what we imagine when we (to repurpose Benedict Anderson's canonized phrase) imagine community. Beginning from disability theorist Tobin Siebers's assertion that art is "the active site designed to explore and expand the spectrum of humanity that we will accept among us" (*Disability Aesthetics* 10), I consider texts that envision nationalism through images of nonnormative bodies and ask if they might expand the spectrum of citizenry that we will accept in our nations. Ngai notes that national sovereignty is often defined as the nation's right to exclude, the "self-proclaimed, absolute right to determine its own membership, a right believed to inhere in the nation-state's very existence" (*Impossible Subjects* 11); the cultural workers discussed in this study challenge us to consider how ideas about national identity might change if they were predicated upon inclusion rather than exclusion. Because the texts examined here refuse the ideal of the healthy, whole body as a paradigm for the nation or the citizen, they provide material through which to explore the ways in which images of disability might open up the idea of national belonging to critical scrutiny.

Instead of envisioning healthy bodies vulnerable to disease, the creators of these texts imagine their political communities as disabled bodies that exist interdependently and act in solidarity with other bodies. Furthermore, because these texts strive toward broader, more expansive, and more just conceptualizations of national belonging, they offer new ways to theorize both citizenship and the representation of disability. Moreover, they do so at times in spite (or even because) of their failure to fully substantiate the inclusive communities they seek. What the texts

I examine here offer—more than a unified or final vision of what a truly accessible form of political belonging might look like—is the beginning of a new framework for re-visioning nationalism and citizenship. In other words, my argument is not that the use of a new bodily metaphor constructs "better" nationalisms, but rather that the use of a different bodily metaphor enables us to ask different questions about our political institutions. This is an important distinction because, as performance scholar Carrie Sandahl notes, disability has long been marshaled in the service of cultural and political work that does not benefit people with disabilities: "Nondisabled artists in all media and genres have appropriated the disability experience to serve as a metaphor expressing their own outsider status, alienation, and alterity, not necessarily the social, economic, and political concerns of actual disabled people" ("Black Man, Blind Man" 583). While it is true that some of the writers and filmmakers included in this study do appropriate disability in ways that can occasionally be troubling, they do so not merely to express their own outsider status but instead to question how political communities define insiders and outsiders, and to link antiracist, feminist, and queer political struggles with struggles for disability rights. As a result, they provide a starting point for imagining accessible political communities.

Enabling Chicanismo

Accessible Citizenships examines Chicana/o literature and film produced after the initial wave of El Movimiento Chicano (or, roughly, from the 1980s forward). In these texts, disability images are used (with varying degrees of success) to expand, reinvent, and critique a range of nationalisms, including those produced and supported by the U.S. and Mexican states as well as Chicana/o cultural nationalism (exemplified in the concept of Aztlán).[2] Chicana/o cultural production constitutes a site of unique theoretical interest for investigating nationhood and citizenship because of the ways in which ethnic Mexicans in the

United States have, according to Ngai, been "racialized as a foreign people, an 'alien race' not legitimately present or intended for inclusion in the polity" (*Impossible Subjects* 138).[3] The effects of this racialization are visible in texts as widely varied as those responding to the nationalisms of El Movimiento Chicano, those addressing the current human rights crisis on the U.S.-Mexico border, and those portraying contemporary Chicana/o identity as postnational or transnational. Furthermore, these texts, produced on both sides of the border by disabled and non-disabled cultural workers, incorporate disability to grapple with the meaning of citizenship in ways that reveal a marked theoretical coherence and demand a comparative analysis.

My focus on disability and Chicanismo as sources of important insights about nationalism and citizenship stems from a belief in the political value of subaltern or minoritized identities. This belief, however, is not universally embraced in either public rhetoric or scholarly discourse. Disability scholar Lennard Davis, for instance, writes against activism and scholarship grounded in identity claims: "Rather than ignore the unstable nature of disability, rather than try to fix it, we should amplify that quality to distinguish it from other identity groups that have . . . reached the limits of their own projects" (*Bending Over Backwards* 26). Davis's critique stems from the fact that identity, once defined, can become normative. For him, the radical potential of disability scholarship and activism lies in the fact that disability—encompassing as it does an extraordinary range of physical, psychiatric, and cognitive attributes—constitutes an exceptionally capacious category that might resist the normalizing impulses of identity politics.

Davis's critique of identity is important, and not lightly set aside. Nonetheless, I emphasize in this project what Michael Hames-García calls "the possibilities of identity politics rather than its limitations" (*Identity Complex* xiv). I suggest that while the potentially normative impulses of identity claims constitute a reason to mobilize them carefully, they are not a reason to eschew them altogether. As Hames-García points out, it is difficult (if not impossible) to engage in activist work without relying on norms of some kind, since claims "about justice, freedom, solidarity, and the like are by their nature 'normative,' that is, they make claims about what things should be like and how people ought to act" (*Fugitive Thought* xx). Indeed, one theorist known for the resistance to norms in her early work, Judith Butler, also concedes this point in her later work: "On the one hand, norms seem to signal the regulatory or normalizing function of power, but from another perspective, norms are precisely what binds individuals together, forming the basis of their ethical and political claims" (*Undoing Gender* 219). It is as a source of ethical and political claims that I invoke identity in this book and insist upon politically marginalized identities as a crucial position from which to reassess nationhood and citizenship.

By claiming disability as a minoritized identity, *Accessible Citizenships* builds upon work by disability scholars like Sandahl and Siebers, who assert the political and cultural value of disability identity. Siebers writes: "While people with disabilities have little power in the social world, their identities possess great theoretical power because they reflect perspectives capable of illuminating the ideological blueprints used to construct social reality" (*Disability Theory* 105). He, like the writers and filmmakers examined in this study, views disability identities as "critical frameworks for identifying and questioning the complicated ideologies on which social injustice and oppression depend" (105). One central hypothesis of this project is that disability images persist in texts that reevaluate the relationship between Chicanas/os and nation-state formations because the perspectives afforded by disability experience provide the kind of theoretical and political insights Siebers describes. Like feminist theorist Paula M.L. Moya, who argues that awareness of our social world depends upon our capacity to "acknowledge and understand the social, political, economic, and epistemic consequences of our own social location" (*Learning from Experience* 43), I contend that disability and Chicanismo, both marginalized in dominant U.S. constructions of national belonging, provide vantage points from which to reassess nationhood and citizenship. Furthermore, these identities' theoretical importance derives from the fact that they have, in different but related ways and in different historical moments, constituted the subordinated specters against which dominant versions of U.S. national identity have produced and maintained the global hegemonic power of the United States.

Given the significance that this study ascribes to minoritized identities, it is important to specify that I do not define disability as a bodily condition or essence. I emphasize this because, although scholarly inquiry in the humanities now accepts race, gender, and sexuality as social constructs, it is still common to think of disability as a medical condition located in the body and not in the society that refuses to accommodate it. As a result, Davis asserts: "We should not go on record as saying that disability is a fixed identity, when the power behind the concept is that disability presents us with a malleable view of the human body and identity" (26). Nonetheless, as Moya points out, the fact that identities are malleable does not mean they lack material effects. She writes: "while identities are not fixed, neither are they random"; indeed, there is a "limit to the range of identities we can plausibly 'construct' or 'choose' for any individual in a given society" (*Learning* 45).[4] More importantly, "the different social categories (such as gender, race, class, and sexuality) that together constitute an individual's social location are causally related to the experiences she will have" (39). In a very different context, sociologist Manuel Castells similarly describes identity as "people's source of meaning and experience" (*Information Age* 6). What Moya and Castells reveal is that the experiences that accrue to specific identities provide knowledge about the world and the way it works. Moya's work is especially important to this study because of her insights about the ways in which the identities of people who are socially and politically marginalized can provide particularly valuable information about the regimes of power that govern a society.

A more detailed discussion of Baca's *Hitting the Wall* will illustrate how political claims grounded in marginalized identities can promote a rigorous interrogation of the idea of national belonging. As stated previously, the mural was created through the 1984 Olympic Arts Festival, an event funded by the Olympic Organizing Committee (OOC) and designed to present Los Angeles as a cosmopolitan, egalitarian city—a model for the democratic ideal of equality that forms an enduring part of U.S. national mythology. As OOC Vice President and Olympic Arts Festival Director Robert Fitzpatrick describes it, the event was guided by the premise that "art is . . . an instrument of truth, an opportunity to put aside differences and rejoice in being alive" ("Olympic Arts Festival" 248). Certainly, the mural depicts a diverse group of women "putting aside their differences" through their shared participation in a rigorous athletic event; an interpretation of the mural that emphasizes this would not, therefore, be entirely inaccurate. Yet despite the OOC's vision of Los Angeles as a site of harmonious equality, the experience of many of its residents is quite different. Los Angeles is a highly segregated city; while Fitzpatrick might truthfully claim that the city's "identity lies in its diversity" (248), it is also important to acknowledge the tensions that accompany that diversity. These tensions, moreover, reflect larger struggles over national identity and political belonging.

The OOC's vision of Los Angeles, which implies equality among its residents, leaves out the legacy of inequality that remains inscribed in the city's built environment. This legacy has been formed by events ranging from the 1959 displacement of the residents of Chavez Ravine to the 1913 anti-begging ordinance that was, according to Susan Schweik, designed to remove working-class people with disabilities from public view. In other words, the OOC's vision of Los Angeles is most easily adopted by those whose lives are unaffected by this history. If art is "an instrument of truth," one might ask: *Whose truth?* Does Baca's mural reflect the OOC's truth of Los Angeles as a city defined by its diversity, or does it reflect the more complete truth of a site formed by national and local efforts to manage and hierarchize diversity? I argue the latter, positing that Baca's mural does not merely depict the temporary "putting aside" of differences but forces viewers to consider the social transformation needed to create a world in which difference is not structurally linked to inequality.

For example, an undocumented woman without a California driver's license who depends on the city's cumbersome public transportation system might not share the OOC's view of Los Angeles as a site in which difference is valued. Viewing the mural, she might see the runners' freedom as a contrast to the barriers imposed by automobile-centric urban design on her life. She might see not a depiction of what Los Angeles *is* but what it *should be* (a place where women of color, with and without disabilities, possess the ability to move freely and are adequately represented in the public sphere). From her perspective, the mural might appear as a statement that the built environment of Los Angeles, which is inconvenient and unsafe for people (especially women) without cars, is unjust. If she navigates Los Angeles in a wheelchair, she might also appreciate the image of a disabled athlete even while critiquing the fact that the woman in the wheelchair is relegated to the background. Such a viewer might note the effort to be inclusive but still wish for more representations of women with disabilities in the public landscape of her city. As a result, from her perspective the mural might reveal something important about the society in which it was created and the position of people with disabilities within that society. In neither interpretation is the depiction of women "putting aside their differences" most salient; rather, both emphasize the mural's effort to imagine a more democratic city. Even as I invoke this hypothetical viewer, however, it is important to note that she might not ever see the mural at all. The art historian Shifra Goldman has critiqued the Olympic mural project because the placement of the murals along freeways has made them difficult to see, particularly for residents of the city who do not own cars and rarely travel by freeway; the placement of the murals also resulted in dangerous working conditions for the muralists and their crews while the murals were being painted. The fraught context of its production, then, makes the political intervention of *Hitting the Wall*—and its claim for the right to free movement in public space—all the more important.[5]

The final point I wish to make about the political intervention made by *Hitting the Wall* has to do with its sophisticated reformulation of Chicana/o nationalism. This becomes apparent when we examine the mural as an artifact of Chicana/o visual culture. Drawing upon the iconography of Mexican cultural nationalism and inspired by the vibrant mural tradition of postrevolutionary Mexico, in which artists like Diego Rivera, José Clemente Orozco, and David Alfaro Siqueiros used murals to celebrate the everyday lives of Mexico's working people, Chicana/o artists in the United States began producing murals in the 1960s and 1970s as El Movimiento Chicano gained momentum. Many of these murals contained overtly nationalist themes, depicting Chicanas/os as the rightful occupants of Aztlán. At the same time, as cultural critic Richard T. Rodríguez points out, many images emerging from El Movimiento, including its murals, depict the heteronormative Chicana/o family as a stand-in for the nation, so that "Chicano/a cultural nationalism and notions of la familia continue to be codified by dominant articulations of masculinity" (*Next of Kin* 20). In particular, a mural entitled *La Familia* (1975), painted by the Royal Chicano Air Force (RCAF)[6] art collective on a freeway pylon in San Diego's Chicano Park, exemplifies what Rodríguez identifies as a visual archive that reifies "la familia as a sacred institution in which gender roles are fixed in the name of tradition" (*Next of Kin* 54). The mural depicts a nuclear family consisting of a father, mother, and son. The father stands with muscled arms wide open (as in a crucifix) against a backdrop consisting of the United Farm Workers' eagle logo; his wife, considerably shorter, stands in front of him embracing their son, who stands in the foreground clutching a schoolbook. While the image celebrates the working-class Chicano family, the placement and size of the family members' bodies both reinforce gender hierarchies. Furthermore, the future of the Chicana/o nation, embodied in the image of the child with a schoolbook, is gendered male.[7]

By contrast, *Hitting the Wall* embraces the possibility of a cultural nationalism without patriarchal gender politics. *Hitting the Wall* also features a person with muscular arms outstretched as the central image; the similarities between the body of the principal runner in *Hitting the Wall* and that of the father of *La Familia* are striking. Yet Baca's mural is both a tribute to the RCAF mural and a feminist reply to it; as striking as the similarities between the two works are the differences between them. The connotations of martyrdom implied by the crucifixion pose are replaced with a corporeal stance (still with arms outstretched) representing athletic triumph. The social hierarchy implied by the positioning of the family members is subverted as collective groups of runners take the place of the patriarchal family. Finally, the fit, strong, able bodies of the RCAF mural, while not entirely supplanted by disability images, are reframed by the inclusion of the runner in the wheelchair. Baca places herself firmly *within* the Chicana/o nation (employing its best-known art form and invoking one of its most canonized images) while also imagining that nation from a perspective that is explicitly informed by feminism and disability. In other words, she expands the body politic of Los Angeles and the dominant U.S. national narrative as well as that of Aztlán.

By discussing how Baca's mural produces different meanings for different viewers, I reinforce a point made by Moya and Ramón Saldívar, who assert that "every interpretive framework simultaneously illuminates certain salient facts about its objects of study even as it obscures others" ("Fictions" 3). The mural's cultural value lies in its ability to produce a multiplicity of meanings when viewed from different interpretive frameworks. At the same time, the mural also reveals certain frameworks to yield richer and more nuanced meanings than others. The perspective of the OOC—one that affirms, instead of challenging, the Los Angeles built environment—is not as complete as those informed by disability activism or Chicana feminism. The latter perspectives turn a critical eye on the society in which the mural was produced and attend to Baca's position in activist Chicana/o visual culture. They illuminate how Baca—like other Chicana/o cultural workers—motivates viewers of her art to consider how the world might be made more just. These frameworks account for the ways in which the mural's utopian content hits the wall of the unequal social and political landscape in which it was made. Furthermore, because the mural invites interpretations grounded in both Chicana/o and disability studies, it reveals how the two critical frameworks might speak meaningfully to one another.

Just as I note a productive tension between the title of *Hitting the Wall* and its content, I now wish to explore the tensions contained in the title of this book: *Accessible Citizenships: Disability, Nation, and the Cultural Politics of Greater Mexico*. These emerge from the use of the following terms: *Accessible/Citizenship* and *Nation/Greater Mexico*. These terms are intended to provoke a set of questions. What does it mean to make citizenship accessible? Is it politically desirable to make it so? Is the concept so overdetermined by its own legacy of exclusion that finding a new institution through which to claim membership and rights in a political community might be more appropriate? What is the relationship between citizenship and nationalism? If citizenship is an institution that links an individual to the state, how might non-state-sponsored nationalisms—like Chicana/o nationalism—provoke new ways of thinking about political belonging? Finally, the terms *nation* and *Greater Mexico* also exist in tension, as the term *Greater Mexico* indicates a transnational community of people of Mexican origin that exceeds the geopolitical boundaries of a single nation-state. These issues are crucial for the project's overarching argument; therefore, the following two sections of this introduction will address them in detail by locating this study within current scholarly conversations about access to citizenship and about the idea of Greater Mexico.

Citizenship and Political Access

Theoretical inquiry in Chicana/o studies and disability studies demands a reassessment of citizenship as a political ideal. This is because both fields emerge from activist social movements aimed not solely at securing a more advantageous position within an unjust society but instead, and much more broadly, at large-scale social transformation. For Robert McRuer, the goal of the disability movement is nothing less than "a newly imagined and newly configured public sphere where full participation is not contingent on an able body" (*Crip Theory* 30). McRuer's language echoes that of the Americans with Disabilities Act, which asserts that disability should not interfere with a person's "right to fully participate in all aspects of society." At the same time, McRuer's notion of *access* extends well beyond the legal mandate of the ADA: "An accessible society, according to the best, critically disabled perspectives, is not simply one with ramps and Braille signs on 'public' buildings, but one in which our ways of relating to, and depending on, each other have been reconfigured" (*Crip Theory* 94). McRuer envisions a society that privileges interdependent relationships among its members instead of one that idealizes the singular political agent, interrogating the liberal emphasis on the independent subject that constitutes the foundation of Western democracy and remains the privileged subject of political rights. In other words, he presents for critical scrutiny the subject that is perceived as a viable candidate for citizenship. McRuer thus critiques a discourse of subjectivity that, as María Josefina Saldaña-Portillo writes in a very different context, "requires the subject to become an agent of transformation in his own right, one who is highly ethical, mobile, progressive, risk taking, and masculinist" (*Revolutionary Imagination* 9). Although Saldaña-Portillo is not a scholar of disability, her choice of words puts her work into conversation with McRuer. Saldaña-Portillo suggests that both neo-imperialist development projects and revolutionary resistance projects in the Americas are "animated by a particular theory

of subjectivity" (6) that privileges the individualism of the liberal citizen and relies upon a notion of "human perfectibility"
(7). Both Saldaña-Portillo and McRuer, then, critique the ways
in which the construction of citizenship rests upon a discourse
privileging individualism and independence over collectivity
and interdependency.

The fact that citizenship is so intertwined with the ideal of
the sovereign individual is not the only reason scholars question
its usefulness as a political goal. For Asian American cultural
critic Lisa Lowe, the concept of citizenship has two additional
flaws. The first is the fact that it is always predicated on exclusion, separating those who "belong" in a given national territory from those who do not. Lowe writes: "in a political system
constituted by the historical exclusion and labor of racialized
groups, the promise of inclusion through citizenship and rights
cannot resolve the material inequalities of racialized exploitation" (*Immigrant Acts* 23). In this critique she is joined by anthropologist Renato Rosaldo: "Even in its late-eighteenth-century
Enlightenment origins, citizenship in the republic differenti-
ated men of privilege from the rest: second-class citizens and
noncitizens" ("Cultural Citizenship" 27). Lowe's second objec-
tion lies in the fact that citizenship is inherently tied to the state:
"the civil rights project confronts its limits where the pursuit of
enfranchisement coincides with a refortification of the state as
the guarantor of rights" (23). For these reasons, Lowe determines
that citizenship is at best a "site of contradiction for racialized
Americans" (24).

The racializing logic of citizenship is deeply intertwined
with a logic of able-bodied supremacy. Anthropologist Aihwa
Ong observes that "liberal conceptions of citizenship" are
often codified through "popular notions about who deserves
to belong in implicit terms of productivity and consumption"
("Cultural Citizenship" 739). This results in a "human-capital
assessment of citizens" that weights "those who can pull themselves up by their bootstraps against those who make claims on
the welfare state" and results in a definition of citizenship as

"the civic duty of individuals to reduce their burden on society" (739). Although for Ong this approach to citizenship aligns the institution with "the process of 'whitening'" (739), there are important disability resonances to her critique as well, since the imperative to be "productive" rather than a "burden" is often used to portray people with disabilities as a drain on a society's resources and, thus, as unfit for citizenship. Even the metaphor of "pulling oneself up by one's bootstraps" is, after all, an ableist one. Furthermore, as Ong points out, such a construction of citizenship is heavily aligned with "neoliberalism, with its celebration of freedom, progress, and individualism" (739)—an economic model that not only relies ideologically upon an ideal able-bodied subject but that also, as disability scholars point out, produces physical impairment. Michael Davidson, for instance, reminds us that neoliberalism, "far from improving access to healthcare, medicines, and sanitation has increased disabilities and disease by privatizing healthcare, exposing workers to industrial waste, and denying access to cheap, generic drugs" ("On the Outskirts" 737). Neoliberalism, then, exacerbates the racializing and disabling effects of dominant constructions of citizenship.

The concerns of the scholars cited above point to the need for more substantive inquiry into the substance and significance of citizenship. Indeed, Lowe's argument that recourse to citizenship ultimately refers us back to the state brings us to an unresolved paradox described by Hannah Arendt in the aftermath of World War II. As Arendt notes, the nation-state remains the only entity in our current social world that has the power to guarantee rights, making *human rights* indistinguishable from those of the citizen: "The Rights of Man, supposedly inalienable, proved to be unenforceable . . . whenever people appeared who were no longer citizens of any sovereign state" (*Origins of Totalitarianism* 293). Arendt argues that the loss of political status has "become identical with expulsion from humanity altogether" (297). This parallels a more recent observation from Latina sociologist Suzanne Oboler that "noncitizenship is paradoxically a much more meaningful and immediate life experience in structuring perceptions of belonging than is citizenship itself" ("Redefining Citizenship" 22–23). From the viewpoint of the citizen, the concept of *human rights* appears as a given; from that of the noncitizen, for whom no state agrees to protect these rights, such rights appear nonexistent. This leads Arendt to conclude: "We are not born equal; we become equal as members of a group on the strength of our decision to guarantee ourselves mutually equal rights" (301). Citizenship, at present, remains the institution by which we "guarantee ourselves mutually equal rights," yet its alliance with the state makes it a decidedly imperfect institution, one that leaves many out of its fold. In fact, it might be said that citizenship is the means by which we collectively decide *not* to guarantee equal rights to certain people (those deemed noncitizens). Precisely for this reason, the need is more urgent than ever to interrogate citizenship with the goal of expanding its accessibility or of replacing it entirely with a new mechanism for asserting political belonging and claiming rights.

If for Arendt the need to open citizenship to critical scrutiny arose from the dilemma of stateless people in the aftermath of two world wars, a pressing concern today is the number of undocumented migrants across the globe. In many cases, the undocumented migrant—who is often a citizen of a state but is prevented by political and economic forces from living within its territory and enjoying the rights it provides—is, unlike the stateless people Arendt describes, apparently made vulnerable by an *excess* of state affiliations. The state where she lives, works, and pays taxes refuses to guarantee her rights because her citizenship is perceived to lie elsewhere; the state that legally sponsors her citizenship fails to guarantee her rights because she has been forced to relocate her body and her labor. In response, scholars have theorized new forms of citizenship capable of accounting for subjects whose lives, labor, and civic obligations are not contained within a single nation-state. Two of the most influential are

Ong's notion of *flexible citizenship* and Rosaldo's concept of *cultural citizenship.*

Ong's theory of flexible citizenship emerges from an analysis of how individuals and governments respond to globalization by developing "a flexible notion of citizenship and sovereignty as strategies to accumulate capital and power" (*Flexible Citizenship* 6). Although she acknowledges *flexibility* as "the modus operandi of late capitalism" (3) and notes that late capitalism promotes an enormous power differential between "mobile and nonmobile subjects" (11), her theory remains most useful for describing subjects with a relatively high degree of mobility. By contrast, people with disabilities, people of color, those Ngai calls *alien citizens,* and the undocumented are not merely "nonmobile subjects" but are subjects actively *immobilized* by the disempowering and discriminatory sociopolitical landscapes they navigate. If, as Ong argues, "strategies of flexible accumulation have promoted a flexible attitude toward citizenship" (17), this "flexible attitude" is a double-edged sword. On one hand, a flexible attitude toward citizenship is a luxury enjoyed by those who live with the security that at least one state will sponsor their citizenship. At the same time, others live with the knowledge that the state has taken a "flexible attitude" toward the protection of their rights; for them, citizenship appears inflexible indeed.

To address how people assert their rights when states flexibly deny them, Rosaldo has developed the concept of cultural citizenship. For Rosaldo, the exercise of cultural citizenship entails "using public space to claim public rights and recognition" ("Cultural Citizenship" 36); the concept encompasses a range of everyday activities through which people claim political and social belonging within the national territory they inhabit. William V. Flores and Rina Benmayor describe why the concept of cultural citizenship is so crucial: "immigrants who might not be citizens in the legal sense or who might not even be in this country legally, but who labor and contribute to the economic and cultural wealth of the country, would be recognized as legitimate political subjects claiming rights for themselves and their children, and in that sense as citizens" ("Introduction" 11). An understanding of cultural citizenship, then, illuminates not only the economic and aesthetic contributions of marginalized groups, but their political contributions as well.

The most important of these political contributions may be an enriched understanding of the concept of rights, which results in an enriched concept of democracy. In a later, solo-authored essay, Flores extends Rosaldo's work to suggest that benefits from the exercise of cultural citizenship extend beyond immigrants. He notes that when groups historically denied citizenship—including women, people of color, and people with disabilities—claim rights, their claims actually result in the creation of new rights: "These new rights not only extend participation but reframe the context of that participation in terms of the needs of the new citizen groups" ("New Citizens" 88). In this way, civil rights struggles benefit society as a whole, not just the specific group of people they seek to liberate, because they make available to everyone an expanded framework for conceptualizing rights. For instance, current efforts by undocumented immigrants in the United States to establish cultural citizenship can broaden the idea of basic rights to include the right to labor outside one's nation of origin or the right to live in the same territory as one's children or life partner. Michael Bérubé makes a similar point when he reminds us that the rights of people with disabilities "were invented, and implemented slowly and with great difficulty" ("Citizenship and Disability" 55). For Bérubé, the claiming of rights by minoritized groups makes possible a new understanding of democracy: as we seek "to extend the promise of democracy to previously excluded individuals and groups," he writes, we discover that "our understandings of democracy and parity are infinitely revisable" (56).

In titling this book *Accessible Citizenships*, my goal is to bring to the concept of citizenship (or political belonging) this sense of "infinite revisability" that Bérubé sees as essential to democracy. Citizenship in this study functions as a way of making the distribution of rights more equitable, not as a fixed relationship to a defined nation-state. In this sense it functions analogously to what Butler describes as norms that are "useful" to social transformation: "norms that no one will own, norms that will have to work not through normalization or racial or ethnic assimilation, but through becoming collective sites of continuous political labor" (*Undoing Gender* 231). More than simply adding another term to the rapidly proliferating theoretical lexicon on citizenship, then, I bring together a set of texts that help us think rigorously about the idea of citizenship—juridical citizenship, cultural citizenship, and all of the flexible and inflexible citizenship forms that marginalized people with and without legal status must navigate—and about the kind of body politic we wish to inhabit. These texts offer not a new "kind" of citizenship but a new set of questions with which to approach citizenship in order to maintain it as a site of "continuous political labor." As Arendt writes: "Human dignity needs a new guarantee which can be found only in a new political principle, in a new law on earth, whose validity this time must comprehend the whole of humanity" (ix). I leave open the question of whether this "new political principle" might include a reformulated, accessible version of what we presently call *citizenship,* or whether the institution itself must be eradicated in order to create a more accessible means of guaranteeing human dignity for the whole of humanity. As my textual analyses in the body chapters of this book will show, the cultural objects I examine offer diverse answers to this question, even as they all begin from the premise that the body politic in its current shape is unjust and must be redefined.

Greater Mexico and the Possibility of the Postnational

The second term from my title that merits discussion is *Greater Mexico,* which I employ to underscore the theoretically consistent ways in which cultural producers from both sides of the U.S.-Mexico border have employed disability images to reexamine nationalism and citizenship. As a result of this consistency, I have found it both ethically and theoretically impossible to limit my study to Chicana/o-authored texts from the United States.[8] Instead, although the cultural producers discussed here are predominantly Chicana/o, they also include an Anglo (film director Tommy Lee Jones), a Mexican (screenwriter Guillermo Arriaga), and a writer who identifies as both Mexican and Chicano (novelist Alex Espinoza). Although this might appear to make this study fit uneasily within currently available disciplinary categories, Chicana/o cultural production has long addressed a range of national identities, including those of the United States, Mexico, and the nation of Aztlán. To a lesser but still noticeable extent, Mexican cultural production is also concerned with the social and political status of ethnic Mexicans in the United States, as canonized texts like Octavio Paz's *El laberinto de la soledad* (1950) and Carlos Fuentes's *La frontera de cristal* (1995) attest. The field of Chicana/o studies has grown increasingly transnational in the last two decades, with the publication of numerous scholarly monographs focused on the border region and beyond.[9] Given the geographical proximity between the United States and Mexico, the circular routes of migration that unite them, and the economic and political asymmetries that differentiate them, it is not surprising that Mexican-origin writers and filmmakers from both nations have addressed questions of citizenship and nationhood in similar ways. What I have found more surprising—and therefore of significant theoretical interest—is that their work also contains similar approaches to the representation of disability, approaches that urge us to imagine the kind of accessible political community that McRuer and other disability scholars advocate.

The term *Greater Mexico* was coined by the Chicano public intellectual Américo Paredes, whose ethnographic writings on the border culture of the Lower Rio Grande Valley in the 1950s constitute some of the earliest scholarly writings in what is now the academic discipline of Chicana/o studies. As Ramón Saldívar defines it, Greater Mexico refers to the "Mexican labor diasporas north from the border, as well as the social, economic, political, and symbolic overlap between those contiguous worlds" (*Borderlands of Culture* 5). He expands the theoretical applications of the term, elaborating how Greater Mexico can serve as a "far more complex imaginary site for the emergence of new citizen-subjects and the construction of new spaces for the enactment of politics outside the realm of the purely national" (59). While I have employed the term *Greater Mexico*, following Paredes and Ramón Saldívar, other scholars have coined other terms to write about the same transnational imaginary. For instance, Rosa Linda Fregoso uses the elegant neologism *MeXicana* to describe cultural work that is not confined to the territorial boundaries of Mexico or the United States. For José David Saldívar, the transnational turn in Chicana/o studies enables scholars to participate in "a trans-American and even global cultural studies that attends to the multiple and overlapping levels of cultural production and critique that circulate in the new global marketplace" (*Trans-Americanity* xxiii).

Even as I position this study in relation to the transnational turn in Chicana/o studies, however, I also wish to emphasize that the national remains a topic of great theoretical significance within the field. As Ramón Saldívar puts it, "both social structures, a nationalist and a transnationalist one, can be vitally present in the same historical moment. . . . We have to live with the one (the nation) even as we see something else (the post-nation) emerging" (*Borderlands of Culture* 59–60). For me, the concept of Greater Mexico proves useful because although the writers and filmmakers whose work I analyze imagine their (and our) lives in ways that exceed national boundaries, they also live (as do we) in a world of deeply entrenched nationalisms and therefore must contend with the political reality of the nation-state. The narratives I examine treat both the ideal of the nation as a whole, nondisabled body to protect from foreign disease/disability and the ideal of the independent, individual citizen as discursive formations that reinforce inaccessible forms of political community.

I have been suggesting that more attention to the representation of disability might enrich our interpretations of Chicana/o and Mexican cultural production, but I wish to emphasize as well that more attention to Mexican and Chicana/o narrative might enrich disability studies. David Mitchell and Sharon Snyder observe that intellectual alliances between disability studies and ethnic, LGBT, or feminist studies appear obvious: The "socially imposed relationship between marginalized populations and 'inferior' biology situates disability studies in proximity to other minority approaches. Like these other identity-based areas of inquiry, disability studies challenges the common ascription of inferior lives to persons with physical and cognitive differences" (*Narrative Prosthesis* 2). Nonetheless, this alliance has not proven as easy to sustain as one might hope: "As feminist, race, and sexuality studies sought to unmoor their identities from debilitating physical and cognitive associations, they inevitably positioned disability as the 'real' limitation from which they must escape" (2). This is an important observation that certainly applies to many texts. However, as my study reveals, other texts aiming to contest relations of domination do so by emphasizing similarities, not differences, between people with disabilities and other minoritized groups.[10] This does not make these texts invulnerable to critique, but it does mean that different theoretical frameworks are required to understand them.

What the writers and filmmakers examined in this project reveal is that the oppression of people with disabilities, the marginalization of Mexicans and Chicanas/os in the United States, and the political and economic subordination of Mexico to its northern neighbor all operate according to a logic of what Siebers calls *human disqualification*—a process in which people are portrayed as "lacking, inept, incompetent, inferior, in need, incapable, degenerate, uneducated, weak, ugly, underdeveloped, diseased, immature, unskilled, frail, uncivilized, defective, and so on" (*Disability Aesthetics* 23). These texts, then, show us how human disqualification invokes "disease, inferiority, impairment, and deformity to disqualify one group in the service of another's rise to power" (27–28). They invite dialogue between Chicana/o studies and disability studies and demonstrate how the theories developed in each field might help the other to contest more effectively the "rise to power" of unjust social systems.

As my analyses of the individual texts make clear, however, not all of the texts discussed in this study offer "positive" disability imagery. (In fact, I discuss one literary form—the overcoming narrative—that is particularly objectionable to disability activists in my fifth chapter.) As I noted in my discussion of *Hitting the Wall,* although the image of the woman in the wheelchair competing in a marathon is empowering, she remains in the background of the mural. Nonetheless, I do suggest that even in cases where the texts I examine contain problematic or marginalizing representations of disability, these texts still offer important insights about the value of disability within our ableist, racist, sexist, and homophobic social world. In this sense, *Accessible Citizenships* aligns with Nicole Marcotić and Robert McRuer's insistence on the need to exceed "the project of simply classifying particular cultural representations of disability as 'positive' or 'negative'—or relatedly, of assessing them in terms of whether they advance or impede a unitary disability movement" ("Leading With Your Head" 168). Furthermore, in none of these representations does disability function merely as a metaphor for a social problem experienced by nondisabled people. With greater and lesser degrees of success, all of the texts reveal disability to be what Mitchell and Snyder call "a mode of experience-based knowledge" (*Narrative Prosthesis* 61) about what it means to live in a world in which our economies and our labor are increasingly transnational while the protection of our rights remains firmly in the realm of the national.

Making Citizenship Accessible: An Overview of the Argument

Accessible Citizenships focuses upon three salient moments in the recent history of Greater Mexico: Chicana/o cultural nationalism, usually associated with the peak of El Movimiento Chicano in the 1960s and 1970s but still visible in Chicana/o activism today; the emergence of the U.S.-Mexico border as a source of anxiety about national identity in both the United States and Mexico, and therefore as a site of increased public surveillance, state-sanctioned violence, and scholarly analysis; and recent neoliberal challenges to the nation-state as a sovereign entity. The book is organized into three sections that correspond to each of these moments and trace how Chicana/o and Mexican cultural workers have collectively responded to them. As I argue throughout, disability functions *not* as a metaphor for the failure of nationalism in each of these moments, as dominant readings might suggest, but as a social location from which to imagine forms of political community that might fulfill the nation's democratic obligation to its citizens.

The book's first part, *The Body Politic of Aztlán,* examines how disability has functioned in feminist and queer reformulations of Chicana/o cultural nationalism. Chicana/o nationalism is a powerful response to the U.S. state's failure to guarantee the rights of ethnic Mexicans living within its territory; as a result, activist cultural workers continue to invoke it as a powerful discourse for asserting civil rights claims. *The Body Politic of Aztlán* explores the implications of ongoing investments in cultural nationalism on the part of Chicana/o cultural workers and specifically analyzes the function of disability in their efforts to queer nationalism. Like the work of Rodríguez, who rejects "the now-common move in Chicano/a and other ethnic studies scholarship to heavy-handedly render cultural nationalism the enemy that inherently generates sexism and homophobia" (*Next of Kin 7*), these chapters take seriously the political significance that cultural nationalism has had for queer Chicana/o writers. Chapter One, "Enabling Aztlán: Arturo Islas Jr. and Chicano Cultural Nationalism," examines two novels by the gay, disabled Chicano writer Arturo Islas. *The Rain God* (1984) and *Migrant Souls* (1991), which Islas began writing during the 1970s, depict the body of their queer, disabled protagonist Miguel Chico as the privileged body of Aztlán. They offer an early instantiation of what Cherríe L. Moraga would later call "Queer Aztlán" and therefore reveal how reconfiguring nationalist representations of the body can redefine Chicano nationalism itself. Chapter Two, "'My Country Was Not Like That':' Cherríe Moraga, Felicia Luna Lemus, and National Failure" examines Cherríe Moraga's play *The Hungry Woman* (2001) and Felicia Luna Lemus's novel *Like Son* (2007). These texts constitute a "cripping" of Queer Aztlán that provides a more nuanced, accountable nationalism than what is offered in Moraga's initial elaboration of the concept, suggesting that disability plays a crucial, yet unexamined, role in the theoretical constitution of Queer Aztlán.

The second part, *Immobilizing the Border,* examines how the U.S.-Mexico border is discursively tied to disability in ways that are both theoretically generative and politically dangerous. One particularly well-known example is Gloria Anzaldúa's frequently cited description of the border as a "1,950 mile-long open wound" (*Borderlands/La Frontera* 24); meanwhile, representations of the suffering migrant body are often invoked in news reports as pundits on both sides of current immigration debates rely upon disability and pain for their rhetorical impact. Furthermore, the fields of border studies and disability studies share a concern with the ways in which social landscapes are built to restrict freedom of movement. *Immobilizing the Border* reveals the political and ethical significance of this connection between the two fields. Chapter Three, "So Much Life in the Still Waters: Alex Espinoza and the Ideology of Ability in the U.S.-Mexico Borderlands" examines Alex Espinoza's 2007 novel *Still Water Saints*. This novel presents characters with a range of disabilities and bodily anomalies—obesity, infertility, wounds sustained during unauthorized border crossings—to reveal the ideology of body normativity that the border produces and supports. Chapter Four, "No Nation for Old Men? Racialized Aging and Border-Crossing Narratives by Guillermo Arriaga, Tommy Lee Jones, and Oscar Casares," examines the Tommy Lee Jones film *The Three Burials of Melquiades Estrada* (USA, 2006), a transborder collaboration with Mexican writer Guillermo Arriaga, and the novel *Amigoland* (2009) by Chicano writer Oscar Casares. These texts depict return journeys from the United States to Mexico, making visible the political interventions of what Schmidt Camacho calls *migrant melancholia* through the representation of masculine-gendered bodies in the process of aging.

The final section, *Beyond Citizenship*, engages with texts that confront the changing role of the nation-state in the face of neoliberalism. These include two Chicana novels that look beyond nationalism, attempting to imagine forms of political belonging that go beyond citizenship in a world in which citizenship remains the only guarantee of rights. Davidson describes the current post-NAFTA reality as one "in which the illusion of mobility and expanded communication masks the re-consolidation of wealth and the containment of resistance within a totalized surveillance regime" ("On the Outskirts" 737–38). The texts discussed in this section, which include both pre- and post-NAFTA works, reveal how the situation Davidson describes extends throughout the Americas, including areas not directly included in NAFTA, and came into being before the official beginning of NAFTA. Chapter Five, "Overcoming the Nation: Ana Castillo, Cecile Pineda, and the Stakes of Disability Identity," examines two novels by Chicanas that follow the form of what disability activists call "overcoming narratives": stories about people with disabilities who triumph over their so-called misfortune. Ana Castillo's *Peel My Love Like an Onion* (1999) depicts a Chicana flamenco dancer with post-polio; Cecile Pineda's *Face* (1985) tells the story of a Brazilian man living in a favela who loses his face in an accident and, unable to afford cosmetic surgery, reconstructs his own face using needles, thread, plastic from discarded toys, and procaine. Reading the two novels together, I reveal how this use of the overcoming narrative form comments upon the continued presence of the national in what Ramón Saldívar calls the "transnational imaginary" of globalization.

Working against the assumption that disability always functions as a metaphor for social decay or political crisis, the texts discussed here seek ways to imagine community that circumvent the exclusionary tendencies of the nation-state and juridical citizenship, beginning from a perspective informed by activism for racial and gender justice, LGBTIQ equality, and immigrant rights, as well as by the disability movement's opposition to bodily norms. Although the texts are not always successful in resisting the ideology of body normativity that undergirds the nation form, the ways in which they mobilize disability in their interrogations of citizenship and nationalism nonetheless allow us to ask new questions about both institutions, thereby prompting us to theorize them in new ways. In this way, my analysis of these texts reveals potential political alliances between people with disabilities and racialized minority groups. *Accessible Citizenships* elucidates the role played by representations of disability in making the rights and benefits of citizenship (both cultural and political) more accessible. Furthermore, it provides an account of how and why the communities we create look radically different when we envision disability as a central part of them.

PART ONE

THE BODY POLITIC OF AZTLÁN

1 / Enabling Aztlán: Arturo Islas Jr. and Chicano Cultural Nationalism

Like some of my characters, I often find myself on the bridge between cultures, between languages, between sexes, between nations, between religions, between my profession as teacher and my vocation as writer, between two different and equally compelling ways of looking agape at this world. . . . Still on the bridge, I run toward my fictions, to the balm of art, knowing that even the most vituperative piece of writing can serve the healing process. And even if I am made uncomfortable by my own imagination and prose, I remember that all art worthy of the name ought to make us uncomfortable. Discomfort often forces us to think and grow.

—ARTURO ISLAS JR., ERNESTO GALARZA COMMEMORATIVE
LECTURE, STANFORD UNIVERSITY, 1990

The fiction of Arturo Islas Jr. is profoundly discomforting. One of a very small number of gay Chicano writers to receive critical attention before the mid-1990s (and an even smaller number of self-identified Chicana/o writers with disabilities to publish at all), Islas unflinchingly depicts the effects of substance abuse, infidelity, gay bashing, suicide, unrequited love, medical malpractice, religious fundamentalism, and political corruption. His first two novels, *The Rain God* (1984) and its companion volume *Migrant Souls* (1990), are saturated with the physical pain of the character Miguel Chico, who (like Islas himself) experiences polio as a child and a colostomy as an adult.[1] They also record the psychic anguish of Miguel Chico and those he calls the "sinners" of his family, who defy family and community norms even as they also internalize dominant ideologies of race, sexuality, gender, and ability in harmful and destructive ways. As a result, critical reception of the novels tends to emphasize the pain they depict.[2] Nonetheless, this chapter is not exclusively about pain; rather, it is also about the healing, thinking, and growing that Islas describes as its outcome in the opening epigraph. The agony that features so prominently in his novels serves the process of unification and community formation, bringing together Mexico and the United States, Spanish and English, Spaniard and Indian, straight and queer, saint and sinner, soul and body, gut and colostomy bag.

In this chapter, drawing from disability theory and from Chicana/o feminist and queer theory, I argue that Islas's acts of synthesis produce a vision of Chicana/o community that circumvents the exclusions upon which cultural nationalisms are often predicated. I read his work, in other words, as an early instantiation of what Chicana lesbian writer Cherríe L. Moraga would later term *Queer Aztlán:* a Chicana/o homeland "strong enough to embrace a full range of racial diversities, human sexualities, and expressions of gender" (*Last Generation* 164). *The Rain God* and *Migrant Souls* reveal the racism and homophobia that undergird U.S. national identity while also inscribing their author's uneasiness with the patriarchal tendencies of Chicano cultural nationalism and the racial intolerance of white gay communities. Unlike some of the more directly activist texts of Islas's era, his novels refuse to idealize pre-Columbian cultural practices or to romanticize notions of gay unity. At the same time, Islas's focus on cultural family places his work within the very cultural nationalist tradition he often critiques. His novels embrace the drive toward community that lies at the core of nationalist impulses. As José David Saldívar notes, they take up the work of "incorporating migrant souls in relation to the body politic, generating other spaces and sites of meaning, and producing new border spaces of political antagonism and unpredictable forces for political representation" (*Border Matters* 84–85).

Reading Islas as a representation of Moraga's Queer Aztlán might seem counterintuitive to readers familiar with the scholarly bibliography on his work and, more generally, on gay

Chicano literary history. Although feminist and lesbian responses to Chicano nationalism emerged as Islas was writing both novels and began receiving critical attention around the same time as the publication of *The Rain God,* critics have often assumed that gay Chicano critiques did not emerge until much later. For instance, in an essay initially published in 1991 in the prominent feminist journal *differences* and later anthologized in the highly influential *Lesbian and Gay Studies Reader* (among other collections), Tomás Almaguer claims: "Unlike the rich literature on the Chicana/Latina lesbian experience, there is a paucity of writings on Chicano gay men" ("Chicano Men" 256). He goes on to cite Islas as an example of gay Chicano writers who "fail to discuss directly the cultural dissonance that Chicano homosexual men confront in reconciling their primary socialization into Chicano family life with the sexual norms of the dominant culture" (256). Furthermore, Moraga herself has written, somewhat dismissively, that Islas's "writing begged to boldly announce his gayness" but contains only "vague references about 'sinners' and tortured alcoholic characters" (*Last Generation* 163).

However, recent work by gay Chicano literary critics has challenged the commonly accepted narrative that Almaguer and Moraga offer in these critiques, a narrative that presents Chicano gay literature largely in terms of absence, lack, and failure. For Antonio Viego, the "lamentation which mourns the fact of gay Latino invisibility at the same time also serves to discipline and punish those gay Latino writers . . . who . . . have failed in their work to inscribe the gay Latino subject" ("Place of Gay Male Chicano" 92–93). According to Viego, this effort to "discipline and punish" coincides with a common discursive move in which gay Chicanos are "figured as the weak links in political movements for Latina/o ethnic and racial empowerment" (93). Meanwhile, Richard T. Rodríguez notes that the self-representations of Chicano gay men before the mid-1990s "form an archive all too often said not to exist" ("Carnal Knowledge" 114); he therefore calls for a critical reexamination of "Chicano gay men in various social and cultural contexts (such as literature and film) to unveil their positionings therein" (117). Following Viego and Rodríguez, this chapter seeks to reevaluate the work of a canonized, yet widely misread, figure in Chicana/o literature.

Although Islas's fiction is often read as more personal than political, or as less directly oppositional than other Chicana/o or gay literatures of its time, I suggest that the representation of disability in *The Rain God* and *Migrant Souls* complicates this perception. Almaguer writes of the need for accounts of how Chicano gay men "negotiate the different ways these cultural systems [U.S. and Mexican] stigmatize homosexuality and how they incorporate these messages into their adult sexual practices" ("Chicano Men" 256); Islas provides precisely such an account, revealing how life in a triply stigmatized body—queer, racialized, and disabled—might offer access to a profoundly different conceptualization of community. Because Islas's notion of community finds expression through images of disability, however, critics have not always recognized the construction of community as one of his principal concerns as a writer. After all, disability is often presumed to represent only political failure and decline. Islas's use of disability to represent the construction of a political collectivity therefore means that his fiction provides an opportunity to contemplate how disability might modify and expand the construction of concepts like the nation, the family, and the citizen. Reading Islas as a queer response to Chicano cultural nationalism helps us to see his work as an early effort to expand what Lee Bebout calls the "restricted cultural citizenry of a Chicano nation" (*Mythohistorical Interventions* 5). This, in turn, positions his work as a project allied with the important Chicana feminist publications of the 1980s[3] and contributes to the effort to interrogate established understandings of Chicano gay literary history. By reframing Islas's work in this way, this chapter reveals how attention to disability might contribute to scholarship about the role of nationalism and citizenship in ongoing struggles for racial justice.

Islas and Chicano Nationalism[4]

In the early 1970s, as Islas was writing the manuscripts that would become *The Rain God* and *Migrant Souls,* Chicano nationalism was defined by *El Plan Espiritual de Aztlán,* a manifesto composed in 1969 at the First National Chicano Liberation Youth Conference. Collectively authored by the poets Alurista and Rodolfo "Corky" Gonzales, along with other attendees, *El Plan* offers a radical vision for Chicana/o liberation, invoking the pre-Columbian Mexica (Aztec) homeland of Aztlán as the basis for Chicana/o claims to cultural and political self-determination: "Before the world, before all of North America, before all our brothers in the bronze continent, we are a nation, we are a union of free pueblos, we are *Aztlán*" (1). *El Plan* exemplifies the importance that Frantz Fanon attributes to nationalism in the process of decolonization: "A national culture is the whole body of efforts made by a people in the sphere of thought to describe, justify and praise the action through which that people has created itself and keeps itself in existence" (233). Given systemic political, economic, and cultural threats to the existence of the Chicana/o people, the necessity for such a manifesto to "describe, justify, and praise" a Chicana/o national culture remains evident even today.[5]

Yet *El Plan* also exemplifies a theoretical problem that haunts decolonial nationalisms: how to counter the oppressive nature of dominant, state-sponsored nations without defining the subjects of the counter-hegemonic national movement so restrictively as to undermine the emancipatory project. The manifesto thus encapsulates both the accomplishments and the problems of cultural nationalism. It makes a territorial claim for Chicanas/os, situates contemporary U.S. racism within a 500–year history of colonization, and envisions a more just social order. At the same time, as Yvonne Yarbro-Bejarano notes in a different context, Chicano nationalist texts like *El Plan* tend to "critique the ideal white body of 'American' identity by positing a quintessential Chicano body that is conceived as male, working-class, heterosexual and racially marked as Indian/mestizo" ("Laying it Bare" 277). To Yarbro-Bejarano's description I add *able-bodied*, for *El Plan* also privileges those with the capacity for physical labor: "Aztlán belongs to those who plant the seeds, water the fields, and gather the crops" (1). It thus defines the body politic of Aztlán in a way that contests the race and class ideology of U.S. culture but fails to address misogyny, heteronormativity, and able-bodied dominance.

As a writer who focuses upon queer, disabled, and otherwise marginalized Chicana/o characters, Islas has a vexed relationship to Chicano nationalism. He employs many of its privileged images—land, *familia,* and pre-Columbian cultural practices— even as he harshly critiques nationalist literature. As faculty advisor during the mid-1970s for *Miquiztli,* a literary magazine published by Chicana/o students at Stanford University, Islas wrote scathing critiques of prominent Chicano writers. In one, he opines: "Much of what is passed off as literature is a compendium of folklore, religious superstition, and recipes for tortillas" ("Writing from a Dual Perspective" 2). While the language Islas wields here is excessively sharp, these pieces reveal his desire for representations depicting the full diversity of Chicana/o identities and experiences. Of Alurista's work, he writes: "Brotherhood of man becomes brotherhood of Mexicans only; then just of those Mexicans who stress their Indian, not their Spanish, heritage; and then just of those Mexicans born in this country; and finally, brotherhood of those who are not *vendidos* but *real* Chicanos because they have not sold out" ("Writing" 2). Islas proposes, against Alurista, that "every Mexican born in this country is a Chicano, like it or not. Even if he is *agringado,* even if he has become successful in *gabacho*land" (2). In a later piece for *Miquiztli,* Islas urges his students to prioritize their individual voices over the collective voice of the community:

Imagine a window. Ignore the howling at the doors and concentrate on that window. Imagine it in any shape you wish. Look out of the window. Open it.

What do you see?
Describe it. Describe it as best you can in Spanish or
English or both. ("Afterword" 24)

Here his emphasis on personal expression directly contradicts
the injunction in *El Plan* for writers and artists to create "literature and art that is appealing to our people and relates to our
revolutionary culture" (3). Yet despite his refusal to envision the
writer as a vehicle for a singular, essentialized communal voice,
and despite his brutal criticisms of Chicano nationalist writers,
these essays reveal Islas to be struggling with the role of literature
in the formation of community. They show his commitment to
forging a new space alongside Alurista and his contemporaries
in the Chicana/o literary canon, not only for himself but also for
the students he mentors. These *Miquiztli* essays thus illuminate
the vision of Chicana/o community and cultural family that
emerges from Islas's novels.

Given Islas's tense relationships with the writers of his day
who were most visibly aligned with Chicano nationalism, critics generally do not interpret his work as nationalist or describe
Islas as a Chicano Movement writer. For example, Frederick Luis
Aldama describes Islas as "never the type to march in the streets"
(*Dancing with Ghosts* 135). Rosaura Sánchez praises his scrutiny
of Chicana/o family life but concludes that his work presents
"counterdiscourses which although critical of family relations
of power do not question the larger economic and political
structures of power in which they arise" (*Ideological Discourses*
125). Recent work by Suzanne Bost on illness and body politics in
Chicana feminist literature helps to illuminate why this apoliti-
cal perception of Islas may persist, even as the Chicana/o literary
canon has expanded to embrace feminist and queer writers. Bost
observes that scholarship in the field of Chicana/o studies has,
to date, privileged "identifications that are communal, culturally configured, and politically interpellated" (*Encarnación* 7),
with the result that "illness and feeling might seem to be private,
individual, temporary, and perhaps also trivial, untheorizable,

or politically irrelevant" (7–8). Nonetheless, Bost concludes that "provocative theoretical and political propositions" (8) are visible—if often unrecognized—in Chicana feminist writings on illness. Islas's representations of disability yield a similar (and similarly unappreciated) potential for theorizing new political identifications.

In the analysis that follows, I will elaborate how *The Rain God* and *Migrant Souls* depart from the project of *El Plan,* which privileges the able, laboring bodies planting the seeds, watering the fields, and gathering the crops, to propose instead a vision of Aztlán predicated on disability. In this way, the novels exemplify Tobin Siebers's assertion that "the inclusion of disability changes the definition of the political unconscious in surprising ways" (*Disability Aesthetics* 58). Expanding the work of Fredric Jameson, Siebers argues that "the political unconscious may also regulate aesthetic forms, excluding those suggestive of broken communities and approving those evocative of ideal ones" (57–58). Aesthetic objects, then, foment a preference for healthy, whole bodies over diseased or disabled bodies; nondisabled bodies are believed to indicate robust, sound communities while disabled bodies signify social decay or political crisis. One result of this correlation is an implicit justification for the political exclusion of people with disabilities and others whose bodies do not fit a narrow national ideal (often due to racialized or gendered corporeal attributes). Building upon Siebers's analysis, it becomes clear that Islas's novels prompt new theoretical inquiry into the body politics of decolonial nationalism. What might it mean that Islas imagines a more inclusive Chicana/o national community through images of disability? How might a vision of Aztlán predicated on disability images avoid the exclusionary norms visible in the nationalist literature against which Islas positions his work? Instead of signaling political crisis or the decline of Aztlán, disability in *The Rain God* and *Migrant Souls* provides a vision of Chicana/o community that, like Moraga's Queer Aztlán, strives toward the full inclusion of Chicanas/os of all gender identifications, sexualities, and abilities.

The Rain God: Dismantling la Familia

The Rain God and *Migrant Souls* focus on the Angel family residing in the border city of Del Sapo (a fictional city whose description in *Migrant Souls* calls to mind Islas's hometown of El Paso, Texas) and its authoritarian matriarch Mama Chona. *The Rain God* revolves around Mama Chona's death, while *Migrant Souls* recounts the familial power struggles that take place among her descendants after she passes. Because Mama Chona adheres to Catholicism, to the race and class ideologies of prerevolutionary Mexico, and to the assimilationist discourses of the pre–Civil Rights Movement United States, her death and the ensuing struggle for familial authority function as an allegory for Chicana/o history: *The Rain God* stages the collapse of the pre–Chicano Movement Mexican American family struggling for a space within the so-called American Dream, while *Migrant Souls* depicts the post–Movement reconstruction of the Chicana/o cultural family. Both novels are narrated from the perspective of characters who refuse Mama Chona's strict religious doctrine and ideals of bodily purity, who reject her emphasis on the family's "Spanish" (not indigenous) lineage, and who defy her upper-middle-class aspirations. In this sense, the novels reflect Moraga's assertion that "since lesbians and gay men have often been forced out of our blood families, and since our love and sexual desire are not housed within the traditional family, we are in a critical position to address those areas within our cultural family that need to change" (*Last Generation* 159). In other words, like Moraga, the novels indicate that those most excluded from the family's fold (or its "sinners") are those best positioned to imagine the cultural family in a more just and democratic way, and, also like Moraga, they depict the family as a microcosm of the larger cultural family or nation.

The Rain God begins with Miguel Chico in the hospital recovering from his colostomy, thinking "about his family and especially its sinners" (4), and ends with his decision to write an honest history of his family that openly addresses its homophobia, racism, and misogyny. The novel thus represents the struggle to understand the family in more inclusive terms, privileging its queer, disabled, and female members as well as its indigenous heritage. The nationalist component to this struggle is made explicit in the novel's title, which evokes the Mexica deity Tlaloc and links contemporary struggles to define the cultural family with indigenous resistance to the Conquest of Mexico. At the same time, the novel predicates its vision of the Chicana/o nation on the broken, fragile, and mutilated bodies of the family "sinners," including Miguel Chico and his uncle Felix. By incorporating Miguel Chico and Felix as central characters, *The Rain God* proposes an alternative framework for Aztlán, one that privileges imperfect bodies and families. It thus reinforces Paula M.L. Moya's notion that "people who have been oppressed in a particular way . . . have experiences—experiences that people who are not oppressed in the same way usually lack—that *can* provide them with information we all need to understand how hierarchies of race, class, gender, and sexuality operate to uphold existing regimes of power in our society" (*Learning from Experience* 38, original emphasis). It suggests that the family "sinners," those who deviate from the family's official narrative and whose bodies are visibly marked as different, are in the best position to identify and contest oppressive ideologies circulating within the family's most intimate spaces.

To argue, however, that the novel predicates its reformulation of Chicano nationalism on disability and privileges the queer members of the Angel family is not to argue that its principal character, Miguel Chico, is consistently positive about his ethnicity, his disability, or his queer sexuality. Miguel Chico struggles throughout the text with the impact of internalized racism, homophobia, and able-bodied supremacy. At certain points Miguel Chico's hatred of his body is violently apparent, as in this distressing early passage:

> Miguel Chico did not care whether or not he survived the
> operation they planned for him. When they described it to

him and told him he would have to wear a plastic appliance
at his side for the rest of his life—a life, they were quick
to assure him, which would be perfectly "normal"—they
grinned and added, "It's better than the alternative."

    "How would you know?" he asked. "Let me die." (*Rain
God* 6–7)

Miguel Chico here articulates the kind of individualism that
some critics see in the novel—a desire to escape his own racialized, disabled, queer embodiment at the expense of contesting
the sociopolitical forces that cause him to devalue his body.
Indeed, this passage is especially disturbing from a disability
studies perspective because, as John Alba Cutler astutely points
out, these "early pages of the book . . . characterize the body
as bearing a triple burden in terms of sexuality, ethnicity, and
disability, but they do so by placing the onus of that burden on
disability" ("Prosthesis" 12); after all, it is because of the appliance that Miguel Chico asks to die. However, the novel quickly
undermines this troubling sentiment. Less than a paragraph
later, Miguel Chico reinterprets his desire to die as an unhealthy
remnant of his grandmother's worldview: "Only later, when he
survived . . . , forever a slave to plastic appliances, did he see how
carefully he had been schooled by Mama Chona to suffer and,
if necessary, to die" (*Rain God* 7). The emphasis of this episode,
then, is not Miguel Chico's wish to destroy his body, but a critique of the social narratives (represented by Mama Chona) that
devalue his body and treat it as meant for suffering.

    Although the novel privileges the critical epistemic position
of the family "sinners" as a beneficial site for recognizing and
challenging oppressive family structures, it refuses to idealize
the characters themselves. Yolanda Padilla notes that critics
have found themselves consistently frustrated by the fact that
the novel offers "neither a 'positive image' of Chicano subjectivity nor a figure of oppositional gay pride" ("Felix beyond the
Closet" 15). But it is precisely because the novel refuses to provide unequivocally "positive" images that it is able to give such

a complex assessment of the psychic damage that occurs when marginalized people unconsciously assimilate the discourses that oppress them. One of *The Rain God*'s most crucial political interventions is its depiction of characters in the act of struggling against the harmful dominant ideologies they have come to internalize. As a result, the novel supports Moya's insight that "the theories through which humans interpret their experiences vary from individual to individual, from time to time, and from situation to situation" (*Learning from Experience* 39–40), as Miguel Chico comes to recognize his lack of concern for his own survival as the result of his grandmother's worldview. Renato Rosaldo observes that *The Rain God* and *Migrant Souls* reveal "variegated Chicano efforts to survive under white supremacy" ("Race and the Borderlands" 250). However, as the passage from *The Rain God* describing Miguel Chico in the hospital shows, not all of these "variegated efforts" are equally valorized; Mama Chona's effort to survive under white supremacy by denying her own racialized embodiment, for instance, has injurious repercussions that continue to harm the family for generations.

By placing a critique of social narratives that oppress people with disabilities alongside Miguel Chico's self-destructive impulses, *The Rain God* compels readers to consider the difference between representing in its full disturbing force the effects of internalized racism, homophobia, and ableism, and reinforcing those same ideologies. Throughout the novel, the force of Miguel Chico's anger is directed most powerfully at his grandmother, his father, and their worldview—a worldview characterized by rejection of the body in general and, in particular, of the body that is brown-skinned, disabled, female, or queer. José David Saldívar cites a letter written by Islas to his agent that describes Miguel Chico as "a historical creature who happened to live at a time when he was taught to hate what he perceived himself to be" ("Hybridity of Culture" 164). The words "he was taught" echo the phrase "schooled by Mama Chona" and suggest a cultural script that Miguel Chico recognizes as harmful but cannot escape. By including reminders, subtle as they are, that

Miguel Chico's conflicted feelings stem from living in a society in which his body has little worth (and a family that reproduces the messages of that society), the novel itself critiques larger sociopolitical narratives even when Miguel Chico as its protagonist conforms to them.

Because Miguel Chico's struggle against Mama Chona's hatred of the body is a central conflict of the novel, it is crucial that the opening section of the novel concludes with Miguel Chico's realization that "Mama Chona was still very much a part of him" (*Rain God* 28). At this moment, he imagines his grandmother "grafted" to him, just as a piece of his colon has been grafted to his side after the colostomy: "[P]erhaps he had survived—albeit in an altered form, like a plant onto which has been grafted an altogether different strain of which the smelly rose at his side, that tip of gut that would always require his care and attention, was only a symbol—perhaps he had survived to tell people about Mama Chona" (28). This particular sentence demands critical scrutiny because its convoluted, almost meandering, structure presents a sharp contrast to Islas's otherwise clear, lucid prose. By placing the memory of Mama Chona, the person most instrumental in teaching him to reject his body, onto the part of the body about which he feels the most shame, Islas creates a deep and haunting image of the physical, bodily impact of oppressive discourses. Moreover, by comparing Miguel Chico's grandmother to "that tip of gut" protruding from his abdomen, the novel suggests that both the grandmother and the new artificial colon require his constant "care and attention." In other words, the act of caring for Miguel Chico's body—overcoming his shame and discomfort so that he is willing to do the work that keeps his body alive—requires that he also devote "care and attention" to his grandmother's influence, remaining vigilant to her effects on his mind and behavior even if he cannot completely remove her ideologies from his life. Furthermore, if we read Miguel Chico's body as representing a new national body, the image of the grafted colon indicates that perhaps the most emancipatory way to imagine community is to treat it as a process requiring care and attention, rather than to assume that it is possible to imagine one community that is and always will be a liberated home for all of its members.

The novel's opening hospital bed—upon which Miguel Chico reconsiders his desire to die by contemplating how his grandmother has been "grafted" onto his psyche like the new artificial colon grafted onto his abdomen—is accompanied by a deathbed at the end: that of Mama Chona. Significantly, the opening section of the novel actually takes place long after Mama Chona's death; through its nonchronological narration, the novel links Miguel Chico's survival with Mama Chona's death and suggests that the demise of Mama Chona's repressive ideology is causally linked to Miguel Chico's acceptance of his embodiment. In contrast to the opening, in which Miguel Chico struggles to embrace his disability, Mama Chona cannot overcome her horror of the body. As her distended uterus falls out, she believes that she is birthing a monster. She also refuses to believe that her son Felix is dead, insisting that he prefers instead to visit her sister Cuca, who has "lighter skin" (174). These gendered and racialized hallucinations, which overtake her mind as her life draws to a close, demonstrate the hatred she feels for her own body. The "monster" that she births—which represents a horror of the body that sustains misogyny, heteronormativity, and the oppression of people with disabilities—appears to Miguel Chico in a dream before Mama Chona's deathbed scene (but after her death chronologically). The monster "put his velvet paw in Miguel Chico's hand and forced him to hold it tightly against his gut right below the appliance at his side" (159), urging Miguel Chico to jump off a bridge. Mama Chona's "monster" touching Miguel Chico's gut and compelling him to destroy himself recalls the earlier image of Mama Chona as "grafted" to the site of her grandson's operation. Once again, Mama Chona's hatred of her own racialized, female body is linked to Miguel Chico's discomfort with his racialized, queer, disabled body and, most disturbingly, to his desire to die. And, once again, Miguel Chico must find a way to live with his grandmother's "monster" without destroying himself.[6] Upon awakening, he decides "to make peace with his dead" and "to tell the family secrets" (160). The novel thus opens with Miguel Chico wishing for death on a hospital bed, remembering his grandmother's horror of the body, and ends with him alive, determined to tell his own contestatory narrative, while the most repressive family member passes on.

The fact that The Rain God concludes with Miguel Chico's decision to write a new family narrative indicates Islas's belief in the power of narrative to redefine community—a belief he shares with the Chicano nationalist writers he critiques, even as he imagines a very different community from theirs. Importantly, as part of its project to redefine communal narratives, the novel explicitly critiques narratives that position people with disabilities on the margins of the community. The Rain God self-consciously draws attention to itself as a literary representation of disability—and to the cultural work that such representations perform—when it describes Miguel Chico's childhood attraction to The Hunchback of Notre Dame: "He loved Esmeralda's name and a torture scene that featured a wooden boot, and he was simultaneously repelled and fascinated by Quasimodo" (161).[7] By noting Quasimodo's allure, the novel shows how children are taught by literature to view the disabled body as "repellant and fascinating."

Even as The Rain God invokes canonized disability images like that of Quasimodo, however, it also subtly replaces such images with quotidian descriptions of life with a disability. Miguel Chico, in the act of changing his colostomy appliance, is neither "fascinating" nor "repellant" but simply engaged in an everyday act:

> While the sauce was bubbling, he put on his favorite
> records and went to the bathroom to change his appliance.
> It was a weekly ritual which took him an hour, or a little
> more if the skin around the piece of intestine sticking out
> from his right side was irritated. Without the appliance

and the bags he attached to it and changed periodically
throughout each day, he knew he could not live. . . . This
time, the skin around the stoma looked all right and he fin-
ished the process before all the records had played out. (25)

Placing this action within the context of other daily activities—
making spaghetti sauce, listening to music—gives the bag a
mundane quality. Even more remarkable in its ordinariness is
Miguel Chico's polio. Although we are told in one sentence that
Miguel Chico "would have a slight limp for the rest of his life"
(95) after surviving polio at age eight, the limp is not treated
as traumatic or tragic. The novel thus makes visible the literary and social narratives that treat disability as extraordinary
and sets these alongside images of everyday life with a disability.
The effect of these juxtapositions is to demonstrate that disability is an ordinary part of life that only acquires its "repellant
and fascinating" status in the context of unequal social relations
between nondisabled and disabled people.

Although the Angel family is where Miguel Chico learns to
understand his queer, disabled, Chicana/o body as possessing
little social value, it is importantly not the only institution in
the novel that operates according to this ideology. Indeed, if one
single event dominates the family story, it is the gay-bashing
murder of Miguel Chico's uncle Felix by a white soldier and
the cover-up of that murder by law enforcement officials. Felix's
murder is mentioned at the beginning of the novel, when Miguel
Chico recalls on his hospital bed that "his uncle Felix had been
murdered in such a twilight" (6). The death is later narrated
three times, in excruciatingly violent detail, from the viewpoints
of three different characters. When the story is told by Miguel
Grande, we see the brutal violation of Felix's body: "There was
no face, and what looked like a tooth was sticking out behind
the left ear. Dried blood and pieces of gravel stuck to the skin.
The eyes were swollen shut, bulbous and insectlike. The back of
the head was mushy. The rest of the body was purple, bloated,
and caved in at odd places. One of the testicles was missing" (81).

When it is told by Felix, we learn of the pain and fear that characterize the final moments of his life: "Felix had time to be afraid before he heard his heart stop" (138). Finally, when the story is told by Felix's son JoEl, we learn how his death impacts the next generation: "JoEl understood infinity for the first time.... All of his fears and evil dreams merged and he had no voice to cry out against them" (152–53). Together, these perspectives reveal the violent impact of Felix's death, a death made possible by the practice of racism and heteronormativity, on all members of the Angel family, queer and heterosexual. Moreover, it is Miguel Chico who synthesizes all three voices when he decides to tell the family secrets: his father identifying the body, his uncle suffering as the soldier kicks him to death, and JoEl numbing the memory of his father's murder with narcotics. By emphasizing the story that his family edits out of its official history, Miguel Chico authors a new family history that challenges racism and homophobia.

Because Felix inspires Miguel Chico's new family narrative, he constitutes an important source of resistance to Mama Chona's harmful ideologies—a source of resistance that emerges from within the family itself. Indeed, it is Felix, not Miguel Chico, for whom the novel is titled. When Miguel Grande goes to tell Felix's wife of the murder, he has a vision of his brother as a child: "For a moment, as he walked toward the house, Miguel saw Felix as a child dancing in the rain" (83–84). Felix the "rain dancer" resurfaces in the final chapter as the rain god of the novel's title, and it is the rain god who gives Miguel Chico the authority to write a new family narrative. This occurs when Miguel Chico receives a poem by the Mexica king Nezahualcoyotl, copied out in longhand by one of his ancestors:

> All the earth is a grave and nothing escapes it; nothing is so perfect that it does not descend to its tomb.
>
> Rivers, rivulets, fountains and waters flow, but never return to their joyful beginnings; anxiously they hasten on to the vast realms of the Rain God.

. . .

Nothing recalls them but the written page. (162)

Death, the realm of the rain god, and Miguel Chico's written page are thus linked in the text. It is this passage that imbues the novel with the force of a cultural nationalist vision, for it unifies Miguel Chico's project of recalling the family narratives erased by the family's oppressive ideologies with the project of recalling those pre-Columbian societies erased by colonialism. Moreover, it is an overtly queer cultural nationalism, for it is those queer characters (Felix and Miguel Chico) already situated precariously in relation to the family narrative who are charged with the work of recovery. Fanon writes of the need to reclaim a national past in the process of decolonization: "Colonialism . . . turns to the past of the oppressed people, and distorts, disfigures, and destroys it" (*Wretched of the Earth* 210). Islas adds an extra layer to Fanon's insight, suggesting that heteronormativity engages in its own distortions of history, and that it is not enough to simply reclaim and retell the past if that reclaiming and retelling leaves intact contemporary practices of patriarchy and homophobia.

By basing his cultural nationalist vision on the queer, wounded/disabled bodies of Miguel Chico and Felix, Islas reveals that nationalism need not be predicated upon heteronormativity and able-bodiedness. In this, *The Rain God* coincides with recent observations by Rodríguez, who notes that the liberatory impulses of Chicano nationalism provided a necessary ideological framework for the Chicano Movement. The problem with early Movement texts, in Rodríguez's estimation, is not their nationalism in and of itself but rather the fact that their nationalism was anchored in heteropatriarchal discourses. He writes: "if minority nationalisms endeavor to liberate their purported constituencies from the subordinating forces of the state, they must relinquish their dependency on exclusionary kinship forms" (*Next of Kin* 7). At the end, when he feels himself "free to tell the family secrets," Miguel Chico begins to construct a nationalist vision liberated from exclusionary kinship; as Cutler puts it, he envisions "a familial love that allows for recognition of difference as something other than abnormality" (10). These family secrets (and familial love) ensure that although Miguel Chico is still not free of Mama Chona's ideologies, he is much more attentive to—and thus more capable of critiquing and contesting—their production and transmission. As Mama Chona dies, she is visited by her long-deceased son Felix in the guise of the rain god. When he arrives, Miguel Chico and Mama Chona are the only ones aware that Felix has come into the room. Thus Miguel Chico and Felix—the two queer family members—are given new life at Mama Chona's death. The conclusion of the novel suggests that by queering and disabling the family history, Miguel Chico's new family narrative will be able to provide a better account of the ideological struggles taking place in the constitution of cultural nationalism.

Migrant Souls: Rewriting La Familia

Miguel Chico's freedom to author a new family history in *The Rain God* is only the beginning; *Migrant Souls* emphasizes that ongoing debates over the narrative remain an essential part of community formation. On a formal level, the narration of the novel is much more dispersed, although Miguel Chico's cousin Josie occupies more narrative space than any other character. Both Miguel Chico and Josie have similarly ambivalent relationships to the family; they see themselves as family "sinners" but neither is positioned completely outside the family. Miguel Chico fails to adhere to the family's standards for normative masculinity, but he is nonetheless a male child who, after Mama Chona's death, goes on to "receive his doctorate and fulfill [Mama Chona's] dream that a member of the Angel family become a university professor" (*Rain God* 5). Meanwhile, although Josie (unlike Miguel Chico) is nondisabled and heterosexual, she is also divorced, female, and dark-skinned; her mother and grandmother frequently employ the racist insult of "Indian" against her. However, although Josie and Miguel Chico occupy similar roles within the family, they do not occupy similar functions within the novels. Josie does not dictate the plot of *Migrant Souls* as Miguel Chico does in *The Rain God*. She narrates almost the entire first part of *Migrant Souls* but only one segment of its second part; sections of both parts are also narrated by Miguel Chico and his brother Gabriel. The dispersed narration of *Migrant Souls* reflects the fact that the family is in conflict over the new family narrative that Miguel Chico has written (a novel called *Tlaloc*); as Josie puts it, members of "our perfectly happy family . . . think you're telling their terrible secrets to the world and they don't like it" (209). Unlike *The Rain God*, *Migrant Souls* also critiques the white gay community and its exclusions; it thus depicts Miguel Chico's struggle to claim a place in multiple communities. By focusing on Josié—a heterosexual, able-bodied, divorced mother—the novel also reveals how the new family narrative written by Miguel Chico might, in its rejection of heteronormativity and patriarchy, promise a less repressive community for all members of the cultural family.

The first image of disability to appear in the novel surfaces quite early and establishes Josie's character as resistant both to the U.S. national narrative of assimilation and to her family's effort to distance itself from lower-class Mexicans. During the fall of her seventh-grade year, she crosses the border to Mexico with her parents to purchase a Thanksgiving turkey. Josie and her sisters beg to eat turkey like their classmates, despite their father's fear that "[e]ating turkey is going to turn my girls into little *gringas*" (*Migrant Souls* 22). Leaving the turkey farm, Josie's father carefully instructs her how to cross back into the United States: "You just say 'American' when the time comes. Not another word, you hear?" (28). Josie, however, is distracted when they cross the bridge, looking out the window to see indigenous beggars approaching her father's truck. In particular, she identifies with a young woman carrying a blind infant: "Her hair was black and shiny and her eyes as dark as Josie's" (33). Although she obeys her father and does not roll down the window to give the woman the quarter in her pocket, Josie nonetheless feels drawn to the woman and her child. Soon after, her father is interrogated at the checkpoint and the family almost fails to make it back across. As a result, an event that is supposed to facilitate assimilation into the U.S. national body—the purchase of a Thanksgiving turkey—has the opposite effect. It instead reminds Josie of the second-class citizenship afforded to Americans of Mexican descent and strengthens her solidarity with those possessing bodies excluded from the U.S. national narrative, including those visibly marked as indigenous and those with disabilities.

Much later, after Josie's divorce, her identification with her queer and disabled cousin Miguel Chico is also evident. Staying with his parents for the Christmas holidays, Miguel Chico is pictured alone in his bedroom, "adjusting the plastic appliance attached to his side a few inches below and to the right of his navel" (175). The text clearly states that Miguel Chico minds the appliance "less than what the devils were doing to his head" (175), indicating yet again that it is living in a society that devalues disability, not disability itself, that causes Miguel Chico's self-destructive impulses. However, in contrast to this image of Miguel Chico alone in his bedroom with his "devils" and his appliance, the novel also offers a happier image of Miguel Chico at a strip club with Josie and her daughters. They stop at the club for a round of drinks before the family Christmas Eve party because it is their "duty" to be late: "The Angels expect us to be rude and we mustn't let them down" (206). In this setting—a bar that contradicts the family's sexual norms, in the company of a fellow family "sinner"—Miguel Chico refers openly and even affectionately to his disability, excusing himself to the bathroom with the announcement that "I must change bag number 14,792" (207). Josie's early moment of identification with disability, then, sets the stage for this alternative image of family that embraces sexual and bodily difference, providing a sharp contrast with the image of Miguel Chico's isolation in his parents' home.

One key distinction between *The Rain God* and *Migrant Souls* is that, whereas *The Rain God* devotes considerable space to depicting the harmful effects of homophobia, racism, and able-bodied dominance, *Migrant Souls* devotes more space to rectifying such discourses. For example, *The Rain God* contains a detailed description of the body of the white soldier who kills Felix: he is "fair with light-colored eyes" (134) and has "the mouth of a young girl" (135). Padilla suggests that Felix's "attraction to whiteness" ("Felix beyond the Closet" 30) allows *The Rain God* to explore "the idea that feelings of unworthiness and insecurity somehow shape Felix's sexual behavior and the relations of power through which that behavior is expressed" (31). This is crucial because Felix, who demonstrates what Padilla calls a "deep shame about his ethnicity" (30), is an important role model for Miguel Chico. *The Rain God* reproduces this shame in a rather uncomfortable way, for although the actions of the soldier who murders Felix are brutal, the physical description of this "shy and fair god" (*Rain God* 115) records the desire Felix feels for him and treats his body as an object of aesthetic beauty.

   Migrant Souls, on the other hand, resists depicting white bodies as aesthetically beautiful, although it dwells upon Miguel Chico's emotional state after his lover Sam Godwin leaves him. The desire for Sam that runs through the novel is palpable, but Sam's body is never represented, even in memory. In fact, although Aldama's extensive archival research on early drafts of the novel establishes Sam's race as white, his race is not explicitly defined in the published version of *Migrant Souls* (although the reader who knows that he shares some biographical details with a white ex-lover of Islas might infer this). One of Sam's most powerful and poignant appearances in the novel also contains a critique of the white gay community of the San Francisco Bay Area. Here Miguel Chico longingly remembers walking through an improbable snowfall in the Bay Area with Sam, watching "hundreds of snowflakes falling symmetrically into a void" (*Migrant Souls* 208). Although the image is a strikingly beautiful one, it also leaves the reader cold; the symmetrical snowflakes reflect the homogeneity of San Francisco's white, largely nondisabled, gay population in the years preceding the AIDS pandemic (not to mention the white, nondisabled beauty standards that have persisted in that community through the pandemic), and the "void" into which they fall indicates Miguel Chico's feelings of alienation within that community.

Meanwhile, the bodies of Chicanas/os are emphatically present in *Migrant Souls,* and they are represented as desiring and desirable. For example, Josie is "dark and lovely" (119); on her wedding day, her mother and older sisters are struck by "the beauty of [Josie's] figure and skin" (98). She then scandalizes her mother by saying "I'm all flesh, Mother. There aren't going to be any immaculate conceptions in my family" (98); this affirmation of her sexuality is also an affirmation of her racialized, female body. Although Josie marries Harold, a biracial white/ Mexican American man, knowing that "her mother would approve of his high forehead and light skin" (71), the relationship that has the greatest influence on her is a two-month affair with her husband's friend Robert, a dark-skinned man who is "Cherokee with some French thrown in" (186). Josie's desire for Robert represents a challenge to the racism of her upbringing, in which she is taught that her grandfather "had more Spanish than Indian blood in his veins" (8–9) and that her ancestors "claimed their portion of Mexico after surveying it with pure Castilian and Catholic eyes" (9). Growing up, she senses that she and her sisters are "more like the Indians than the Spanish ladies they were brought up to be" (3) and ignores her mother's threats that if she does not behave "the Indians were going to claim her as their own" (3). When Josie returns home after her divorce, she confronts her mother after introducing her daughters for the first time: "Before Eduviges began talking about them, Josie looked into her mother's eyes and asked, 'Aren't my little Indians beautiful?'" (200). She thus transforms her mother's racialized threats into a positive affirmation of her daughters' (and her own) indigenous heritage.

Finally, even as Miguel Chico continues to mourn the loss of Sam, the male body that is represented as the most salient object of desire is that of a dark-skinned Chicano named Manuel

Chavez, husband of Miguel Chico's aunt Jesus Maria. As her name indicates, Jesus Maria is a sternly religious figure, a repressive aunt who attempts to take Mama Chona's place as the family matriarch. Nonetheless, the desire that she feels for Manuel indicates that she has not, like Mama Chona, suppressed all evidence of her own embodiment, nor has she fully internalized Mama Chona's racism. At the novel's end, Jesus Maria recalls seeing Manuel for the first time: "His wavy, black hair was wet and he looked like a dark terracotta angel" (226). In this way, the novel shows that Mama Chona and her efforts to deny the racialized bodies of herself and her descendants have not been successfully duplicated in the next generation. Furthermore, although Jesus Maria's desire for her husband cannot be called queer, it is crucial that Miguel Chico is represented in the act of grieving the end of his relationship with Sam just as Jesus Maria grieves the death of Manuel. By representing Miguel Chico's grief alongside Jesus Maria's grief, the novel gives a carnal immediacy to Jesus Maria's spiritual life and imbues Miguel Chico's relationship to Sam with the cultural force of the heterosexual marriage. By focusing on Manuel's body instead of Sam's, however, it ensures that the desire that circulates in the novel focuses, exclusively, on Chicana/o bodies.

In this way, *Migrant Souls* bears a striking coherence with an observation that Yarbro-Bejarano has made of Chicana lesbian visual art. She writes: "the desire that flows through it does not limit itself to the sexual: It is for social justice, community, and representation in all its meanings" ("Laying it Bare" 283). Indeed, the desire circulating through *Migrant Souls* focuses on the need for community and a non-oppressive means of creating family. The novel concludes with Miguel Chico's brother Gabriel (a priest) in the act of prayer on Christmas Eve, imagining a more inclusive community: "He prayed for the altar boys and the gang members, for the sick and the dead and the dying in and out of his parish, for the poor and hungry, the rich and privileged" (246). This concluding image is similar to that of *The Rain God,* in that it sanctions a vision of family that escapes the repressive ideology that Mama Chona represents. Here, however, the need for a reconfigured Chicana/o family rests not only on the queer son and grandson (Felix and Miguel Chico) but on the entire family, including Josie and Gabriel, and on the larger community that supports the family. Moreover, it reflects Islas's insistence in the early *Miquiztli* essays that all U.S. residents of Mexican descent belong to the Chicana/o community, embracing not only the gang members (the pachucos and cholos venerated as figures of cultural resistance in the iconography of the Chicano Movement) but also the altar boys (figures aligned with the religion of the Conquest who do not have such iconic status). The ending thus suggests that a Chicana/o cultural family that privileges the queer and disabled body will ultimately provide an inclusive family for all of its members. More importantly, it charges *all* members of the family (not only those who are queer and/or disabled) with participating in the reformulation of the cultural family.

The Rain God and *Migrant Souls* counter normative narratives of Chicana/o family; instead of positing the patriarchal family as an idealized representation of the nation, they reveal the violence and trauma that must be edited out of the family history in order for the patriarchal family to present itself as a whole and unified representation of the whole and unified nation. However, the novels do not relinquish the project of imagining a cultural family. Instead, they expose what Bebout calls the "continual tension between the community constituted by identity-based social movements and those who lack access to citizenship within those movements" (*Mythohistorical Interventions* 7). At the very end of *The Rain God,* as Mama Chona dies, she utters the word *familia* directly to Miguel Chico, her queer and disabled grandson. This moment represents the possibility that even Mama Chona experiences a (belated) transformation, signifying the extensive inclusivity of Islas's vision of Aztlán. Yet although all members of the family are included in this new Aztlán, all perspectives are not equally privileged.

Indeed, it is Mama Chona's queer and disabled grandson who is ultimately entrusted with the task of creating a new familial and national narrative, one capable of incorporating the lives and histories of those cut out of the dominant narrative. In *The Rain God* and *Migrant Souls*, Miguel Chico's queer and disabled body thus becomes representative of a new kind of body politic. This occurs not because all members of his community must be queer and disabled, but because his body's noncompliance with norms allows for the possibility of a nationalism predicated on antinormativity. This antinormativity, in turn, benefits not only Miguel Chico but also characters like Josie (whose life is also at odds with the heteronormative family script) and Jesus María (who, although she subscribes to the dictates of Mama Chona and the Catholic Church, clearly does not benefit emotionally or politically from doing so). As a result, the inclusion demonstrated in Gabriel's prayer at the end of *Migrant Souls* shows how a queer and disabled Aztlán provides a broad-based liberatory vision. It functions, in Bebout's terms, as a means "to imagine new citizenships" (8) *within* the larger national construct of Aztlán. As in the epigraph to this chapter, in which Islas describes discomfort as a force that promotes thought and growth, in his fiction bodily discomfort serves as a force that promotes community formation. Islas therefore proposes that reconfiguring cultural nationalist depictions of the body has the potential to redefine—in more just and inclusive terms—the nation itself.

2 / "My Country Was Not Like That": Cherríe Moraga, Felicia Luna Lemus, and National Failure

Aztlán.

Pero, es un sueño. This safety
of the desert.
My country was not like that.
Neither was yours.

—CHERRÍE MORAGA, *LOVING IN THE WAR YEARS*

In 1992, one year after the untimely passing of Arturo Islas Jr., Chicana feminist playwright, poet, and queer theorist Cherríe L. Moraga published her famous call for a new Chicana/o nationalism. As discussed in the previous chapter, that essay, titled "Queer Aztlán: The Re-Formation of the Chicano Tribe," reimagines the Chicana/o homeland of Aztlán in ways that attempt to circumvent the misogyny and heteronormativity that often accompany appeals to cultural nationalism. In the two decades since the publication of "Queer Aztlán," however, even while critics like myself have incorporated the concept into our theoretical lexicon, Moraga herself has occasionally moved away from the nationalism she espouses in it, exploring instead Aztlán's limitations.[1] Taking seriously this shift in Moraga's intellectual project, this chapter examines two texts that represent nonnormative forms of embodiment, including disability (as well as gender transitioning and aging), in ways that critically reassess the liberatory efficacy of queer Chicana/o nationalism: Moraga's own 2001 play *The Hungry Woman: A Mexican Medea* and the younger Chicana queer writer Felicia Luna Lemus's 2007 novel *Like Son*. Where the previous chapter addresses the ways in which the disability images in Islas's work function to construct a version of Queer Aztlán, this chapter shows how later writers—including Moraga—represent disability in ways that open the idea of Queer Aztlán up for critique. I argue that these texts are not merely a "cripping" of the queer Chicana/o nation;[2] instead, they reveal that disability plays a crucial, yet unexamined, role in the very theoretical constitution of Queer Aztlán. In this sense, this chapter is both an extension and a complication of the previous chapter's work.

Even as *The Hungry Woman* and *Like Son* expose the political shortcomings of Queer Aztlán, neither text presents it as a project to be abandoned altogether. Instead, they depict Queer Aztlán as the sort of queer failure that Judith Halberstam has recently theorized: failure as "a way of refusing to acquiesce to dominant logics of power and discipline" (*Queer Art of Failure* 88), failure as a recognition "that alternatives are embedded already in the dominant and that power is never total or consistent" (88), failure as a means of exploiting "the unpredictability of ideology and its indeterminate qualities" (88). In other words, for Halberstam failure functions more as a point of departure than as an ending. Halberstam's theorization of failure draws extensively from the work of Latino queer theorist José Esteban Muñoz and has particular resonance with his notion of a concrete utopia—a utopia that is "relational to historically situated struggles" and reflects "the hopes of a collective, emergent group, or even the solitary oddball who is the one who dreams for many" (*Cruising Utopia* 3). In the work of Moraga and Lemus, disability is connected to the failure of the national project, but not through a tired ableist metaphor that links the nonnormative body to political crisis and, thus, to the impossibility of utopian nationalism. Instead, the nation's failure to fully recognize and accommodate corporeal variation is posited in both texts as the impetus for a sustained interrogation of the political usefulness of nationalism. In other words, bodily difference exposes the nation's failure to fully incorporate its citizens and, thus, to achieve its utopian promises, with the result that disability becomes the starting point for reevaluating queer cultural nationalism.

Like utopianism, nationalism is subject to charges of naïveté from scholars who see it as a theoretically impoverished concept. As Muñoz observes, it "is certainly difficult to argue for hope or critical utopianism at a moment when cultural analysis is dominated by an anti-utopianism often functioning as a poor substitute for actual critical intervention" (4). Along similar lines, cultural nationalism is often seen as a throwback to the political rhetoric of the 1960s. To many cultural critics, nationalism relies upon essentialist identity politics that reify categories of race, gender, sexuality, and ability. Moraga's work responds to this critique, depicting the search for a nationalism grounded in identity-based civil rights movements without glossing over the ways in which even counter-hegemonic nationalisms can reinforce boundaries and perpetuate logics of exclusion. Disability and bodily variations, moreover, function in Moraga's work as forms of difference that make nationalism's exclusionary tendencies impossible to ignore. Within mainstream rhetoric, meanwhile, cultural nationalisms are seen as divisive and separatist in a "post-race" society privileging ideals of "color blindness." Lemus, in response, reveals how race and racism remain salient even in a social environment that refuses to name them, challenging what Ramón Saldívar calls "the sanitized, casual, mainstream racism without racists of the postrace era US" ("Historical Fantasy" 576). In her work, disability is central to the project of remembering the continued injustices of a post–Civil Rights-era United States. For both writers, Queer Aztlán remains a necessity even as the danger of its failure looms. It is by addressing the possibility of its failure that they are able to retain Queer Aztlán as a politically significant, concrete queer utopia.

"A Failure Worth Knowing":
Moraga's Ambivalent Nationalism

The Hungry Woman is set in a "muy Blade-Runner-esque" (7) future, in which the United States has splintered into five smaller nation-states resulting from different ethnonationalist movements: the United States (or Gringolandia), Africa-America, the Mechicano Nation of Aztlán, the Union of Indian Nations, the Hawai'i Nation, and the confederacy of First Nations Peoples. In the border zone between Gringolandia and Aztlán is Tamoachán (formerly Phoenix, Arizona), to which the outcasts of each nation have been exiled. The Aztlán of *The Hungry Woman* is not Moraga's liberatory Queer Aztlán but the masculinist, heteronormative Aztlán of the early Chicano Movement, the Aztlán that writers like Islas and Moraga critique. Rather, if any of these fictitious territories is meant to stand in for Queer Aztlán, it is Tamoachán. The play's protagonist, Medea, is a former revolutionary, ex-wife of the nationalist leader Jasón; she has been exiled with her son Chac-Mool, her partner Luna, and her grandmother Mama Sal. As Patricia Ybarra describes her, Medea "is a warrior woman fallen by the wayside after being pushed out of her homeland. . . . Her fallenness is attitudinal rather than situational. Medea no longer has the optimism necessary to believe in the possibility of revolution, transformation, or incremental social change" ("Revolution Fails Here" 68). The play is staged largely in flashbacks, with the current action taking place in a psychiatric prison where an incarcerated Medea recalls the events leading to her imprisonment: Jasón has demanded the return of Chac-Mool to Aztlán; Chac-Mool has decided to go; and Medea has killed her son to avoid surrendering him to the patriarchal rule of Aztlán. At the end, Chac-Mool returns to assist Medea in her suicide.

The character of Medea—revolutionary warrior struggling with the loss of Aztlán and aging lover clinging to the memory of her youthful beauty—coalesces two concerns that surface throughout Moraga's intellectual trajectory, now in its fourth decade: nationalism and bodily difference. Her engagements with both have occasionally led to controversy. Moraga's nationalism, embraced for its bold queer claiming of the legacy of a major civil rights movement, El Movimiento Chicano, has also been read as essentialist. As Sandra K. Soto, a friendly reader of her work, has observed, it has resulted in her "occasional objectification of race, reification of binary oppositions, refusal to critique models of authenticity, and modernist-inflected concepts of power and resistance," aspects of her work that "can seem misguided" ("Cherríe Moraga's Going Brown" 238) to some critics. Christina Sharpe, a less friendly reader, charges that the nationalism of Moraga's writings from the 1990s onward abandons the woman-of-color coalitional feminism of her earlier work and specifically uses Black women to draw the boundary lines of her nation.

Similarly, the representation of disability in Moraga's work has been ambivalently received. For instance, her "Queer Aztlán" essay expresses the desire for a nation with "no 'freaks,' no others to point one's finger at" (164)—a passage that might be read not only as the desire for a nation with no "othering" ideologies but also, as the anonymous disability scholar who peer-reviewed my first publication on Moraga astutely pointed out to me, as the desire for a nation without disability.[3] Telory Davies has also argued that Moraga's commitment to an intersectional analysis of oppression ultimately collapses when "race takes precedence" over disability in her play *Heroes and Saints,* thereby "making disability more a metaphor than a reality" ("Race, Gender, and Disability" 29). Finally, although disability and transgender identity are not conflatable, scholars working on these issues have drawn from each other's theoretical frameworks, and as a result it is important to acknowledge here some of the controversial comments about gender transitioning that appear in Moraga's most recent book: "I know I *am* scared; scared that the political agenda of the transgender movement at large, and plain ole peer pressure, may prevent young people from simply residing in that queer, gender-ambivalent site for as long and as deeply as necessary. . . . I am scared when yet another student comes into my office to announce their planned breast removal over summer break" (*Xicana* 184, original emphasis). Before analyzing Moraga's critical engagement with bodily norms in *The Hungry Woman,* then, I will discuss the complicated representations of disability and nationalism in her work as a whole.

From the beginning, Moraga's writing has been shaped by an uneasy preoccupation with Chicano nationalism. Her essay "A Long Line of Vendidas," the most frequently cited piece from her first solo-authored book *Loving in the War Years: Lo que nunca pasó por sus labios* (1983), describes her exclusion from El Movimiento Chicano:

> During the late 60s and early 70s, I was not an active part of la causa. I never managed to get myself to walk in the marches in East Los Angeles (I merely watched from the sidelines); I never went to one meeting of MECHA on campus. No soy tonta. I would have been murdered in El Movimiento at the time—light-skinned, unable to speak Spanish well enough to hang; miserably attracted to women and fighting it; and constantly questioning all authority, including men's. (104)

The word *Aztlán* appears only twice in the first edition of *Loving,* once in the poem "Passage," from which the epigraph to this chapter is drawn, and once in the "Vendidas" essay.[4] Neither reference contains much nationalist idealism. "Passage" describes Aztlán as an unrealized dream ("es un sueño"), while "Vendidas" notes the danger of believing in Aztlán "so thoroughly and single-mindedly that finding solutions to present-day inequities loses priority, or we attempt to create too-easy solutions for the pain we feel today" (120). Yet Moraga also insists on her rightful place in the movement: "I fully knew that there was a part of me that was a part of that movement, but it seemed that part would have to go unexpressed until the time I could be a Chicano and be the woman I had to be, too" (104).

The contradictions in Moraga's early engagement with nationalism are exacerbated, not resolved, in her later work. Her 1989 play *Heroes and Saints*—the most frequently staged of her oeuvre—is read by numerous critics (including me) as her first overtly nationalist text.[5] The "Queer Aztlán" essay, published four years later in *The Last Generation* (1993), makes this nationalism explicit: "I cling to the word 'nation' because without the specific naming of the nation, the nation will be lost (as when feminism is reduced to humanism, the woman is subsumed)" (150). Less than a decade later, however, *The Hungry Woman* depicts the nation in collapse; Ybarra notes that the mood of the play, often perceived as "pessimistic" (84) by audiences, "contrasts sharply with the celebratory tone and projected future imagined in [the] 'Queer Aztlán' essay" (74). I argue, however, that despite its pessimistic tone, *The Hungry Woman* appears not as a repudiation of Queer Aztlán but rather as a confrontation with the body politics of nation-building that expands Queer Aztlán's theoretical and political possibilities. Yvonne Yarbro-Bejarano has insightfully observed that the "essay and the theater perform different functions in Moraga's work: the essays attempt to make sense of the contradictory aspects of her identity, especially the intersections of race and sexuality; her theatrical characters embody these contradictions" (*Wounded Heart* 27). Yarbro-Bejarano thus helps to explain how Moraga's plays can seem at times to work against her essays, since embodying contradictions can certainly turn out to be much messier than examining them in an essay. Indeed, *The Hungry Woman* reveals that the ruptures between queerness and nationalism that are apparently resolved by the phrase "Queer Aztlán" are not so easily sutured.

Like her representation of nationalism, Moraga's depiction of disability also resists easy classification. Her most widely read texts all contain prominent disability images. *Loving,* in particular, seeks political alliances among antiracist, feminist, and disability activists: "What the oppressor often succeeds in doing is simply *externalizing* his fears, projecting them into the bodies of women, Asians, gays, disabled folks, whoever seems most 'other'" (48). However, the mere mention of able-bodied discrimination does not necessarily mean that a text affirms the rights of people with disabilities, and other passages in Moraga's work are not so inclusive. Her memoir *Waiting in the Wings: Portrait of a Queer Motherhood* is a particularly salient example. Written at the same time as *The Hungry Woman*, it describes Moraga's pregnancy and the premature delivery of her son Rafael Angel. The text inscribes Moraga's fear that her son may not be "perfectly normal genetically" (31); at one point, she reports without critique the following statement from her mother: "When I was pregnant, I thought it wasn't even good to look at a deformed child" (59). Disability critics who embrace Moraga's work ignore these passages. For instance, Suzanne Bost argues that *Waiting* "suggests that we shift our desires from the self-defensiveness of health to the permeability of caregiving" (*Encarnación* 118). Yet in these passages, which Bost does not discuss, the "self-defensiveness of health" clearly supersedes "the permeability of caregiving." Despite these problems, Moraga's work represents a crucial set of texts for disability analysis because of its insistence on grounding political concerns in human bodies. As Moraga has noted: "my writings have always had bodies" (*Xicana* 36). The corporeal nature of her writing allows it to explore (even if imperfectly) the links between different forms of oppression and the resulting potential for political coalition.

Instead of criticizing Moraga (as in Davies) or uncritically celebrating her (as in Bost), the reading I propose seeks to account for *both* the productive uses of disability and the occasionally disquieting images that surface in her work. As Lisa Tatonetti succinctly reminds us, "Moraga's theoretical project is not about comfort" (228). With this in mind, I argue that Moraga's depictions of corporeal variation—what she calls "bodies of revolt, bodies in dissent against oblivion" (*Xicana* 41–42)—are intimately tied to her nationalism, which is both profoundly liberatory and potentially exclusionary. In *The Hungry Woman*, Moraga depicts Queer Aztlán as a political failure that nevertheless contains instructive possibilities. Muñoz suggests that even the work of politically flawed theorists can "create an opening in queer thought" (2); his investigations of queer utopias therefore makes the provocative gesture of engaging controversial theorists like Heidegger, whose work he describes as "a failure worth knowing, a potential that faltered but can nonetheless be reworked" (16). Moraga, even more provocatively, invokes *her own* theoretical concept as a "failure worth knowing," depicting Queer Aztlán as a concept that requires ongoing revision, expansion, and critique if it is to function as a truly liberatory political project.

The Hungry Woman draws simultaneously from the Greek myth of Medea, who kills her children, and from the story of Mexica/Aztec moon goddess Coyolxauhqui. For Moraga, both stories represent the "desire to kill patriarchal motherhood" (*Loving* 147). According to Mexica cosmography, Coyolxauhqui's mother, Coatlicue (the earth/fertility goddess) is cleaning a temple when she finds some feathers and places them in her apron. The feathers gestate, and Coatlicue becomes pregnant with Huitzilopochtli, the war/sun god. To prevent war from entering the world, Coyolxauhqui plots with her four hundred siblings to kill Coatlicue.[6] Huitzilopochtli learns of the plan and bursts forth from the womb in full warrior regalia, decapitates his sister, and dismembers the four hundred siblings. He throws Coyolxauhqui's head into the sky, where it becomes the moon, followed by the severed body parts of his other siblings, which become the stars. As Paula M.L. Moya describes it, the Coyolxauhqui story is both "a story of a mother who betrays her daughter by giving birth to her murderer" and also a story "of a daughter who betrays her mother by attempting to control, through matricide, her mother's fecundity and/or unsanctioned sexuality"; furthermore, "the rift between the mother and the daughter in this story symbolized the inauguration of Aztec warrior society . . . and affirmed an ideology of male dominance" ("Another Way to Be" 499). Coyolxauhqui's story is invoked in the prelude to *The Hungry Woman*:

This is how all stories begin and end
the innocence of an eagle feather
stuffed inside a mother's apron.

The birdboy growing there
taking shape.
The warrior son waiting in the wings
taking flight.

So, too begins and ends this story.
The birth of a male child
from the dark sea of Medea
at the dawning of an age. (9)

Although Coyolxauhqui's story is not told until the second act, the prologue establishes the birth of the "birdboy" into a culture privileging the "warrior son" as its central problem, critiquing a nationalism that "begins and ends" with the male warrior and not the mutilated daughter.

Coyolxauhqui appears (in various guises) in most of Moraga's writings. In the foreword to the second edition of *Loving,* she writes: "In 1977 when I wrote the first poems of what later would become part of *Loving in the War Years,* I had never heard of Coyolxauhqui, severed into pieces in the war against her brother, but I knew her brokenness" (iii). She defines the desire that animates her work: "Maybe I could re-member Coyolxauhqui at least in this writing, this teaching, this praying, this home" (vii). As Yarbro-Bejarano notes, Moraga often represents the mestiza lesbian body through "its fragmentation and the partial redefining of its parts, yet with a vision of a new way to be whole" (*Wounded Heart* 10). However, Moraga never fully reconstitutes this dismantled body but instead enacts "a process of making sense out of the rifts and splits of our shifting and multiple identity" to create "diverse disconnections and connections" (Yarbro-Bejarano, *Wounded Heart* 20). The re-membering of Coyolxauhqui is not a seamless recomposition of severed parts; rather, her "new way to be whole" leaves visible the scars of patriarchy.

The fact that Moraga begins *The Hungry Woman* with an invocation of Coyolxauhqui places the injured female body at the center of her interrogation of nationalism. To illuminate the significance of this gesture, it is helpful to compare Moraga's broken Coyolxauhqui to another prominent Chicana feminist rendering of the goddess: her image on the *Maestrapeace* mural adorning the San Francisco Women's Building in the Mission District of that city.[7] This image draws from the ancient Coyolxauhqui Stone on display at Mexico City's Templo Mayor, in which the dismembered body parts of the goddess are arranged on a circular stone, but depicts Coyolxauhqui whole with the stone shattered behind her. While the feminist implications of this rendering are clear, this restoration of corporeal wholeness resonates quite differently in a disability context than do Moraga's images, which do not strive to reinstate bodily completeness but leave visible the goddess's wounds. Indeed, while Moraga is not unique in her use of Coyolxauhqui as a symbol (the goddess is an important figure in Chicana feminist iconography), she is noteworthy for her consistent representation of the goddess *in her broken state*. For Moraga, the scarred or disfigured female body is a privileged site from which to envision a more just social order. As a result, the presence of Coyolxauhqui in Moraga's work—from her earliest, still-nameless appearances in *Loving* to the staging of her story in *The Hungry Woman*—puts Moraga in alliance (uneasy as that alliance may at times be) with feminist disability scholars, activists, and cultural workers seeking to represent the full variation of women's bodies as they are formed and de-formed by heteropatriarchy, racism, and able-bodied supremacy. Her work, moreover, calls not for a facile healing of the wounds (physical and emotional) that result from injustice, but rather for a community that can embrace the wounded.

The difference between a community that can incorporate bodily differences and emotional damages resulting from injurious oppression and one that cannot is visible in *The Hungry Woman*'s two primary settings: the prison psychiatric ward and Tamoachán. As Bost notes, the prison ward's function as "hospital, insane asylum, and prison" exposes the heteropatriarchal management of women's bodies and social roles, reflecting "the normalizing, juridical function of medicine as well as the . . . demonization of any female role beyond that of 'good' mother" (*Encarnación* 134). Tamoachán, meanwhile, is described in the play's opening notes as "the dumping site of every kind of poison and person unwanted by its neighbors" (6). The city resembles Gloria Anzaldúa's famous description of the Borderlands: "*Los atravesados* live here: the squint-eyed, the perverse, the queer, the troublesome, the mongrel, the mulato, the half-breed, the half dead; in short, those who cross over, pass over, or go through the confines of the 'normal'" (*Borderlands/ La Frontera* 25). Tamoachán seems to have little resonance with anything that might be described as utopian. Yet although its potential is unrealized, Tamoachán represents a site of potential alliance among its "unwanted" inhabitants. Medea's grandmother Mama Sal offers a description of the city that resonates with Muñoz's conceptualization of a concrete queer utopia: "Y los homos became peregrinos . . . como nomads, just like our Aztec ancestors a thousand years ago. . . . And the seeking itself became home" (24). This notion of *seeking as home* reflects what Muñoz calls "a kernel of possibility within a stultifying heterosexual present" (*Cruising Utopia* 49). Tamoachán is *not* a full-fledged utopia because its residents remain restricted by the laws of Aztlán and Gringolandia, but within their potential to forge a new collectivity in the wake of their shared exclusion exists a latent utopian possibility. As the home of the "unwanted," Tamoachán represents the site of a potentially disabled *and* queer future.

Medea, however, is unable to recognize Tamoachán's potential; throughout the play, she clings instead to a melancholic longing for Aztlán and for the young, perfect body she possessed when she lived there. The play's first scene depicts Medea in the prison ward, lamenting the signs of her age. She describes herself as "red-eyed, crows feet drooping," and mourns that her "chin is dropping," that her "face is falling into my throat," and that her "eyelids are falling" (Moraga, *Hungry Woman* 12). Medea's vanity is discussed repeatedly throughout the first act of the play. She reminds Luna of her fading beauty, recalling her "hair the silky darkness of a raven's" (41) and "spectacular thighs" (42). This nostalgia for corporeal perfection parallels her nostalgia for the dream of a whole, perfect Aztlán: "I had always imagined we'd return to Aztlán one day with my son grown. I thought they'd change their mind, say it was all a mistake" (43). Medea repeatedly expresses unhappiness with what she calls the "wasteland" (15) of Tamoachán, "with all of this . . . failure" (49). Here she echoes Jasón, who calls Tamoachán a "wasteland of counter-revolutionary degenerates" (69), indicating that although she has left Jasón and Aztlán behind, she has not fully abandoned the ideology of ability to which they adhere.[8] Crucially, the only bodily imperfections she voluntarily displays are wounds sustained in fighting for Aztlán, her "trail of scars from shoulder to wrist bone" (27); the scars that link her to the patriarchal nation remain a source of pride, while the bodily markers that reveal her age (declining fitness as a warrior and loss of the ability to birth more warriors for the nation) are a source of shame. Medea's failure, then, ensues not only from her loss of optimism about social change (as Ybarra notes) but also from her inability to accept imperfection of either body or nation. Mary Pat Brady describes Moraga's work as notable for its refusal to "sentimentalize the past" or to traffic in "nostalgia for 'the whole and the one'" (*Extinct Lands* 152). In *The Hungry Woman,* the nostalgia for wholeness is Medea's downfall.

Luna, on the other hand, provides a stark contrast to Medea. Medea describes Luna as "born" to "transgress those boundaries" (Moraga, *Hungry Woman* 46) of sexuality and nation. While Luna resents being forced to "live in the fuckin' colony of my so-called liberators" (48), she does not despise her life in the "queer ghetto" (48) as Medea does; unlike Medea, she does not "hate it here that much" (49). Crucially, too, Luna likes best the bodily imperfections that Medea detests: "I always liked that tiny fold hanging over Medea's eyes. . . . I liked how that little mistake made her face less perfect. There's something to read in that. Nothing's printed in perfection" (14). Luna represents what Muñoz describes as the utopian impulse behind queerness: "Queerness could and should be about a desire for another way of being in both the world and time, a desire that resists mandates to accept that which is not enough" (*Cruising Utopia* 96). For Luna, Medea's imperfections represent the possibility of another way of being, one not defined by the patriarchal, heterosexist norms that govern Aztlán. From this perspective, Medea's aging body represents the possibility of a concrete utopia; the tragedy of the play resides in her refusal to recognize it as such.

The play's depiction of lesbian sex makes clear the political significance of Luna's queer desire for Medea's aging, female, racialized body. As Yarbro-Bejarano notes: "In Moraga's writing, the representation of lesbian sex . . . explores the impact of socially defined power dynamics" (*Wounded Heart* 85). The potential for representations of lesbian sexuality to disrupt regimes of domination is an issue further explored by Moraga herself in an essay from the second edition of *Loving*. Here she describes the experience of seeing Tony Kushner's play *Angels in America* on Broadway and recognizing the absence of colonized women's bodies on mainstream stages:

> I did a little private experiment. Every time I heard the word or a reference to "Jewish dick," I replaced it with "Mexican pussy." Jewish dick . . . Mexican pussy. Jewish dick . . . Mexican pussy. Jewish dick . . . Mexican pussy. And nobody was laughing. That's me on Broadway. That's my people on Broadway. That chilling silence. Nobody is laughing. Pussy ain't funny unless a man tells the joke. Mexican ain't funny unless a gringo's talking. Put a Mexican woman downstage center wanting some pussy and nobody's gonna laugh, unless she is laughed at, i.e., ridiculed, objectified, scorned. *And who the hell's gonna*

translate that Spanglish those Chicanos speak anyway? (*Loving* 157, original emphasis)

For Moraga, the erasure of the colonized woman's body and sexuality from the stage (and the page, and the screen, and the art gallery) is a reflection of the removal of colonized people from the territory they inhabit, visible in the ongoing struggles over Native land rights and in the effort to expel Central American and Mexican immigrants from U.S. national space. It is nothing less than collusion with the violent policing of the contours of the U.S. body politic.

Written around the same time as the essay quoted above, *The Hungry Woman* contains a scene entitled "Before the Fall. Mexican Pussy" (60). This scene puts Mexican pussy onstage and represents that most intimate—and most "ridiculed, objectified, scorned"—part of the racialized female body as a site of utopian possibility. It reflects Yarbro-Bejarano's argument that "fear, pain, and difficulty" are "important in Moraga's writing, even as she retains the utopian impulse necessary to imagine alternative sexualities and social relations" (*Wounded Heart* 90). The scene is a flashback, interrupting another in which Luna is stopped at the border after going to Aztlán. By framing the sex scene in this way, the play makes clear that female sexuality—including lesbian sexuality—is always circumscribed by heteropatriarchal social relations (represented by the border controlling Luna's access to Aztlán). *The Hungry Woman* thus depicts the sex between Luna and Medea as revolutionary without idealizing it. The scene begins when Medea finds Luna examining her vulva with a mirror and continues with the women describing their most intimate body parts to each other as worthy of love. It is quite explicit: Luna tells Medea, "I love your pussy" (61), and Medea describes Luna's sex to her by saying "I see beauty" (61). Their dialogue exemplifies Moraga's commitment to representing devalued bodies as valuable, rejecting the body politics of exclusionary nationalism. Yet this moment is fleeting. At the end of the scene, Luna's consciousness shifts abruptly back to the border where she is detained. In response to the border guard's demand that she confess her lesbianism, Luna states: "By the end, it was a mindless reflex. The desire was gone from us months before or was it years? We fought about it. We slept as sisters" (62). This is not, however, the failure of their woman-centered desire but rather an acknowledgement of the power of the heteropatriarchal social norms that threaten it. The memory of the desire—and the hope of reclaiming it—ensure the continuation of utopian potential, even in the face of that power.

The Hungry Woman concludes, as mentioned, with Medea killing her son and then herself; she does not return triumphantly to Aztlán with Chac-Mool. As a result, the play appears to end with the political failure of both Aztlán and Tamoachán: Aztlán because its inhabitants have refused to recognize the error of policing its body politic to the point of casting out warriors (like Medea), Tamoachán because of the nostalgia for wholeness that haunts its residents (like Medea). The ending of the play thus echoes a question Moraga poses in the "Queer Aztlán" essay, one that also reflects an urgent concern at the heart of disability studies: *"how will our lands be free if our bodies aren't?"* (*Last Generation* 173, original emphasis). *The Hungry Woman* exposes the consequences of leaving this question unanswered, of attempting to decolonize without facing the question of what it might mean to fully embrace the bodies (and body parts) most rejected and wounded in an oppressive social order. If the work of Halberstam and Muñoz together suggests that imagining liberation is futile without adequately theorizing queer utopia and addressing the possibility of its failure, Moraga reveals how paying attention to bodies and bodily norms forces an acknowledgment of the ways in which liberatory nationalism continues to fail. Furthermore, in order for the queer utopian potential of Queer Aztlán to be realized, a disability sensibility must also help to shape it.

Even at its most nationalist, Moraga's work treats Aztlán as potentially dangerous and always at risk of failure. The "Queer Aztlán" essay, for instance, characterizes the dominant version of Chicano nationalism as marred by "its institutionalized heterosexism, its inbred machismo, and its lack of a cohesive national political strategy" (*Last Generation* 148–49); it acknowledges nationalism's "tendency toward separatism [that] can run dangerously close to biological determinism and a kind of fascism" (149). In a frequently cited passage from *Waiting*, she writes: "Nation. Nationality. I am to be the mother of a Mexican baby. I am the worst and best of those macho Chicano nationalists. I picked a man for his brains and dark beauty. And the race continues" (39). What critics often fail to note in their analyses of this passage, however, is that even here Moraga retreats from uncritically claiming this nationalism by the end of the paragraph, which concludes with a much less frequently cited disclaimer: "We try to get what we can on paper, to protect ourselves against pain, against loss, but the papers don't protect us. Neither can a nation" (39). Moraga thus represents her own nationalism in a self-critical way, as an unrealized (and possibly unachievable) utopian possibility that may disappoint but nonetheless presents a continued effort to envision a liberated future. Wounds, scars, and bodily imperfections are a central component of Moraga's nationalism; it is the consistent privileging of nonnormative and vulnerable bodies, bodies in chronic pain, bodies that show signs of age, bodies with visible scars, that gives Moraga's nationalism its potential for radical inclusivity. This is the case even when (as her critics charge) that potential is not fully realized within her work.

Genderqueer Aztlán: Lemus's Post-Punk Nationalist Nostalgia

Lemus does not pepper her prose with "typical" Chicano nationalist literary tropes. Her characters listen to 1990s hardcore-influenced bands like Fugazi and Bikini Kill, clothe themselves in "post-teen skater slop" (*Like Son* 14) purchased at thrift stores, eat "tofu scramble" (118) for breakfast, and live in neighborhoods like Los Angeles's Silver Lake and New York's East

Village; their social milieu is middle-class, mostly college-edu-
cated, and (on the surface at least) effortlessly racially integrated.
The gentrified Los Angeles full of queer punk bars and UCLA
grad students pictured in her first two novels—2003's *Trace Elements of Random Tea Parties* and 2007's *Like Son*—is markedly
different from the East L.A. depicted in more canonical (and
more nationalist) Chicana/o texts like Luis Rodríguez's 1993
memoir *Always Running* or Gregory Nava's 1995 film *My Family*.
(Indeed, it is quite unlike Moraga's own Califas, Aztlán.) Nonetheless, a hallmark of Lemus's work is its queer appropriation of
figures from Mexican cultural history (La Llorona in *Trace Elements,* Nahui Olin in *Like Son),* and her novels subtly interrogate
the construction of Chicana/o identity by rejecting facile notions
of Mexican cultural authenticity. Although she does not explicitly engage with Moraga's Queer Aztlán, then, Lemus provides
an opportunity to consider the concept's usefulness as a her-
meneutic for examining the work of younger queer Chicana/o
writers. *Like Son,* with its emphasis on both transgender identity and disability, significantly extends and expands the work of
earlier queer Chicana/o writers; it reimagines not only the body
politic of Aztlán (as in the work of her queer predecessors Islas
and Moraga) but also that of Queer Aztlán. In fact, its focus on
a transgender protagonist makes it a particularly appropriate
case study for considering the possibility of expanding Queer
Aztlán's liberatory potential, given Moraga's own controversial
statements on the subject; it provides an opportunity to consider
how a concept like Queer Aztlán can be employed in ways not
necessarily imagined by its author.

Both of Lemus's novels focus on queer romantic relationships,
most of them interracial; in this, her work seems to depart from
that of Moraga, which has moved away from representations of
interraciality.[9] Yet from Islas to Terri de la Peña to Michael Nava,
interracial desire has played a central role in Chicana/o queer
fiction.[10] While interraciality might seem to signal a rejection
of Chicano nationalism, the work of Stefanie Dunning on Black
queer interraciality suggests something more complicated: "In

all the texts I analyze, an interracial experience functions to stage blackness for the protagonist. In some texts, racial essentialism is disavowed and the interracial relationship operates in positive ways; others stage the interracial relationship, critique it, and then reject it. . . . But they are all in dialogue with black nationalism about the place of the black queer subject in the nation" (*Queer in Black and White* 8). Lemus's characters navigate an ostensibly "post-racial" queer landscape but also negotiate the legacy of Mexican American history, including the Bracero Program and the racial inequalities of the military draft. In this way, Lemus's characters reinforce Dunning's sense that although the idea of interraciality as harmonious blending "has been both the fear and the hope of all kinds of people on either side of the issue" (12), its representation in cultural texts often functions instead to reify racial difference. This is particularly true of *Like Son*, in which racial identities are mediated through characters' starkly differing experiences of gendered and (dis)abled embodiment. As a result, although Lemus's work does not directly address Chicana/o nationalism, its concern with the social salience of race (especially within intimate, romantic settings) engages with a long-standing ethnonationalist preoccupation.

Like Son follows its protagonist, FTM transgender Chicano Frank Guerrero Cruz, from his early 20s to age 30. During this period, Frank reunites with his dying father, parts ways with his abusive mother, leaves Los Angeles for a fresh start in New York City, and falls in love with the "gorgeous, addictively engaging, ballsy" Nathalie (98). Throughout, Frank is accompanied by the spirit of Mexican revolutionary poet Nahui Olin, who also turns out to be his grandmother's ex-lover: "Communist. Radical feminist. Fucked whomever she wanted to. . . . Scandalized her barrio" (109). Just before his death, Frank's father gives him a portrait of Nahui Olin and a book of her poems, "making sure I'd have a retablo of a surrogate saint to turn to in my sadness" (31). Although he initially wonders if he will ever love "a fire-eyed girl like Nahui" (32), Frank soon recognizes "Nahui's stare"

(98) upon meeting Nathalie. Like the seven-year relationship between Medea and Luna, the seven-year relationship between Frank and Nathalie contains moments of utopian possibility: "So yes, *duh,* it made little sense that she basically moved in the night we met, but logic to hell, being together felt more right than anything either of us had ever known. And so, happy brick by brick, we built a fantasy fort to live in together. Our fort had invisible walls. We were absolutely everything in our fort. We needed nothing else" (102). As in *The Hungry Woman,* however, this utopian possibility is eventually disappointed: "we woke one day to find that the fantasy fort we'd built and mortared with repetition had been smashed by a wrecking ball as we slept" (117). Nathalie twice abandons Frank with no warning and pretends to have the same degenerative eye condition as Frank's father. The novel ends with Frank and Nathalie reuniting after Nathalie's second disappearance, but offers no reassurance that their reconciliation is permanent.

Through Frank's relationship with Nathalie, which seems to repeat Nahui Olin's relationship to his grandmother and his father's relationship to his mother, *Like Son* establishes issues of heritage and inheritance as central themes. The novel examines these three relationships in order to explore the links between personal family history and the political history of the nation. It opens with a prologue that takes place chronologically at the end of the narrative, depicting Frank waiting for Nathalie at the Temperance Fountain in Tompkins Square Park in New York City. The fountain is a "distant cousin to the crumbling WPA fountain my father courted my mother at before they totally hated each other" and is also "not so entirely unlike the Mexico City fountain where my father's mother sat when she broke Nahui Olin's heart" (9). The novel thus sets itself up as a "family cycle come full circle" (9). It begins in 1995 on Ash Wednesday, with the 22-year-old Frank reunited with his dying father, vowing to be "the perfect son" (25) for the rest of his father's days; it ends on Ash Wednesday in 2003 with Frank trying to stay with Nathalie. In this way, the text suggests a kind of political futility—a family legacy of crumbling monuments, broken hearts, and affairs that end with the lovers "totally hating each other," a legacy unaffected by political upheavals like the Mexican Revolution and the New Deal. The novel's title, evoking the phrase "like father, like son," suggests a destructive political cycle secured by patriarchal social relations and maintained by what Lee Edelman famously calls reproductive futurity. Yet, as Yarbro-Bejarano observes in her analysis of *Trace Elements,* the complex temporalities employed in Lemus's fiction subvert this facile interpretation, for her novels engage two simultaneous trajectories, "the linear one moving forward from beginning to end, and the one bringing past events into the present of the narration" ("Queer Storytelling" 74).

Therefore, I will argue here that the novel does not depict Frank's continuation of the family legacy but rather his struggle to escape it. The similarities between Frank and his father go beyond their history of attraction to dangerous women like Nahui Olin and Nathalie. First, both share the experience of nonnormative embodiment: Frank as a transgender man; his father as a blind man. Second, both share a complicated relationship to the idea of national belonging and to the documents that regulate it. The relationship between Frank and his father suggests that citizenship and national belonging are governed, expressed, and enacted not only by sexual norms (as Moraga's "Queer Aztlán" essay argues) but also by bodily norms. However, just as the sexuality Frank inherits from his father (the attraction to fiery, destructive women) proves harmful, so too does the relationship to norms of embodiment, institutionalized through citizenship, that Frank's father also passes on. Frank, as a result, is charged with finding a way to love his father while avoiding his legacy—in other words, with seeking a new way of securing political belonging that does not require capitulating to the harmful bodily and sexual norms that regulate citizenship. I argue, then, that the novel's title should be read not as an invocation but rather as a truncation of the expression "like father, like son." Just as Lemus breaks the expression in half to create the title *Like Son*, Frank breaks the family cycle. At the end, Frank is definitively not "like father."

Both Frank and his father believe themselves to be "failed" by their bodies. Frank's father has the degenerative eye condition retinitis pigmentosa, which causes his blindness, as well as intestinal cancer, which causes his death; Frank, who is masculine-gendered, is born female. In fact, it is Frank's female body that prevents him from inheriting his father's blindness: "The blindness affected only males, my father said. But female offspring of the blind generation carried the gene and could pass the blindness to their male children" (23). Despite a lifetime of experience that might seem to suggest otherwise, Frank's father believes in the perfectibility of the human body through medical intervention, proclaiming that Frank need not pass the condition on to his children: "Really, Paquita, it's amazing what science can control" (25). His declaration, however, is belied by the feminine-gendered nickname he uses for his son. Because Frank has not revealed his gender identity to his father, his father does not comprehend the irony of proclaiming to his biologically female son that "science can control" the human body. Frank, therefore, cannot share his father's faith in the possibility of corporeal perfection: "There we were, living proof to the contrary. My chromosomes defined me as a daughter. And cancer was irreversibly sabotaging my father on the most essential of cellular levels. Our bodies were failing us in ways science could never entirely repair" (25). What Frank must learn in the course of the novel—and what his father never learns—is how to live with the "failure" of the human body instead of expecting science to control or repair it.

Frank and his father represent what disability theorist Lennard Davis calls two different "ethics of the body" (22)—one predicated on overcoming its limitations and one predicated on accommodating its limitations and recognizing them as the basis for a new form of political belonging. The difference between these approaches to embodiment are exemplified in a scene in which Frank assists his dying father with his colostomy bags.[11] Frank's father objects: "I can't do this. I can't. . . . You shouldn't have to do this either" (26). Frank acknowledges his distaste for the task but nonetheless accepts it: "I loved my father. Dearly. And I wanted to help. In any way possible. I'd take as many days off work as I could without getting fired. I'd fucking get fired if I had to. I'd really do anything" (27). To use Davis's terminology, Frank's father subscribes to an ethics of the body that emphasizes "care *for* the body" (27)—the management and control of disease and disability through submission to the health care industry. Frank, on the other hand, is guided by an ethics of "caring *about* the body" (28), which leads him to recognize "how all groups, based on physical traits or markings, are selected for disablement by a larger system of regulation and signification" (29). Although Frank does not completely reject the troubling idea of his body as "failed," then, he sees that failure as cultural and political, as rooted in the refusal of his society to accommodate his body, instead of as scientific or biological—in other words, he does not see his body as a flaw that he must fix.

In addition to their nonnormative embodiment, Frank and his father also share a conflicted relationship to citizenship and to the documents that regulate it. For Frank's father, this conflict stems from the fact that he grows up in Mexico, unaware that he is a U.S. citizen until he is drafted to fight in the Vietnam War: "And, unbelievable as it may have seemed, it was true—he really hadn't known he was a U.S. citizen until he was drafted. He also hadn't known until he was eighteen that when his mother was pregnant with him, his family had gone north as *braceros* to build railroads" (19). U.S. citizenship for him entails not a set of rights and benefits but a troubled relationship that commences when "the U.S. government took the farm tools from [his] hands, forced him to report to San Diego for processing, taught him how to shoot a rifle, and shipped him to a jungle in Vietnam" (21). Frank, for very different reasons, is similarly accustomed to having his identity questioned. Presenting his driver's license to a Wells Fargo bank employee, he finds that the document that is supposed to prove his legal identity offers very few guarantees:

"As he stared at it, his thick face pinched into a confused mess of wrinkles. He looked up at me. Then back at my license. The photo had been taken when I was sixteen and far less of a man. The name on that little laminated plastic card read: *Francisca Guerrero. Sex: F*" (46). Both Frank and his father, then, share the status of what Mae Ngai calls alien citizenship—"a condition of racial otherness, a badge of foreignness that could not be shed" (*Impossible Subjects* 8) regardless of citizenship status. *Like Son* suggests that gender and disability, like race, constitute "conditions of otherness" that function as mechanisms of political exclusion.

Through meticulous descriptions of each character's clothing (a source of particular pleasure for fashion-conscious readers), *Like Son* also reveals the quotidian ways in which Frank and his father seek to mitigate the effects of alien citizenship. After the war, Frank's father decides "to embark on his newfound birthright: the American Dream" (21), but even years later the traces of his uncertain relationship to the country of his birth remain visible. He dresses "like a Hitchcock flick leading man" (14) in a three-piece suit, fedora, and wingtips; he goes to the barber once a week and shaves twice daily. When Frank, as a child, asks his father why he dresses so formally, his father replies: "Don't ever let anyone call you a lazy wetback" (15). Frank's father's clothing, then, is a way of claiming the cultural citizenship that racism continues to deny him. Although Frank's clothing is much more informal than his father's, he, too, dresses to convey his claim to a social category in which he is believed not to belong. Frank refers to his clothing as a "careful staging" (18) designed to render his gender identity consistently legible: "a baggy long-sleeved black T-shirt over a tight Hanes undershirt over a wifebeater over an extra-small binder; boxers peeking out from under low-slung over-sized black Dickies cinched with an Army surplus belt; a bulky dark gray hoody sweatshirt, hood down" (18). Although it might be tempting to read the novel's emphasis on clothing solely as evidence of race and gender as performed social categories, I would suggest that this elaborate costuming on the part of both characters reveals instead the materiality of discriminatory social practices. Because of the ways in which their bodies are (to use Davis's terminology) "selected for disablement" by a social environment that refuses to accommodate the differences they represent, both characters are profoundly attentive to the social norms that govern self-presentation and self-fashioning. In effect, then, the attention placed on clothing by Frank and his father demonstrates the profound social salience of the bodily norms that classify people according to race, gender, and ability.

These bodily norms have a crucial impact on Frank's relationship with Nathalie. Although Nathalie's race and ability are never definitively named in the text, numerous clues suggest that she is an able-bodied, cis-gendered white woman. She has freckled skin that flushes easily, auburn hair, and a Jewish mother; Frank is surprised to learn that she speaks Spanish. These traits alone, however, are not definitive markers of race, especially considering that Frank does not consider himself to "look 'Mexican'" (57). More revealing of Nathalie's social identity than her physical description, ancestry, or linguistic ability is this revelation:

[F]or all of Nathalie's wanting and needing everything
to be so fantastically hyperbolic and transgressive all the
time, for all her perpetual 1920s party attire and zany
observations and bizarre take on etiquette, no matter how
much she wanted to think she and I and her life entire
were some sort of brilliant freak show, I'd come to learn
exactly what Nathalie was. She was normal. Just plain ol'
potentially boring N-O-R-M-A-L. Seriously, strip away all
the pyrotechnics and you'd find nothing truly revolutionary about Nathalie's revolution. She wanted a happy home.
She wanted a man to love. And she wanted her man to love
her. Passionately. Devotedly. She wanted that day in and
day out. But, I also knew with absolute certainty, nothing scared Nathalie more than how thoroughly normal she
really was. (110–11)

Unlike Frank and his father, who dress in ways that mitigate the bodily markers that exclude them from the category of the "normal," Nathalie dresses to distance herself from it. They fear the repercussions of being seen as *not* normal; she fears being seen as normal. Her character in many ways reflects Michael Warner's critique of the "embrace of the normal" (60), which results in "the betrayal of the abject and the queer in favor of a banalized respectability" (66) and which ultimately "desexualizes the [queer] movement and depoliticizes queer sex" (66). However, while Nathalie is right to fear the normal, what she fails to note is how an uncritical embrace of the "not-normal" can also be a depoliticizing gesture when it fails to recognize the specific histories through which the lines of normal and not-normal are drawn. In other words, Nathalie embraces the nonnormativity of 1920s party attire, zany observations, and her partner's gender-nonconforming, racialized body without sufficient attention to the effects of her antics or her partner's experience in his body.

As the novel progresses, Frank grows increasingly impatient with Nathalie's insistence on "transgression," as evidenced when she decides that she and Frank will march with the Socialist delegation of a peace march: "Since when were we Socialists? I mean, I know marching with the proto-Commies sounded sexy, but wouldn't it have been more honest to march with Democrats or the Green Party or even just the Lower East Side contingent? Whatever" (175). Frank's resistance to marching with the Socialists here might appear conservative. However, Karen Tongson's critique of hipster aesthetics is helpful for understanding not only this response but also Frank's general discomfort with Nathalie's facile disavowal of normalcy. Tongson's work examines queer-of-color cultural workers who, "instead of using humor or irony to make themselves distinct, or to stand out and apart from the popular mainstream, ... cull from the popular to forge unlikely sociabilities, relationships, and alliances between themselves and the spheres of living and referentiality they are meant to be excluded from" (*Relocations* 15). Indeed, by inhabiting spheres that are predicated on exclusion, queers of color and people with nonnormative bodies can in their very presence transform them. This is the initial insight behind Moraga's "Queer Aztlán" essay, which suggests that Aztlán becomes something different when it embraces its queerfolk. Frank's frustrated "whatever" to marching with the Socialists, then, is not a disagreement with their politics but discomfort with Nathalie's tendency to embrace and appropriate difference without actually attending to its societal implications, as well as with her refusal to understand inhabiting less conspicuously "transgressive" spaces as also potentially radicalizing.

Despite Nathalie's fear of her own normalcy, she continues to enjoy the privileges it affords, a fact that becomes viscerally apparent during a moment of national crisis. The first sign of trouble in the lovers' relationship surfaces on September 11, 2001, when Nathalie's sense of national belonging asserts itself: "Nathalie leaned on my side, she huddled into me. And she shook. She rattled, actually. And sobbed. She cried enough for the both of us. This was her job, I guess, because I couldn't cry. Tears and emotions were nowhere forthcoming for me" (118). Although the novel never explicitly addresses the reason for this disparity in their responses to the national tragedy, it is not difficult to trace Frank's lack of response back to his memories of his father's rants "about how Vietnam had never been his war to fight, about how he'd grown up in Mexico with no clue he'd been born in the States, so why should he have had to go to war for this country?" (19). Nathalie, who does not question her national identity, feels a much more personal investment in mourning the national tragedy; Frank, whose father's military service never guarantees the sense of national belonging that citizenship purports to provide, does not. Frank's discomfort grows when Nathalie decides to adopt the Mexican custom of creating a Day of the Dead altar for the 9/11 victims: "Untraditional Mexican-descendent jerk that I was, I'd never even thought of making an altar for my father. . . . She wanted to set up an altar in our apartment for people she didn't even know" (121–22). Frank, who has never experienced an unequivocal sense of belonging in either the United States or Mexico, is uncomfortable with both the state-sponsored post-9/11 national mourning rituals and Mexican domestic mourning practices, while Nathalie feels comfortable assuming both.

Frank's discomfort with Nathalie's fear of normalcy grows when Nathalie finds his father's dark glasses and begins to use them (along with his cane) as ironic hipster fashion accessories: "I wasn't angry exactly, but I felt violated on a cellular level somehow" (173). Here he uses the same phrase ("cellular level") that he employs to describe the cancer that kills his father. However, there is a crucial difference in this usage. Frank's father feels his body invaded on a cellular level by disease; he fears his own body. Frank feels invaded on a cellular level by Nathalie, by her fetishization of the not-normal and its unintended reinforcement of the privilege of the normal. Frank is particularly disturbed when Nathalie insists on using the glasses and cane in public: "The entire way I was terrified we might cross paths with an actual blind person. Obviously, they wouldn't be able to see us if we did, but man, talk about rude. It would have been a seriously shameful moment" (178). Nathalie fails to see how the differences between her embodiment and that of Frank's father are attached to social relations, power, and privilege. Her blithe use of the glasses coincides with her refusal to recognize Frank's bodily difference. She begins to ask Frank if they can have a baby, willfully ignoring the fact that he cannot father children: "Did she really want me to delineate the obvious out loud? . . . Nathalie knew that having a baby wouldn't just be prenatal vitamins from the corner pharmacy and don't use a condom for a few months" (174). Against Nathalie's desire to portray as negligible the effects of race, nationality, disability, and gender, a desire characteristic of a society that defines itself as postracial and post-oppression, the text reveals how these categories continue to have a very real effect on the most intimate of personal relationships.

Although Frank and Nathalie never explicitly discuss the differences of race, gender expression, and ability that differentiate them, *Like Son* therefore reinforces an observation Dunning

has made about interracial Black queer texts: "we can understand interraciality as a metaphor which works to consolidate
black identity rather than compromise it, exposing the black
subject's location *within* blackness" (*Queer in Black and White*
16, original emphasis). Despite Frank's uneasy relationship to
Chicana/o identity—his previously cited sense that he does not
"look Mexican" and characterization of himself as an "untraditional Mexican-descendent jerk"—he nonetheless possesses a
set of experiences that are very different from Nathalie's. The
Chicana/o identity consolidated in the text, however, is not
an essentialized, inherited identity but one acquired through
the accumulation of experience. It is, furthermore, an identity
mediated through sexuality, gender expression, and disability.
As a result, despite the fact that Frank himself never overtly
claims an identity grounded in Queer Aztlán (and despite the
fact that he himself would likely greet the concept with a post-
teen, skater-slang pronouncement of *"whatever"*), his search for
an identity that simultaneously locates him within Chicanismo
and accounts for his nonnormative embodiment represents precisely the political impulse behind Moraga's initial theorization
of Queer Aztlán.

Nonetheless, despite Frank's apparent embodiment of Queer
Aztlán, the end of the novel appears to repudiate the concept.
Confronted with Nathalie's second disappearance, Frank goes
to California before returning to meet Nathalie at the Temperance Foundatain and take her home. While in California, he
buries his father's cane and glasses on the beach: "I dug a hole
three feet deep in the moist sand near the ocean's edge. And in
that hole I placed my father's glasses and folded walking stick.
Handfuls of sand patted over his things in the small grave, I
buried the ill-chosen tokens" (261–62). Frank literally abandons
and buries the family history that has not only fomented conflict
in his relationship with Nathalie but has also provided him with
a link to his identity. Leaving his father's prosthetics buried in
the sand, he appears to foreclose the possibility that his father's
legacy might play a positive role in his future—in other words,

to bury the potentiality of Queer Aztlán. Nathalie, meanwhile, relinquishes nothing as she merrily totters back into Frank's life on her fabulous vintage heels. The ending of *Like Son*, in other words, appears at first glance to fail, and so too does Queer Aztlán.

Another way to read the ending, however, is to see Frank's burial of his father's effects as a way of safeguarding them against Nathalie's mis-use. In this reading, Frank allows Nathalie back into his life, but only on the condition that she stop using him and his father to turn her life into "some sort of brilliant freak show." This reading would emphasize Frank's words to Nathalie as they meet by the fountain: "'Nat,' I took a deep breath, 'don't leave again'" (265). Here we might emphasize that instead of uncomfortably acquiescing to Nathalie's bizarre whims—as he does when she uses the glasses and cane—Frank is now asserting his own agency and identity within the relationship.

Still a third way to read the ending—not entirely incompatible with the alternate reading proposed above—is to emphasize that it is extremely difficult to be happy with the ending of *Like Son*; Frank's return to Nathalie after all of her actions (many of which could be construed as emotional abuse) is distressing.[12] If we read the ending—containing as it does the possibility that Frank and Nathalie will stay together—as an intentionally unhappy one, we might see Frank's final act of burying his father's belongings as emblematic of the consequences of abandoning the utopian possibility of queer and decolonial nationalism. A truly liberatory movement predicated on a queer and disabled Aztlán is foreclosed in order to secure the happy endings of Nathalie's *normalcy*; what remains in its place is an emotionally unsatisfying relationship. Read in this way, *Like Son* functions as a cautionary tale about the consequences of prematurely abandoning—instead of working to redefine and reformulate—the liberatory possibility of Queer Aztlán.

Because of the potential for nationalism to coincide with exclusionary or essentialist forms of identity politics, the concept of

Queer Aztlán has sparked some debate within Chicana/o queer studies. Chicano nationalism has endured feminist and queer critique since the circulation of its best-known manifesto *El Plan Espiritual de Aztlán*,[13] and these critiques have led some to question whether the concept is worth reformulating and reclaiming. Catriona Rueda Esquibel explains the complex relationship between Chicana lesbian cultural representations and Chicano cultural nationalism: "In some instances, this representation poses a strong challenge to nationalist ideology. In other instances, it attempts to reconfigure the nation, and often it is itself created in and through nationalist desire and longing" (*With Her Machete* 148). As Esquibel notes, queer women of color have been some of the earliest and best-known theoretical architects of the rejection of "nationalist rhetoric that continues to be used against women, against gays and lesbians, and in the service of male privilege" (148), making the "nationalist desire and longing" of writers like Moraga surprising and even controversial.

Yet Chicana/o nationalism retains its urgency—and continues to function as a framework for reading the work of younger writers, including Lemus—because the injustices that prompted its formation continue into the present. Indeed, the queer theorist Heather Love, describing the need for radical queer politics in the present moment, also offers an explanation of the urgency of ethnonationalisms at a time when minoritized subjects (including LGBTIQ people, racialized minorities, and people with disabilities) see their very existence subjected to a "continuing denigration and dismissal" (*Feeling Backward* 10). Love, who objects to a teleological, progressive account of queer history, observes: "Although many queer critics take exception to the idea of a linear, triumphalist view of history, we are in practice deeply committed to the notion of progress; we just cannot stop dreaming of a better life for queer people" (3). Love critiques this desire to dream, which Moraga and Lemus certainly demonstrate; at the same time, Moraga and Lemus also partake in what Love calls "feeling backward," for their work is predicated on the recognition that turning "away from past degradation to a present or future affirmation . . . makes it harder to see the persistence of the past in the present" (19). Their texts therefore strive toward what Muñoz calls a concrete utopia, but they do so while making clear that this utopia may continue to hold traces of exclusion and injustice. Indeed, Muñoz defines disappointment as crucial to theorizing utopia: "utopian feelings can and regularly will be disappointed," he writes, but they "are nonetheless indispensable to the act of imaging transformation" (9). Oppositional struggle need not be successful to provide ideological infrastructure for imagining a more just world; indeed, it is sometimes the *failure* of a political project that incites greater scrutiny of (and thus more informed resistance to) injustice. For Moraga and Lemus, that failure occurs when nationalisms (even queer nationalisms) capitulate to the normativizing impulses of exclusionary nationalisms.

The potential dissolution of Queer Aztlán depicted in the work of Moraga and Lemus preserves its utopian possibilities by affirming political work aimed at creating a future in which disability and queerness are accommodated instead of eliminated or tolerated. Lemus's work seems a radical departure from Moraga's, depicting multiracial hipster scenes in New York and Los Angeles and irreverently deploying the nationalist tropes of her Chicana/o literary predecessors. Yet just as Moraga's nationalism is more complex than many critics acknowledge, so too is Lemus's work more reliant on nationalist impulses than it initially appears. These authors reveal the profound theoretical work remaining to be done on decolonial and queer nationalisms—work that is foreclosed when critics too hastily dismiss the nation as what Benedict Anderson so famously called an "imagined political community" (*Imagined Communities* 6). By holding on to Aztlán as a radical possibility in the midst of a profoundly neocolonial historical moment, Moraga and Lemus suggest that utopian nationalism grounded in queer and disabled liberation remains a crucial element of oppositional political struggle. The next two chapters, dealing with contemporary political struggles on the U.S.-Mexico border, will further reveal how the struggles of the Chicano Movement—which have sought to contest the denial of full cultural citizenship to ethnic Mexicans living in the United States—retain their urgency in the present historical moment.

PART TWO

Immobilizing the Border

3 / "So Much Life in the Still Waters":
Alex Espinoza and the Ideology of Ability
in the U.S.-Mexico Borderlands

On December 22, 2010, officials at Chicago's Advocate Christ Medical Center forcibly repatriated an undocumented Mexican patient, Quelino Ojeda Jiménez, who had become a quadriplegic four months earlier after falling at his roofing job. Although U.S. law prohibits hospitals from releasing patients if they cannot find an adequate facility to provide ongoing care, the Mexican hospital to which Ojeda was sent (located four hours from his family) did not offer rehabilitation nor could it change his ventilator filters regularly. As disability rights advocate Horacio Esparza put it: "They threw him out like a piece of garbage."[1] Yet while the incident angered many, the *Chicago Tribune*'s coverage of it also displeased some readers, who were infuriated to discover not that Ojeda was illegally deported, but that he received any care at all. Reporter Judith Graham sums up these readers' opinions: "Advocate Christ should not have been expected to pay for this young man's medical needs indefinitely . . . . Nor should American taxpayers be expected to shoulder that burden."[2] The following week, *Colorlines,* a national online magazine covering racial justice issues, featured a report on the *Tribune* readers' responses to the incident in which writer Mónica Novoa links "the dehumanizing way in which we discuss immigrants today and the increasingly brutal treatment immigrants receive even at places like hospitals."[3] In other words, responses to the story exemplify what Joseph Nevins calls the belief "that the illegal deserves nothing from the United States, regardless of what his or her contributions to society might be and of what his or her rights are as outlined in the U.S. Constitution, in the wide body of American law, or in various international human rights covenants" (*Operation Gatekeeper* 177).[4]

What Novoa's analysis does not address are the pejorative attitudes about disability that also permeate reader responses to the *Tribune* story. One reader writes: "He wanted to stay here until he recovered? That woud [sic] most likely be the rest of his life." Another writes: "Would it have been cheaper just to pull the plug than to fly him back to Mexico?"[5] These readers base their negation of Ojeda's right to medical treatment (and, indeed, to life itself) not only on his legal status but also on his newly acquired disability. They assume that the "rest of his life" will amount to nothing more than a costly burden. These ableist biases, moreover, are not limited to the *Tribune* readers' responses but also surface in the initial report, which is largely sympathetic to Ojeda's predicament. The report concludes with these lines: "Without rehabilitation, he knows progress is unlikely. But still, he imagines a better future, saying, 'I want to get up from here . . . and back at work.'"[6] Here, the subtle implication is that it is Ojeda's desire and ability to work—not his status as a human being—that justifies his wish to receive medical care.

I begin this chapter by discussing the coverage of Ojeda's deportation because it exemplifies my central concern in this second segment of *Accessible Citizenships*: the rhetorical function of disability in public discourse surrounding boundary enforcement in the United States and the place of immigrants in U.S. society. Indeed, as the prior paragraph shows, even pro-immigration discourses can (and often do) fail to address their own underlying ableist biases.[7] My argument is not simply that current debates about immigration in the contemporary United

States rely upon what Tobin Siebers calls the *ideology of ability*, or the notion that the able body and mind constitute the baseline criteria for acceptance into the human community; I also propose that challenging this ideology might promote more democratic public discourse about the border, which is crucial for the enactment of a more humane immigration policy. In other words, I argue that a nuanced understanding of how disability functions in the discursive reinforcement of the U.S.-Mexico border is as essential for border scholars and activists as it is for disability scholars and activists.

In order to concretize this latter claim, this chapter examines Alex Espinoza's 2007 debut novel *Still Water Saints*, a text that convincingly reveals (and thoroughly rejects) the preference for normative embodiment that undergirds exclusionary conceptualizations of national belonging. Unlike the gay, disabled writer Arturo Islas (the subject of this study's first chapter), Espinoza—a gay, disabled writer who identifies as both Mexican and Chicano—does not confront these issues by presenting characters who share his sexuality, disability, or citizenship status. Instead, his novel includes characters with a range of corporeal attributes, national affiliations, and sexual desires/practices. What makes *Still Water Saints* a particularly useful case study for my argument is that—like the *Colorlines* and *Tribune* reports about Ojeda—it does not present itself as being principally about disability. At the same time, the many different kinds of bodies, people, and stories represented in the novel prompt a broader interrogation of how embodiment is linked to social and political value in the dominant political imaginary.

This chapter and the one that follows mark a shift in focus from the previous two, in which I have scrutinized the liberatory potential (and shortcomings) of queer cultural nationalisms. These next two chapters, on the other hand, are concerned with dominant, state-supported nationalism—and, more specifically, with the ways in which U.S. nativism reinforces an exclusionary construction of the U.S. national body that is mobilized to justify brutal immigration restrictions. In a study that interrogates the continued political, social, and emotional power of the nation form, I have found it imperative to look at both cultural nationalisms and state-sponsored nationalisms, but also to treat them as fundamentally different kinds of political collectivities.

As the previous chapters show, the heteropatriarchy and able-bodied supremacy of early Chicano nationalisms negatively impacted their efficacy in sustaining a broad-based social justice movement; meanwhile, this chapter and the next will show that U.S. boundary enforcement policies have had similarly deleterious implications for the practice of officially proclaimed democratic principles in the United States. These consequences, however, are not equivalent and therefore require distinct analyses. In other words, the desire that surfaces in the work of Arturo Islas, Cherríe Moraga, and Felicia Luna Lemus for a social movement predicated on community and cultural family (as outlined in the previous section) cannot be conflated with the desire that surfaces in the work of Alex Espinoza (and, as the next chapter shows, of Guillermo Arriaga, Tommy Lee Jones, and Oscar Casares) for state recognition of the rights and contributions of undocumented residents and their descendants, even as both desires entail a critical scrutiny of the terms under which cultural and political belonging or citizenship is conferred. I begin this chapter by elaborating the connection between boundary enforcement and the ideology of ability, proceed by examining two formal elements of the novel (its botánica setting and its unique narrative structure) that underscore this connection, and conclude by tracing how specific characters in the novel reveal why challenging the ideology of ability is necessary to contesting exclusionary practices of boundary enforcement.

The U.S.-Mexico Border and the Ideology of Ability

As anthropologist Jonathan Xavier Inda points out, U.S. immigration policy essentially functions as an expression of collective decisions about "the value and nonvalue of life, distinguishing between those lives that deserve to be lived and those that can be disallowed to the point of death" ("Value of Immigrant Life" 149). Concerns about which lives do and do not deserve to be lived, of course, also motivate disability activists, who have long argued against the idea that physical, psychological, or cognitive differences necessarily equate to a less valuable life. *Still Water Saints* unites concerns about immigration policy with concerns about corporeal norms by focusing on a botánica that provides healing and spiritual guidance to the fictional community of Agua Mansa.[8] As public health scholars Alfredo Gomez-Beloz and Noel Chavez argue, the importance of a botánica is not only that it "offers a legitimate health care service for treatment of illnesses and provides this service in a culturally appropriate manner" ("The Botánica" 545) but also that it fills a health care void when medical services available to unauthorized (and, increasingly, even to authorized) immigrants are eroded by anti-immigration policies. At a historical moment when legal scholar Kendra Stead identifies immigration and health care as "two of the highest profile and most contentious domestic policy issues within the United States" ("Critical Condition" 310), the botánica setting of *Still Water Saints* underscores how disability and immigration are linked by the ideology of ability.

Siebers defines the ideology of ability as "the preference for able-bodiedness," which "defines the baseline by which humanness is determined, setting the measure of body and mind that gives or denies human status to individual persons" (*Disability Theory* 8). Because this ideology inflects "nearly all of our judgments, definitions and values about human beings" (8), its impact is not solely felt by people with disabilities. Examining the corporeal metaphors that surface in what Leo Chavez calls the Latino Threat Narrative, scholars have uncovered substantial evidence for Siebers's argument.[9] As Otto Santa Ana argues: "In public discourse, to put it bluntly, Latinos are never the arms or the heart of the United States; they are burdens or diseases of the body politic" (10). Such discourses portray immigrants, particularly those from Latin America, as responsible for a number of social ills (from high unemployment to the declining quality of public education) and thus as pathological. As a result, Inda argues, U.S. immigration policy rests on the logic that "if one expels the pathogen, the illness will go away, the nation will be cured" ("Foreign Bodies" 47). The fact that the image of the unauthorized immigrant as a danger to the health of the national body carries such rhetorical force is a direct result of the ideology of ability; it is because bodies deemed unhealthy or disabled are seen as unsuited for political inclusion that the invocation of a disease attacking the body politic is so effective at mobilizing anti-immigrant sentiment.

Just as Louis Althusser famously asserts that ideology is most at work when it is least apparent,[10] my analysis of *Still Water Saints* exposes the ideology of ability in situations that do not appear immediately to be about disability. For instance, the novel concludes with its protagonist, Perla, attending a vigil for a Latino teen killed in a hit-and-run car accident in her borderlands community.[11] The boy's sister blames government officials for refusing to install a traffic light, proclaiming: "If there'd been a stoplight here my brother wouldn't have been killed. Nobody'll do nothing, though. Just watch" (236). She denounces city administrators who determine which neighborhoods are (and which are not) worthy of public expenditures. Meanwhile, the neighborhood protests the government's neglect by turning the bloodstained pavement into an altar:

> Seven-day veladoras surrounded it, one lined up next to the other, forming the outline of a body. Nuestra Señora de la Caridad del Cobre, La Mano Poderosa, San Martín de Porres, and Santa Marta outlined part of his left arm. There was San Judas Tadeo on the heel of his left foot, La Anima Sola near his inner thigh, and El Santo Niño de Atocha by one knee. El Sagrado Corazón, El Cristo Rey, and San Martín Caballero crowned his head and shaped part of a shoulder. (236–37)

These community witnesses to the boy's death recognize it as a *corporeal* devaluation, rooted in systemic disregard for the lives of people with racially marked bodies, and they symbolically reconstitute his body as a sacred object. In so doing, the boy's community resists race and class oppression by responding to the ideology of ability that sustains them.

By itself, my assertion that institutional racism is fundamentally linked to a preference for nondisabled bodies is not new; Cynthia Wu, for instance, notes that at least since 1882 (when both the Chinese Exclusion Act and the Immigration Act of 1882, which barred people with diseases and disabilities from entering the United States, took effect), U.S. immigration policy has reflected a perception of the racialized body "as already impaired, already compromised, and already diseased" (*Chang and Eng Reconnected* 8). What is new about *Still Water Saints*—and what makes an analysis of it so politically urgent—is the way it affirms corporeal difference as a social good in its effort to imagine a more just and humane border policy. Eithne Luibhéid describes how "immigration control practices implicate citizens who have historically been excluded from full belonging in the nation-state," particularly those whose "bodies are . . . marked as racial, sexual, cultural, and class outsiders" ("Introduction: Queering Migration" xviii). In *Still Water Saints,* imagining a U.S. national community that recognizes those with "marked" bodies as deserving of full rights and personhood—regardless of legal status—requires confronting and rejecting the ideology of ability, replacing it with a body politics grounded in the valorization of corporeal diversity.

Still Water Saints and Narrative Form

LA BOTÁNICA OSHÚN: SETTING OF RESISTANCE

One of the two formal elements of the novel that make it particularly useful for examining the relationship between the ideology of ability and border policy is its setting in a botánica, a community alternative to formal health care services: "When doctors failed, when priests and praying were not enough, the people of

Agua Mansa came to the Botánica Oshún, to Perla. The shop sold amulets and stones, rosaries and candles. They bought charms to change their luck, teas to ease unsettled nerves, and estampas of saints" (3). This description emphasizes that Agua Mansa's residents are neglected by (and therefore mistrust) the institutions charged with protecting them, including the state, the corporate health care system, and organized religion. It prompts readers to consider why doctors might "fail" (lack of access to their services or inability to pay for them) and why priests and praying might not be "enough." Yet the novel also does not idealize the botánica. Its opening passage reveals the economic and social marginalization of Perla's community by alluding to community members' encounters with the health care system, the drug trade, police surveillance, and the gambling industry: "As thanks the customers brought her booklets of coupons and long strips of lottery tickets.... They showed her pictures of aunts and uncles she had helped see through heart surgeries and hip replacements. They brought in the children she had saved from drug addictions and prison sentences. They told her of the abusive husbands and gambling wives she had chased away for good" (3–4). Here the novel reinforces Perla's importance in the community by revealing how she fills in where resources for services like domestic violence intervention and drug rehabilitation are scarce. At the same time, for the reader skeptical of Perla's power, this passage raises the question of whether a botánica is the most appropriate entity to confront these situations. In this way, it also critiques the more formal political institutions that have willfully neglected the people of Agua Mansa.

The botánica setting of *Still Water Saints* functions as an allegory for other informal community institutions that respond to the needs of undocumented immigrants and other targets of border violence. Scholars who study violence on the border have emphasized the importance of cultural representations in holding the U.S. and Mexican states accountable for their negligence. Among these scholars I include not only those who study migration but also those examining the murders of women (or feminicides) in border cities like Ciudad Juárez, Mexico. I draw from both bodies of scholarship because although the deaths of migrants crossing the border and the large-scale murders of women for being women are certainly not conflatable, studies of the Juárez feminicide expose the criminal neglect on the part of two states who permit these deaths to continue unabated because the victims (poor, gendered female, and often dark-skinned) are seen as disposable in both the United States and Mexico. Scholarship on migrant deaths and border violence similarly reveals willful state neglect anchored in racism and classism. Writing about the feminicide in Juárez, Steven S. Volk and Marian E. Schlotterbeck observe that "it is precisely because the state has failed so abjectly in stopping these murders that 'fictional' narratives have become both the site where victims are mourned and the means by which justice can be restored"; they determine that cultural representations fill "the vacuum left by state officials" ("Gender, Order and Femicide" 54). Pablo Ramírez makes a similar argument about the role of Chicana/o literature dealing with themes of migration that reflects "two competing realities: a borderlands reality and an authorized, legally legitimate reality" ("Toward a Borderlands Ethics" 53–54). Like Volk and Schlotterbeck, Ramírez cites cultural production as an antidote: "Since there is presently no place in the law to hear the ethical call of U.S. Latina/os, Chicana/o and Latina/o fiction provides one space in which an ethnic community and a nation can begin to imagine a democracy that laws and borders have made unthinkable" ("Toward a Borderlands Ethics" 65). Ramírez, Volk, and Schlotterbeck simultaneously affirm the political interventions performed by cultural representations and caution us to consider the limitations of these representations as agents of reparative justice when (as Ramírez reminds us) the reality of these texts is neither approved by mainstream rhetoric nor legitimized by current immigration law.

Given the lack of reparative justice for violence against undocumented migrants and other border dwellers, the strategies that cultural producers employ in the representation of border violence have profound implications for how such violence is understood, justified, challenged, or tolerated in the larger political imaginary. As Latina feminist philosopher Linda Martín Alcoff observes, representing others is always politically fraught: "In both the practice of speaking for as well as the practice of speaking about others, I am engaging in the act of representing the other's needs, goals, situation, and in fact, *who they are.* I am representing them *as* such and such, or . . . participating in the construction of their subject-positions" ("Problem of Speaking" 9, original emphasis). In creating texts that contest border violence, artists and writers can risk constructing subject-positions for the people they represent as abject victims lacking in agency. As Volk and Schlotterbeck observe, many cultural producers who protest the Juárez feminicide "express a profound sympathy" for the women they represent, yet they nonetheless "narratively revictimize Juárez's women by representing them within a framework of male dominance and female submissiveness" (58). Similarly, cultural representations can condemn violence while reaffirming the ideology of ability that provides its support. As a case in point, the *Tribune* report about Ojeda's deportation, which is sympathetic to his case, critiques the dehumanization of migrants while leaving unchallenged the fundamentally ableist and xenophobic belief that it is a migrant's ability and desire to work that justifies her presence in the United States.

The Botánica Oshún is, like the cultural representations that the above-cited scholars have examined, a stand-in for legally sanctioned, formal protections for the people of Agua Mansa. The novel directly alludes to the problems of relying solely upon informal, non-state-sanctioned entities by recording Perla's own concerns about her ability to serve her community:

> Perla could not do what they said or believed, could not float through walls and utter strange words, could not speak with the spirits of the dead. She never could, and she knew she never would.
>
> But Darío had said she had el don, the gift. It was strong

in her. He had said so. And there were times she even
believed him. (11)

Given that Perla doubts her own capacity to perform the feats
ascribed to her, the novel poses the question of whether the
Botánica Oshún is enough for a community lacking adequate
political representation or health care. In other words, it depicts
a negotiation between the protections offered by formal institutions (the state, the health care system, organized religion) and
the benefits afforded by an informal community presence like
the botánica. On a larger allegorical level, it also draws attention
to the insufficiency of cultural responses alone—like the novel
itself—to issues that demand state intervention.

The novel's representation of organized religion and health
care reinforces the case for access to *both* the botánica and the
institutional protections afforded by the state. The novel's characters need informal spirituality *and* inclusive religious institutions; alternative medicine or home remedios *and* adequate
health care from established medical professionals; state recognition *and* community networks through which to exercise their
rights more informally. For instance, although the botánica
serves people for whom "priests and praying were not enough,"
Perla herself is a devout Catholic who maintains a strong relationship with the local priest. The priest, for his part, tells Perla
that he refers his parishioners to her: "I tell them to go see you
for novenas and scapulars. I tell the mothers you sell the baptis-
mal candles. . . . I try to give you business" (35). Similarly, one of
Perla's most faithful clients is also her doctor, Teresa Martínez,
who comes to the botánica for valeriana tea and asks Perla to
light a candle for her new romance. I interpret Perla's doubts
about her role in the community, then, not as the novel's rejection of informal entities like the botánica but rather as its affirmation that such informal establishments must be paired with
more formal, institutional, or state-sponsored safeguards and
guarantees if they are to effectively safeguard people's dignity
and ensure that their rights are protected.

These interactions between the formal and informal mechanisms through which the people of Agua Mansa exercise their rights offer a useful framework for thinking about both immigration and disability. With regard to immigration, the novel legitimates the life of the migrant who, as Nevins observes, "lives her life more as a citizen of a nonbounded society than as a citizen of a bounded territorial state," thereby challenging "the legitimacy of nation-statism" (*Operation Gatekeeper* 215) and prompting the creation of more just and open forms of political collectivity. Rather than merely valorizing this important cultural contribution of the undocumented migrant, however, the novel also recognizes the extreme social and political vulnerability that she experiences. From a disability studies perspective, the novel's depiction of the need for better health care in low-income communities exposes disparities in the health care system that disproportionately affect low-income people, people of color, and people with disabilities. Yet by also valorizing home remedies, *Still Water Saints* resists the impulse to pathologize all corporeal difference, demonstrating that bodily difference can have diverse social and cultural meanings and that not all nonnormative bodies require a medical cure. As a result, it is significant that the novel's most striking image of a person inhabiting *both* a formal institution of social protection and the more informal protection represented by the botánica is a Mexican-Cuban immigrant with a disability. This is an image of Darío, Perla's mentor and the original owner of the botánica, in church: "Every Sunday they saw him at Mass, sitting up front, a cane neatly folded between his legs, always the first in line to receive the Host, always first to shake the priest's hand" (72).

NARRATIVE STRUCTURE: PERLA AND HER CLIENTS

The other formal element of *Still Water Saints* that is crucial to my argument is its narrative structure, which integrates stories from characters with a range of race, gender, national, and disability identifications. The novel is divided into eight sections, each themed around the feast day of a saint. Of these sections, seven are made up of two chapters, one narrated by a limited third-person narrator who speaks from Perla's perspective and one narrated in the first person by one of her customers. These customers, usually (but not always) Mexican or Chicana/o, often possess bodies that defy social norms; they include an obese teenager, a young professional overwhelmed by grief, a transgender dancer, an interracial couple, a white working-class drug addict, and others. The final section, unlike the previous seven, includes only a chapter narrated from Perla's perspective. The novel thus incorporates multiple perspectives from the community, highlighting events from their lives while following Perla's story in a more sustained way. The short, first-person community narratives (which function like interlocking short stories embedded within the novel) and Perla's extended third-person story each have important functions in the text, one revealing people's positioning in relation to dominant ideologies about the body and the nation and the other revealing how people's relationships to dominant ideologies might change.

First, by incorporating diverse voices from Agua Mansa, *Still Water Saints* reveals how the social locations occupied by citizens and noncitizens, authorized and unauthorized immigrants, and people with and without disabilities prompt different relationships to the ideology of ability. The novel reveals how these categories and distinctions serve regimes of power that delegitimize certain lives in order to legitimize others. Finally, it demonstrates how different characters' perceptions of the world around them are linked to their ability to recognize their own position within the hierarchical social landscape they inhabit. In other words, *Still Water Saints* invites its readers to imaginatively occupy a range of social positions with different relationships to issues of public health and border enforcement; as a result, readers are able to examine these issues from different ideological vantage points and, thus, to consider the implications of their own social locations.

Second, by focusing on Perla's life over a period of several months, the novel models a transition from what Karen

Tongson calls "a suburban, 'model minority' sensibility of individual uplift through entrepreneurship" (*Relocations* 146) to a subjectivity that exists in opposition to the ideology of ability as it shapes the experience of migration across the U.S.-Mexico border. This occurs through a series of interactions between Perla and Rodrigo, an undocumented teenager who is brought to the United States after being sold into sexual captivity by his employer in Mexico (a nightclub owner). Ultimately, Perla comes to an insight very similar to one described by Inda, who interrogates the notion of the unauthorized immigrant as a "parasite" in the national body: "the nation and the immigrant are each parasite and host for the other, they feed on each other, thus helping to keep each other alive, and, at the same time, by draining each other of nutrients, they are a threat to each other's well-being" ("Foreign Bodies" 58). In this way, she challenges both the exclusion of unauthorized migrants like Rodrigo from the national body and also the ideology of ability that reinforces that exclusion.

A crucial premise of both Chicana/o studies and disability studies is that by learning to recognize and critically evaluate the oppressive ideologies that shape social relations, people can resist these ideologies. Ramón Saldívar asserts: "Chicano narrative is not content with merely reproducing the world but also attempts to reveal the ideological structures by which we continue to create that world" (*Chicano Narrative* 9). The collective stories of Perla's clients, particularly the story of Rodrigo, demonstrate the ideology of ability to constitute a particularly crucial "ideological structure" operating on the U.S.-Mexico border, one that produces exclusionary effects for people with and without disabilities. Siebers, meanwhile, argues that "because [the ideology of ability] is discriminatory and exclusionary, it creates social locations outside of and critical of its purview, most notably in this case, the perspective of disability" (*Disability Theory* 8). For Siebers, then, subjects who are marginalized by particular ideological structures—and who recognize and contest their marginalized positionality—can position themselves in opposition to that ideology and work to contest and transform it. The ideology of ability, then, is neither necessary nor inevitable; it can be countered by paying attention to the perspectives of people who are harmed by its exclusions. As a result, literary texts (like *Still Water Saints*) that require their readers to imaginatively occupy spaces outside of (and actively excluded by) the ideology of ability have a crucial role to play in challenging its effects. The final, and most extensive, section of this analysis will explore how this happens: first in the individual stories of Perla's clients, and finally in the extended narration of Perla's interactions with Rodrigo.

Against the Ideology of Ability: Community Narratives of Agua Mansa

ROSA, JUAN, SHAWN, AND LLUVIA

As one might expect in a novel about a healer, *Still Water Saints* contains numerous characters with disabilities and diseases. Surprisingly, however, the focus of its stories is not a depiction of Perla helping her clients to cure or overcome their ailments. Perla's most important role in Agua Mansa is not ridding it of disease and disability but helping her community to see disease and disability as ordinary parts of life. David Mitchell and Sharon Snyder argue that disability often takes on a hypersymbolic function by which literature "serves up disability as a repressed deviation from cultural imperatives of normativity, while disabled populations suffer the consequences of representational association with deviance and recalcitrant corporeal difference" (*Narrative Prosthesis* 8). In *Still Water Saints,* by contrast, it is the unmarked body that constitutes a deviation. Disability surfaces during the most ordinary of situations, as just another part of everyday life; for instance, one character recalls being separated from his mother in a department store as a child and watching as "a man in a motorized wheelchair maneuvered around the racks of slacks and shirts my mother had rummaged through"

(Espinoza, *Still Water Saints* 47). By presenting disability in diverse and yet thoroughly mundane contexts, the novel treats bodily variation not as a "device of characterization" (Mitchell and Snyder, *Narrative Prosthesis* 9) but as a variegated yet commonplace aspect of life. Furthermore, although I am emphasizing here the stories' engagement with bodily norms (rather than U.S. immigration policy), in all of the stories the presence of Mexican economic and cultural contributions to the community are also significant. In the stories I discuss here, these elements include mariachi and cumbia music, Mexican grocery stores, Day of the Dead celebrations, racially integrated social circles, and murals. As a result, these stories all subtly align the rejection of the ideology of ability with their U.S.-Mexico border setting and with an affirmation of the presence of Mexican-origin people and Mexican cultures within the United States.

The first story told in the novel is that of Rosa, an obese teenager whose mother brings her to the botánica for weight-loss remedies: "My great-grandfather used to call my mother 'Gorda' because she was chubby when she was a young girl. . . . It was embarrassing, and it wasn't until after my mother gave birth to me and started exercising that she lost the weight. And it's because of her 'victory over obesity' that my mother's decided to help me with my battle" (14). Rosa and her sister recognize the harm in their mother's view of Rosa's body as something to "battle," something over which to declare "victory"; Rosa's sister repeatedly assures her that she is pretty, but Rosa acquiesces to her mother. Rosa becomes emboldened, however, when she begins dating a coworker at Las Glorias Market named Miguel Angel who, like her sister, tells her that she doesn't need the tea her mother purchases. Eventually Rosa goes to the botánica and tells Perla that her mother's preoccupation with her weight "doesn't make sense to me" (28). When Perla replies that Rosa's mother doesn't want to see her hurting, Rosa objects: "I'm not. . . . I'm not hurting" (28). Rosa's statement here is a powerful repudiation of one of the ideology of ability's most prevalent assumptions: that those who possess nonnormative bodies necessarily suffer the pain of social rejection, so that their bodies must be altered to alleviate this pain. Perla, for her part, recognizes her error in ascribing "hurt" to Rosa, and gives back her money. Perla's act of healing in this story, then, is to *deny* Rosa a cure, suggesting that an important function of the botánica is to create a space in which the harm created by narrow beauty standards is subject to critical scrutiny.[12]

Juan is a young professional overwhelmed by grief after the death of his father. He takes out his grief on his girlfriend Deborah, who decides to give him space from their relationship, and on his mother Evelyn, an avid collector of Elvis memorabilia. His grief erupts after he accompanies Evelyn on her annual trip to the botánica to purchase a sugar skull for her Day of the Dead altar to Elvis. Juan lashes out at his mother, accusing her of grieving Elvis's death but not his father's. Later, at an Elvis impersonation concert, he watches his mother dance: "Here's my mother, Evelyn. She's just lost her husband to emphysema. . . . Standing on a chair in an Indian casino, Evelyn's clutching the hand of a woman she's just met. Wearing a lavender poodle skirt that she pulled out from deep within her closet, Evelyn dances" (57–58). At this moment, Juan recognizes his mother's right to express her grief differently and also to go on living after her husband's death. This recognition incites him to try to reconcile with Deborah. In this episode, by selling the sugar skulls to Evelyn and Juan, Perla prompts the mother and son to confront their different ways of expressing their grief, and ultimately forces Juan to recognize and accept the frailty of the human body. As Rosemarie Garland Thomson observes, the "fact that we will all become disabled if we live long enough is a reality many people who consider themselves able-bodied are reluctant to admit"; she notes that this makes disability "threatening" (*Extraordinary Bodies* 14) to many nondisabled people. Juan's story, then, represents the necessity of understanding and accepting not only the mutability of the body but also its mortality.[13]

Shawn is one of the novel's few white characters, a drug addict who has grown up among the Mexican-origin people who are a statistical majority in the town of Agua Mansa. He lives with his best friend Beady, to whom he is profoundly attracted (although he does not appear to identify as gay), works in an electronics store, and is generally happy with his life. He has no intention of giving up speed (although he also refuses to shoot it): "Here's what it felt like and why I'm still doing it. It felt electric. Like volts of energy making my blood boil, turning everything inside me on all at once.... I know I'm not doing it no justice. So there's no point in even trying to describe it except to say it's good" (142). Of Beady he asserts: "I know Beady. Know him so good I can practically get into that head of his. I know his ways and he knows mine. We're family, Beady and me" (153). Trouble starts, however, when Beady starts sleeping with a coworker and fellow addict named Daisy: "we don't need someone like her coming in and messing up what we got, what we've always kept for ourselves" (154). Shawn goes to the botánica looking for a religious image for a new tattoo, but instead purchases a candle to expel a negative presence, hoping to drive Daisy away. This story does not glorify Shawn's life, but it also resists a simple cure narrative that would portray drug addiction as a mere failure of personal will. It reveals the larger circumstances that have contributed to Shawn's addiction, such as homophobia and a lack of substantive opportunities for young men in working-class communities, as well as the lack of viable options for rehabilitation. Furthermore, by focusing on Shawn's desire to be rid of Daisy, the novel represents Shawn's unrequited love for Beady (rather than his drug addiction) as the issue in his life that he perceives as his most urgent problem.

The final story I will address here is that of Lluvia, a young artist known in Agua Mansa as the rebellious daughter of Enrique Medina: "He's a real together guy, they say. Takes great care of that family of his. . . . But the daughter. She's a problem. Was in a few fights when she was in high school and got suspended. Just paints murals around town. Riding around on that chopper of hers. A studded leather jacket and combat boots like some thug" (215). Lluvia struggles with the knowledge of her father's infidelity and her mother's refusal to acknowledge it. Perla hires Lluvia to paint a mural of the Virgin of Guadalupe on the wall of the botánica, and Lluvia uses an old photograph of her mother as inspiration for the face: "She's laughing. . . . She's real young. I can tell this was way before my father" (222). Lluvia doesn't show her mother the mural until after her mother is diagnosed with gonorrhea, a diagnosis that finally prompts her to leave her husband. In this vignette, Perla's act of healing is to give Lluvia a vehicle to imagine her mother's happiness, to paint her mother outside the confines of the role of devoted wife. Moreover, while the disease is not treated as unequivocally positive, it functions as a catalyst for Lluvia and her mother to reexamine their lives and ultimately to reject Enrique.

Each of these vignettes presents a view of the body that operates not according to a binary of able-bodied/disabled but that instead attends to the multiple ways in which social norms construct bodies as deviant or noncompliant. They do not treat obesity, emphysema, death, drug abuse, or gonorrhea as happy life events or as definitive social goods, but they do reveal them as important—and common—bodily experiences that can offer new perspectives and knowledge to people who experience them. These experiences, as a result, enable the characters to challenge the ideology of ability. Furthermore, in each of these stories the botánica functions as a space in which the characters are empowered to imagine their lives and circumstances from a position outside this ideology. Finally, each of these stories depicts Mexican contributions to the U.S. national landscape. Ironically, it is Shawn who most explicitly articulates this: "The thing about living around so many Mexicans is that you start to pick up their ways. The streets and cities and mountains around here have Spanish names, so already, right there you learn some words. . . . You wake up hungover and menudo suddenly sounds good. Around Christmastime, you start to crave tamales" (151). Although on its own this passage could be read as a kind of facile embrace of multiculturalism, within the context of the novel as a whole—which (as I will discuss in the next section) offers a direct challenge to U.S. immigration policy—I read this as a statement of the need to conceptualize the U.S. body politic in more inclusive terms, just as the vignettes I just analyzed demonstrate the value of bodily variability.

PERLA AND RODRIGO

While the stories discussed above seem to be primarily about characters who learn to value and understand bodily variation, and less about the nationalist discourses that propel U.S. border enforcement, the story of Perla and Rodrigo seems to be primarily about the consequences of U.S. border policy and less directly about the ideology of ability. However, just as there is a latent but powerful critique of exclusionary conceptualizations of U.S. national identity in the vignettes discussed above, Perla's story is also strongly influenced by her interactions with people whose lives are negatively impacted by prevailing bodily norms. Indeed, while Perla's story on the surface seems to be about a woman who overcomes her fear of an undocumented migrant to recognize his humanity, her ability to do this is predicated on the ways in which she comes to scrutinize the ideology of ability and to actively position herself outside it. Crucial to Perla's interactions with Rodrigo, then, are her memories of her childhood, of the early years of her marriage, and of coming to work at the botánica. As a result, the sections of *Still Water Saints* that focus on Perla's past and on her interactions with Rodrigo represent the novel's most provocative political critique.

In order to grasp how Perla's back-story positions her in opposition to the ideology of ability, it is important to note what Tongson has identified as the novel's resistance to a "critical formulation in which Chicano literature in particular, and 'ethnic' literature in general, are niched by the contemporary publishing economy into the 'magical realist' genre because they offer representations of 'atavistic' superstitions, beliefs, and fantasies" (*Relocations* 141). For Tongson, reading the novel as a magical-realist tale "risks eliding the painstaking historicity of Espinoza's realism" (141). Although she does not address the representation of disability, the political stakes of rejecting a magical realist interpretation are nowhere more urgent than in the scene in which Perla decides to apprentice with Darío, the original owner of the botánica. Although she originally approaches Darío because she and her husband have not been able to conceive a child, Darío convinces her to work with him instead of pursuing motherhood:

> He walked around the counter and pulled his pant leg up. The skin of his left leg was shriveled and pale and scarred just above the ankle. "Polio," Darío said. "It shrunk my leg. It was my price. The woman I learned from, she was burned in a fire. Another man I knew, he was blind in one eye, but his gift of prophecy and his healing powers were strong. You"—he pointed to Perla, to her stomach— "you'll never have children. It's the price you pay. But you do have power. I saw it when you walked in. Shining blue around your whole body. Why don't you let me help you? Teach you to make it stronger? You could be my apprentice. Think about it," he said. "I know it sounds crazy. And I know it's not what you want." (79)

On its own, this passage might bring to mind a critique made by Mitchell and Snyder of disability representations in which "the overdetermined symbolism ascribed to disabled bodies [obscures] the more complex and banal reality of those who inhabit them" (*Narrative Prosthesis* 60), a practice that "has led to the reification of disabled people as fathomless mysteries" (61). Reading the novel as a magical realist text, then, colludes with a long tradition of ascribing special powers and special symbolism to people and literary characters with disabilities. However, the novel itself actually undermines this facile interpretation of disability by making it clear that Perla herself is not disabled; rather, it is her husband who cannot have children.

By locating the source of Perla's power in her husband's body, not her own, the novel makes clear that it is not bodily deviance in and of itself that provides healing power but rather the loss of the ability to pass unmarked through society that possession of a normative body provides. Because of her husband's inability to have children, Perla is forced to reexamine her expectations for her life, as she must choose between leaving the man she loves to create the heteronormative family she wants or finding another purpose for her life. As Tongson puts it, instead of finding a cure for her reproductive failure, "she finds another solution to (re)productivity altogether" (*Relocations* 142). Perla's power, then, stems not from disability itself but more precisely from the experience of living outside social norms. In this way, the novel represents disability not as an innate and inscrutable essence of the body but as a social location critical of dominant ideologies (like the imperative to reproduce). By imagining her life outside the conventions with which she was raised, conventions that do not accommodate her husband's body, Perla acquires ideological tools that allow her to help others imagine their own lives outside social norms that devalue women, LGBT people, and people of color. In other words, Perla is forced to begin looking at life from outside the ideology of ability and to learn how to help her customers do so as well. It is noteworthy that she acquiesces not only to her husband's masculinist refusal to seek fertility treatments but also to his patriarchal refusal to adopt; Perla certainly does not instantly reject all harmful norms when she comes to apprentice with Darío. Instead, Perla's rejection of the ideology of ability develops over the course of the novel, as she interacts with and learns from her customers.

Of the clients Perla learns from, of course, the most important (in terms of both the narrative space he occupies and his structural position in the text) is Rodrigo. Unlike Perla's other clients, Rodrigo is a difficult character for the reader to know; he never speaks in the first person, and his presence in the novel is shrouded in mystery. He enters the text at the end of the first chapter as a disembodied premonition when Perla sees an opossum on her patio and believes it to be an omen: "It was a messenger. It was letting her know. Something was out there. It was coming" (12). In the second chapter, Perla sees an adolescent boy outside the botánica as she closes the store. He stands outside the shop knocking on the door, "nervously looking over his shoulder every now and again" (42); when a car approaches, he runs off, his fists leaving "impressions like a baby's footprints on the window glass" (42). In the third chapter he comes to the botánica asking for English lessons, which Perla initially refuses, and in the fourth and fifth chapters Perla misses him when he comes by. It is not until the sixth chapter that we learn his full name and personal history. Rodrigo Abel Zamora is an undocumented immigrant who moves from Michoacán (birthplace of Perla's mother) to Tijuana at the age of fifteen, hoping to work in the United States and to support his family. After performing sex work at a nightclub in Tijuana, he is sold to a white soldier named Dwight, a drug addict who shows symptoms of post-traumatic stress disorder, who smuggles him across the border, keeps him captive, and routinely beats and rapes him. Ultimately, when Perla is unable to convince Rodrigo that she can help him without having him discovered by immigration officials and deported, he stops visiting her. Perla looks for Rodrigo but finds only clues suggesting that he has been murdered, most likely by Dwight. Rodrigo's disappearance from the text, then, is as mystifying as his arrival.

Another point that distinguishes Perla's relationship with Rodrigo from her relationships with other clients is that this one is, for much of the text, marked by mutual distrust. Perla's first encounter with Rodrigo emphasizes the border between them in the form of the locked door to the botánica. As he knocks, Perla tells him that the shop is closed, repeating herself in Spanish, and grips a screwdriver. Even after he leaves, as Perla crosses her parking lot, she clutches her purse and looks behind herself. From the very first encounter between the two characters, the novel reveals their points of commonality as well as the disparities between them. Like Rodrigo, Perla as an elderly woman is vulnerable to violence; like him, she must be vigilant to people with the capacity to do her harm. Yet unlike Rodrigo, Perla has access to doors she can lock against people who might hurt her;

she has the power to enforce boundaries of her own. The second time Rodrigo comes to the botánica, he arrives during business hours, but Perla nonetheless regards him with suspicion: "She stepped behind the counter and made sure the cash register's drawer was shut" (62). Everything we read about Rodrigo, then, is framed by the knowledge that we are learning his story from someone who is, like him, vulnerable to violence but also from someone who has the power to exclude him, to turn him over to the authorities, to refuse to help him. In this way, the novel reveals the complexity of relationships between those with and those without legal standing in the nation they inhabit, attending to the ways in which their stories are linked as well as to the vast differences between their lives.

The second interaction between the characters further emphasizes how the border shapes the conditions of their relationship. After his first encounter with Perla, Rodrigo does not return to the botánica for another month. He shows up on a day when it is pouring rain, as Perla recalls similar rains that devastated Agua Mansa in her childhood. She remembers crossing La Cadena Bridge with her parents in their pickup truck; both the bridge and its name evoke the border, even though the bridge is located within the town of Agua Mansa. After her family has safely crossed, the bridge collapses and a car falls in; Perla's mother covers her eyes and tells her not to look, but Perla cannot avoid confronting the deaths: "Still, Perla heard the man screaming, the loud rush of the water, the sound of things cracking, breaking off, and washing away" (62). Perla remains haunted by the arbitrary fact that her family managed to live simply by crossing a few moments earlier; as her father puts it, "Unos cuantos minutos . . . .. We could have been on that bridge. This troque could have been our tumba" (62). The memory evokes the tension between inclusion and exclusion that the border represents; on the one hand, Perla's mother urges her to look away from the deaths, attempting to render them invisible, while on the other hand her father's words encourage her to identify with the victims.

It is just as Perla is remembering these deaths on the bridge that Rodrigo arrives at the botánica and asks her for English lessons; this is significant because it is this memory that prepares her to treat Rodrigo as a human being, not as a threat to her safety and property, and to try to help him. Nonetheless, she initially resists, insisting, "I'm not a teacher . . . .. I'm a business-woman" (63). Yet she also shows him books, speaks to him in English, and allows him to stay at the botánica until he decides to leave. The next day, when he returns, she allows him to sleep in the shop. She remains afraid of him, especially when he tells her that he lives at Galena Court, a particularly rough part of town: "Maybe there was something going on at the duplexes that he was involved in. *Drugs? Gangs? Maybe he's an illegal. Maybe he's hiding out from La Migra*" (67). However, despite her fear, and despite her use of the politically fraught term "illegal," she notices that he flinches in terror when she reaches for his hands, that his body bears the markers of unspoken violence: "Small round welts dotted the backs of Rodrigo's hands. They looked tender and painful" (68). Perla's recognition of the marks of violence on Rodrigo's body demonstrates her reluctant but nonetheless evident willingness to see him as a human being who deserves protection instead of only as a potential criminal. As a result, she defends him when clients see him in the store and tell her to be careful, searching First Aid manuals for images like the welts on his hands until she determines that they are cigarette burns. Most importantly, during this encounter, Perla begins to picture him as someone with a family who loves him, a person whose life matters to others: "Here was somebody's son, she thought. Alone and invisible. If she could call or write her, Perla would tell Rodrigo's mother, *He's fine. Your baby's fine*" (68). Particularly noteworthy in this passage is the assertion of Rodrigo's value as a subject based upon his relationships with others, particularly his mother, and not solely upon his potential for physical labor.

Rodrigo's story is also distinguished from the others by the formal techniques Espinoza employs in its telling. The first of these is the use of a mediator to tell his story; unlike the story of every character except Perla, Rodrigo's is narrated in the third person. As readers, we have access to his voice only once. This occurs two months after Rodrigo's rest in the botánica, when Perla arrives at work and discovers a note:

> Senora I come to looking for you but you are gone I come back soon. I am needing your help. I am afraid. The cops they wont help me and not even a church because I have feeling they will call the migra.
> Please be here.
> Rodrigo Zamora. (113)

When Rodrigo finally returns to the botánica five months later, the chapter that we (by now) expect to tell Perla's story begins in the third person as usual but instead narrates Rodrigo's story. Initially the reader assumes herself to be learning Rodrigo's story from an omniscient third-person narrator, but this idea is abruptly disrupted when his story ends and we are confronted with the sentence, "He stopped talking after that" (170). We learn here that the story that we think is told by an omniscient narrator is actually being told by Perla's (third-person limited) narrator, and thus that it is relayed entirely from Perla's perspective. We know about Rodrigo only what Perla knows, only what Rodrigo chooses to tell her. In this way the novel emphasizes that the reader's access to the subjectivity of a character like Rodrigo is limited. Instead of attempting to speak on behalf of Rodrigo, the novel draws attention to itself as a representation, forcing its reader to confront the ethical and political dimensions of speaking for a person like Rodrigo, thus attending to the problems of representation that I discussed earlier in this chapter. Furthermore, and most importantly, the reader is put in the ethical position of choosing whether or not to trust Rodrigo and his version of events. In other words, the reader must decide about the trustworthiness of a person whose subjectivity is constructed in the mainstream media through discourses of illegality. Indeed, it is not until the seventh chapter—when Rodrigo fails to return and Perla goes looking for him, finding evidence that not only corroborates his story but also suggests he has been killed—that the text legitimates his story. In this way, the novel forces its readers to take an ethical position in the assessment of Rodrigo.

The final distinction between Rodrigo's story and most of the others is that Rodrigo's story is never resolved. For some of the characters, it is necessary to read the novel several times before discovering how their stories conclude, since the vignettes about Perla's customers often take place chronologically before the Perla/Rodrigo storyline, but the stories do usually have a resolution.[14] For instance, Rosa's story ends with Rosa and Miguel Angel Cabrera just getting to know each other, but Perla's first chapter includes a visit from one of her favorite customers, now named Rosa Cabrera: "She had been in high school when her mother had first brought her to the store. Now she was in her late twenties, married, and taking classes to become a hair stylist" (8). Perla's second chapter, which precedes Juan's chapter, tells us that the couple has worked out its differences through a radio dedication Perla hears one morning while purchasing her morning coffee and donuts at the business located next door to her botánica: "My name is Deborah. I'm calling from Agua Mansa. I'd like to dedicate 'We've Only Just Begun' by the Carpenters . . .. For my fiancé, Juan" (38). The fact that Rodrigo's story lacks such a resolution indicates Perla's inability to solve all of the problems she encounters. As I argued earlier in this chapter, Perla and the botánica function as alternatives to a corporate health care system and as entities that challenge dominant social norms; for many of the characters in the novel, this function is sufficient. Rodrigo, however, needs state intervention to protect his life; he needs the guarantees of political citizenship. Given Rodrigo's undocumented status and the injustices of the legal system and the society in which his story takes place, a satisfactory resolution to his story is impossible.

For Tongson, the lack of resolution in Rodrigo's story is also fundamentally linked to the fact that Dwight is a soldier. She writes: "Espinoza explores the failures of the imperial imaginary to hold itself accountable to what happens *after*. . . . Abroad Dwight fancies himself the American marine whose aim is 'to do good,' whereas at home he is forced to confront his . . . own failure to achieve that category of success as a working-class figure in the American context" (*Relocations* 149–50, original emphasis). Tongson's focus here is not disability, but her analysis of Dwight as a figure produced by the failures of the U.S. state in the aftermath of war allows us to interrogate how the neglect of attention to the mental health of returning soldiers (failure to be accountable for what happens *after*) also functions as a destructive manifestation of the ideology of ability. For although, as Tongson observes, Dwight "profoundly embodies his 'Americanness' as a white soldier" (151), he also responds in a profoundly threatened and threatening way when his embodiment of that ideal is challenged, following his return home from the war. His response to this new reality, in other words, is to reassert his own position within the national body by violently drawing its boundary lines on the body of Rodrigo.

The closest thing to a resolution in Rodrigo's story occurs when Perla reads a newspaper report of an unidentified teenager's body found on the banks of the river. Here she prays that it isn't Rodrigo: "*That wasn't him. He's fine. He's still alive. . . . He'll go to school. Learn things. Grow up and be successful. His parents will be proud.* . . . She wished that life for him, wished it again and again" (211). This moment constitutes a profound resistance to the discursive violence that has made possible the physical violence enacted on Rodrigo's body. In this moment, Perla recognizes and asserts Rodrigo's worth: his place in his family, his potential as a student. Against a social order that sees Rodrigo as disposable, as inconsequential, as nothing more than the dollar value of the labor his body is capable of performing, Perla insists upon the significance of Rodrigo's life. Although she is powerless against the physical violence that has most likely ended that life, she refuses to capitulate to discourses that posit him solely as a body made for working and as a legitimate target of violence. Perla's assertion of Rodrigo's humanity at this moment functions as a staunch indictment of the state and its disregard for migrant life.

Although Rodrigo's story seems to be the least about disability, then, it is also the story that shows the most violent consequences of the ideology of ability. For, as with the deportation of Quelino Ojeda, Rodrigo's body becomes a site at which the ideology of ability is brutally mobilized to police the contours of the national body. In both cases, a more comprehensive understanding of the ideology of ability and its function of disallowing certain lives is critical to contesting these acts of injustice.

While the fictional story of Rodrigo is never resolved, leaving open the possibility that he has escaped and perhaps even gone to school as Perla imagines, the story of Ojeda has a definite and tragic resolution. *Chicago Tribune* reporter Becky Schlikerman reports that just over a year after his illegal and unconscionable deportation, on January 1, 2012, Ojeda passed away at the General Hospital of Juchitán de Zaragoza in Oaxaca, Mexico; the causes of his death were pneumonia, sepsis, and the effects of his spinal cord injury. He was buried in Monte Negro, Oaxaca, two days later. Many of his friends and advocates believe he would still be alive if he had not been deported.[15] The ideology of ability is not simply a flawed discourse but an instrument of violence and even of death. Cultural critic Rosa-Linda Fregoso observes that "the border is a central concept for theorizing a complex web of power relations, the boundaries of exclusion and inclusion, [that] helps to account for the intersection of multiple forces and orders of power in proliferating violence" ("We Want Them Alive!" 110). As both Ojeda's story and my analysis of *Still Water Saints* reveal, the ideology of ability is one of the central elements of this proliferating violence.

Yet the stories of Ojeda and Rodrigo also offer a framework for resisting the ideology of ability, for both also contain evidence of the value of these young men's lives. While the news reports about Ojeda's deportation do inadvertently reproduce the ideology of ability by affirming his desire to return to work, they also demonstrate the existence of a community of family and friends in Oaxaca and Chicago who mourn his death. Friends from Chicago stayed in touch with Ojeda throughout his year at the hospital in Juchitán de Zaragoza, and relatives from Monte Negro consistently made the four-hour journey to visit him there. Like Perla imagining a different future for Rodrigo, these affirmations of Ojeda's value as a subject represent a radical departure from the ideology of ability that devalues immigrant life. These stories—one fictional, one nonfiction—offer a model for reconfiguring what Fregoso identifies as the boundaries of inclusion and exclusion that define U.S. national identity.

Literature and other cultural representations constitute a powerful means of contesting the border violence that the ideology of ability manufactures and maintains. Border theorist José David Saldívar describes cultural production as one means through which "documented and undocumented migrants in the U.S.-Mexico borderlands secure spaces of survival and self-respect" (*Border Matters* 1). By rejecting the ideology of ability used to construct immigrants in the dominant imaginary, *Still Water Saints* serves as one effort to secure spaces of survival and self-respect. The novel thus reveals how a rigorous understanding of the rhetorical infrastructure of disability oppression is central to advocacy for a more expansive conceptualization of the U.S. national body. At the same time, *Still Water Saints* also demands large-scale social transformation, as it points to the fact that new representations, alone, are not enough. The novel thus produces an ethical call to its readers, demonstrating the necessity not only of finding new ways to represent the human rights crisis on the U.S.-Mexico border but also of taking political action to end the crisis. The next chapter will examine how three cultural workers—a Chicano novelist, a Mexican screenwriter, and an Anglo film director—continue this effort in their depictions of aging male bodies that challenge U.S. national bodily ideals.

4 /   No Nation For Old Men? Racialized Aging and Border-Crossing Narratives by Guillermo Arriaga, Tommy Lee Jones, and Oscar Casares

> The U.S.-Mexico border changes pesos into dollars, humans into undocumented workers, . . . people between cultures into people without culture.
>
> —JOSÉ DAVID SALDÍVAR, *BORDER MATTERS*

In the face of increasingly punitive anti-immigration legislation (and the increasingly xenophobic public rhetoric that fuels it), cultural workers, journalists, and scholars have documented the dangers and traumas of crossing unauthorized from Mexico to the United States. Less attention, however, has been paid to how the border *keeps people in*—effectively securing the presence of a racialized, vulnerable, and easily exploited underclass within the territorial boundaries of the United States. As Jorge Durand, Douglas Massey, and Emilio Parrado find, because "migrants are at greatest risk while crossing the border, a buildup of enforcement resources there perversely creates strong incentives for undocumented migrants to stay put" ("New Era" 524), whether or not they intend to live permanently in the United States. In this chapter, I build upon the previous chapter's exploration of how the U.S.-Mexico border defines the shape of the national body; here, however, the objects of study depict crossings from the United States to Mexico. In so doing, these texts (and my analyses of them) work to reverse the dehumanizing effects of the border crossing that José David Saldívar describes in the epigraph to this chapter. By looking at Mexico—and not the United States—as a longed-for repository of migrant hopes and dreams, this chapter explores the effects of what Alicia Schmidt Camacho has identified as "the distortion of civic life in places where large numbers of undocumented migrants work and reside without the rights and privileges enjoyed by the larger society" (*Migrant Imaginaries* 293).

The novel *Amigoland* (2009) by Chicano writer Oscar Casares and the film *The Three Burials of Melquiades Estrada* (USA, 2006), a transborder film collaboratively made by white, Anglo actor-director Tommy Lee Jones and Mexican writer Guillermo Arriaga, both feature aging male protagonists who undertake arduous journeys across the border, traveling from the United States to Mexico. In *The Three Burials,* an Anglo rancher and Border Patrol agent travel to Mexico to repatriate the body of an undocumented ranch worker killed by the Border Patrol agent; in *Amigoland,* an elderly Chicano leaves a nursing home to live his final days at his family's ranchito in Mexico. There are, of course, significant differences between the two texts that must be acknowledged at the outset. In addition to the national and ethnic identifications that distinguish their creators and characters, there are also the important questions of production, distribution, and reception that distinguish a novel from a film, and that therefore demand different analytical methodologies. Nonetheless, there is a significant case to be made for undertaking a comparative analysis of *The Three Burials* and *Amigoland.* At a historical moment when U.S. policies have created a settled population of undocumented residents within its borders— what Schmidt Camacho calls a "coercive" (*Migrant Imaginaries* 298) cancellation of the option of circular migration—the proliferation of texts staging a return migration demands critical exploration. Narratives of reverse migration have the potential to disrupt the fiction of the so-called American Dream, as they depict characters who, upon experiencing the purported benefits of life in the United States, choose to leave them behind. In particular, *The Three Burials* and *Amigoland* both depict this return journey undertaken by men who are dead, dying, or advanced in age, thus demanding an analysis of how they rely upon or disrupt the cultural meanings attached to aging male bodies.

Building on the work of border theorists like Schmidt Camacho and Saldívar, this chapter will argue that both *Amigoland* and *The Three Burials* represent racialized aging as a bodily experience linked to melancholic national identifications. *The Three Burials* examines what Judith Butler calls *national melancholia:* a "disavowed mourning" on the part of U.S. citizens that "follows upon the erasure from public representation of the names, images, and narratives of those the US has killed" (*Precarious* xiv).[1] Where Butler's national melancholic experiences the "prohibitions on avowing grief in public" as "an effective mandate in favor of a generalized melancholia (and a derealization of loss) when it comes to considering as dead those the United States or its allies have killed" (*Precarious Life* 37), the protagonist of *The Three Burials* (an Anglo rancher) finds that not only is his grief over the death of his undocumented ranch hand socially unintelligible, it renders *him* socially unintelligible as well. *Amigoland,* on the other hand, focuses on the historical legacy of what Schmidt Camacho calls *migrant melancholia,* the undocumented migrant's refusal to give up both the emotional attachment to a lost homeland and the political attachment to the rights of state-sponsored citizenship. Although the novel's protagonists are both U.S. citizens, their experiences highlight the extent to which the "psychic wounding" (Schmidt Camacho, *Migrant Imaginaries* 299) of the border crossing is transmitted intergenerationally and lingers long after citizenship is secured. Like the Freudian melancholic subject, who refuses to relinquish a mourned object to integrate herself into the dominant social order, Schmidt Camacho's melancholic migrant refuses to relinquish her humanity to assimilate to a society that devalues her.

Despite the fact that Butler's national melancholia is clearly aligned with a dominant (white, Anglo, U.S. citizen) subjectivity and Schmidt Camacho's migrant melancholia is aligned with a nondominant subjectivity, my analysis of the two texts will treat them as arising from the same social conditions. The work of Anne Anlin Cheng (which predates that of both Schmidt Camacho and Butler) reveals how hegemonic and nonhegemonic melancholias are related. Cheng suggests that melancholia illuminates "two particular aspects of American racial culture: first, dominant, white culture's rejection of yet attachment to the racial other and, second, the ramifications that such paradox holds for the racial other" (*Melancholy of Race* xi). My analysis will suggest, furthermore, that examining national melancholia together with migrant melancholia reveals how representations of immigration in contemporary U.S. public rhetoric are circumscribed by what the philosopher Sara Ahmed, who (independently of Schmidt Camacho) also theorizes what she calls the *melancholic migrant*, calls "the happiness duty" (*Promise of Happiness* 158). Ahmed defines this duty as an injunction for citizens and noncitizens alike "not to speak about racism in the present, not to speak of the unhappiness of colonial histories, or of attachments that cannot be reconciled into the colorful diversity of the multicultural nation" (158).[2] By examining *The Three Burials* and *Amigoland* together, I not only argue that the two texts represent different takes on a singular affect—melancholia—that is politicized in different ways, I also suggest that the anxieties about aging that animate both texts buttress their political interventions.

Where Schmidt Camacho describes the journey of the undocumented migrant as a "passage from citizenship to noncitizenship, authorized status to unauthorized status" (*Migrant Imaginaries* 287), the protagonists of *The Three Burials* and *Amigoland* experience the process of aging as a similar passage. As a result of aging, they lose their authority and political status; they are deprived of their agency, their motivations are questioned, and their actions are perceived as irrational. In this way, the texts employ images of aging men to represent a larger preoccupation with undocumented migration and (non)citizenship. However, the process of aging is not merely a metaphor for the consequences of border-crossing. Instead, both texts also exploit the

intersections between age and unauthorized legal status to reinforce the efforts of scholars and activists who remind the public
at large that we are all at risk of being denied human rights on
the basis of disability or legal attachment to a nation-state. Disability activists have long used aging as an example of why disability is a concern for everyone, not just people with disabilities;
they remind us that everyone will become disabled if they have
the good fortune to live long enough. Meanwhile, writing in
the aftermath of World War II, Hannah Arendt insists that the
dilemma of the *stateless person* is also a concern of the citizen:

> For the nation-state cannot exist once its principle of
> equality before the law has broken down. Without this
> legal equality, . . . the nation dissolves into an anarchic
> mass of over- and underprivileged individuals. Laws that
> are not equal for all revert to rights and privileges, some-
> thing contradictory to the very nature of nation-states. The
> clearer the proof of their inability to treat stateless people
> as legal persons . . . the more difficult it is for states to resist
> the temptation to deprive all citizens of legal status and
> rule them with an omnipotent police. (290)

By using the corporeal effects of aging to meditate on the sociopolitical effects of migration, *The Three Burials* and *Amigoland*
also force us to confront this point of rhetorical commonality
shared by disability and border activism. Examined together,
then, *The Three Burials* and *Amigoland* offer a critical look not
only at the consequences of migrant melancholia and national
melancholia but also at the larger social conditions that create them. By linking a bodily experience—aging—that is both
extraordinarily common and widely feared to concerns about
the human rights of undocumented migrants in the United
States, these texts interrogate the politics and ethics at stake in
the representation of undocumented immigration.

The Three Burials: Tommy Lee Jones, Affective Alienation, and the Refusal of National Melancholia

The Three Burials depicts the journey into Mexico of two men, traveling with corpse in tow, to bury an undocumented immigrant who is recklessly killed by a Border Patrol agent. Melquiades Estrada (Julio César Cedillo) is tending sheep for Pete Perkins (Tommy Lee Jones) while Border Patrol agent Mike Norton (Barry Pepper) surveys the territory nearby. When Melquiades shoots at a coyote that threatens the sheep, Norton thinks he is under fire and responds by fatally shooting him. Pete, recalling a promise he has made to Melquiades that he will bury him in his hometown if he should die in the United States, kidnaps Norton and forces him to help disinter Melquiades's remains as well as to aid his quest to give Melquiades the burial he requested. The plot follows their journey south, charting their efforts to evade law enforcement, preserve Melquiades's decomposing body, and escape the dangers of the desert that threaten the lives of unauthorized border crossers (including snakebites, thirst, hunger, and heat). When he finally locates Melquiades's hometown, however, Pete finds that it is not at all as it was described: the name of the town is not Jiménez (as Melquiades has called it), and the woman Melquiades called his wife (who appears with Melquiades in a photograph he has shown to Pete, and which Pete brings along on the journey) claims not to know him.

For his theatrical-release directorial debut,[3] Jones sought the collaboration of Mexican novelist and screenwriter Guillermo Arriaga, known for his three film collaborations with director Alejandro González Iñárritu (Amores perros, 21 Grams, and Babel),[4] as well as for novels like Un dulce olor a muerte (1994) and La noche del búfalo (1999). In an interview with Salon.com film critic Andrew O'Hehir, Jones describes Arriaga as his "hunting buddy" and characterizes the inspiration for the transborder collaboration as follows: "Arriaga likes to make movies about his country and its history; I want to make movies about my country and its history. If you spend much time along the river [i.e., the Rio Grande], you understand that in many ways the two countries are the same." Indeed, the film emphasizes the geographical similarities between the two countries with frequent wide-angle landscape shots. Yet *The Three Burials* also underscores how U.S. immigration policy attempts to differentiate the two countries culturally and politically. As Joseph Nevins argues, the enforcement buildup on the U.S.-Mexico border has required "the creation of the national 'self' and alien 'other'" in order to mitigate "what many perceived to be an excessive blurring of the social boundaries between 'us' and 'them'" (*Operation Gatekeeper* 92). The screenplay for the film is inspired by a historical event: the 1997 killing of 18-year-old Esequiel Hernández, shot by U.S. marines while herding goats near the border.[5] According to border scholars and activists, deaths like that of Hernández (who was a U.S. citizen) are made possible by rhetoric in which, as Durand, Massey, and Parrado put it, Latin American immigrants are "connected symbolically with invaders, criminals, and drug smugglers, who [are] pictured as poised menacingly along a lightly-defended two-thousand-mile frontier dividing the United States from Mexico and the poor masses of the Third World" ("New Era" 521). Buttressed by such discourse, border enforcement initiatives work to minimize the "sameness" that Jones identifies between the United States and Mexico. Maintaining the fiction of an essential difference between the United States and Mexico is important for border enforcement because policing the border is such violent work. If the devaluation of the lives of undocumented Mexican migrants relies upon the persistent belief that Mexico and the United States are fundamentally different, then Jones's emphasis on the similarities between the two countries constitutes a political act, an affirmation that the undocumented Mexican migrant possesses a life that should be valued and protected.

As politically significant as his insistence on Mexico's "sameness" with the United States is the fact that Jones's recent work as both actor and director has demonstrated a marked focus on the effects and consequences of national melancholia. In *The*

Three Burials, as I will argue, he explores the consequences of refusing national melancholia. In other recent films, like *In the Electric Mist* (USA, 2009), *In the Valley of Elah* (USA, 2007), and *No Country For Old Men* (USA, 2007), he performs the consequences of participating in it. *In the Electric Mist* stars Jones as an aging detective in post-Katrina New Orleans who finds himself haunted by the ghosts of the Confederate past; *In the Valley of Elah* features him as the father of a murdered Iraq war veteran who struggles to recognize and comprehend the brutality of his son's actions during the war; *No Country For Old Men* presents him as a small-town sheriff who is horrified by his confrontation with the violence of the drug trade. In all of these films, Jones's aging, white, male body is used to great effect in an exploration of the consequences of national melancholia, representing a nation that has fallen into decline, ruined by its own disregard for life.[6] Jones's characters in these films mourn the failure of a U.S. national identity in which they have fervently believed, while the spectacle of their aging bodies presents a visual image of national crisis.

In *The Three Burials*—which predates the films described above but which is also the only one of the four to be directed by Jones, thereby giving him greater control over the visual representation of his body—Jones departs from these roles. Here he depicts not a character whose grief is prompted by a sudden confrontation with the crisis of U.S. identity but rather a character profoundly changed by his grief for a victim of that crisis. At its most basic level, *The Three Burials* is about Pete Perkins's efforts (ineffectual and unusual as they might be) to mourn his lost friend Melquiades. To use Cheng's words, it is about the "transformation from grief to grievance, from suffering injury to speaking out against that injury" (*Melancholy of Race* 3). In *The Three Burials*, then, Jones's aging white male body does not represent the decline of national ideals but serves instead to underscore the affective alignment of his character, Pete Perkins, outside of the dominant national narrative. If, as Ahmed argues, the dominant affective mode of citizenship is happiness, making happiness into what she calls a "technology of citizenship" (*Promise of Happiness* 133), these films depict Jones refusing "to see happily" and thereby repudiating the citizen's obligation "not to see violence, asymmetry, or force" (132). In *The Three Burials*, Pete's aging body underscores his radical difference from his social world; corporeal otherness becomes a way of visually representing his status as what Ahmed calls an "affect alien" (123).

The Three Burials was not (by Hollywood standards) successful in the United States (or among English-speaking film audiences in general), barely grossing $5 million at the box office and completely ignored by the Academy Awards. It also received critical reviews from sources like *The Guardian*, where Peter Bradshaw calls it "a strangely self-regarding and self-indulgent contemporary western," and *The San Francisco Chronicle*, where Mike LaSalle describes it as "dreadfully slow without much in the way of rewards." Outside the United States it fared better, winning prizes at Cannes (best actor and best screenplay; nominated for the Palme d'Or), at the Ghent International Film Festival (the Grand Prix), and at Camerimage (the Golden Frog).[7] After winning at Cannes, screenwriter Arriaga was commemorated by the government of the Mexican state of Tamaulipas, where local official Adriana González declared him "one of the most significant personalities in the literature and cinematography of contemporary Mexico" (Aguilar Grimaldo).[8] The film's favorable reception among non-U.S. audiences in general and Spanish-speaking audiences in particular suggests, as John "Rio" Riofrio argues, that the film has been "underestimated and misunderstood" by U.S. audiences, and that it is actually "a sophisticated meditation on the struggle for a post-9/11 American identity."[9] What the remainder of this analysis will explore, then, is how the film uses Jones's aging, white, male body in the service of this meditation.

The Three Burials initially appears to follow the formula of the classic Western in which a cowboy hero goes to great lengths to avenge an injustice committed against a friend or companion.

To reinforce this initial impression, the film relies upon audience familiarity with Jones himself and with the heroes of classic Westerns like the 1989 made-for-television film *Lonesome Dove* (starring a much-younger Jones, whose character also undertakes an arduous journey to give a friend a proper burial). In the beginning, Pete appears to be the stoic, rational hero whose actions are beyond question and whose motives are unassailable. During the first ten minutes of the film, Pete makes an unusual request to the local sheriff: he asks for Melquiades's body to be given to him after the autopsy, so that he can return the body to Mexico. The sheriff immediately asks Pete if he is crazy, and Pete solemnly replies: "No. I'm not." At this moment, early in the film, the viewer's sympathy is firmly with Pete. The conversation is filmed in a classic shot-reverse-shot back-and-forth, so that as Pete replies to the sheriff, the camera faces him squarely, allowing the viewer to look him in the eye as he affirms his psychiatric health. The implication, then, is that Pete's desire to honor Melquiades is rational while the disregard for it shown by law enforcement is not.

It might be possible—though it would require leaving aside much of the film's nuance—to argue that this presentation of Pete (as radically out of step with the small-town Texas social life that surrounds him) persists throughout the film, and that Pete is, in fact, the rational hero of the traditional Western. Using flashbacks, the film shows us the loneliness of Pete's life; his affair with a married waitress who is also sleeping with the town sheriff is his only significant relationship besides his friendship with Melquiades. All of this indicates Pete's lack of fit with the town that surrounds him, which is portrayed as a site of corruption and even depravity (I would cite again the married waitress, who demonstrates both the boredom of life in the town and the sexual depravity of its residents). Furthermore, Pete is the one character in the film who refuses to see Melquiades's death as inconsequential, who insists upon grieving the life that is presented in the town's dominant narrative as unworthy of grief, and who in this way repudiates national melancholia. What is confusing about the film, however, is that it does not seem to take a definitive stance on either the ethics or the rationality of Pete's ultimate response to Melquiades's death. Instead, the film ultimately leaves it up to the viewer to determine whether Pete's affective dissonance with the social world that surrounds him— his refusal to participate in national melancholia—is rational or right. That the film condemns the social circumstances that lead to the death of Melquiades is clear. Whether the film affirms Pete's response to those circumstances is much less so.

As the film progresses, it becomes increasingly clear that Pete's attachment to Melquiades is far above and beyond the healthy concern of a friend, not to mention the healthy concern of an employer for even an exceptional employee. Furthermore, Pete's actions become increasingly erratic. He kidnaps Norton, he disinters his friend, and he sets off on a journey that is not only illegal but is also treacherous and difficult. Meanwhile, he cares meticulously for the corpse of his friend while subjecting Norton's body to harm (for instance, forcing Norton to walk mostly barefoot, except when the terrain is so rough that he allows him to wear tattered boots with no socks) and barely caring for his own. He jolts awake to brush ants off Melquiades's body after Norton tells him that there are ants crawling on it and uses antifreeze to undertake a DIY embalming procedure when the body begins to stink. Eventually, after he discovers that local law enforcement officials are pursuing him, Pete seeks out the help of a coyote to cross into Mexico. Eyeing him suspiciously, the coyote states that he has never helped anyone cross to Mexico before. Later, Norton shouts at Pete that he is crazy, echoing the words of the sheriff at the beginning of the film, and this time Pete does not respond. The fact that Pete's behavior continues to be represented as unintelligible to those around him—even when he leaves his town—means that the film leaves its judgment of his actions unclear.

Because of the ambivalence that surrounds his character, Pete might seem to provide a stark contrast to Melquiades. Where Pete's actions are treated as questionable, Melquiades for much of the film appears as a noble, innocent martyr. Flashbacks in which Melquiades appears are always filmed in soft focus, many taking place outdoors, in sunny natural light and accompanied by sentimental music; this filmmaking style seems to suggest an idealized portrait of a man whose life has been senselessly cut short. By representing Melquiades in this way, the film might appear to follow the formula of what performance scholar Ana Elena Puga has called the *migrant melodrama*: a morality tale depicting the tremendous tribulations that migrants endure in their journeys to the United States. Puga concedes that the migrant melodrama inspires sympathy for undocumented migrants, "helping readers/viewers from the United States to experience them as worthy of our concern rather than our indifference or our hostility." At the same time, such narratives can also be dehumanizing, for they present migrants' humanity as circumscribed and thus reinforces their abjection. Even worse, Puga notes, the migrant melodrama ultimately leaves audiences with the message that it is by experiencing unimaginable trauma that the undocumented migrant comes to "earn" her place in the United States.

Although *The Three Burials* seems for much of the narrative to present itself as a migrant melodrama, however, the ending of the film disrupts this formula. Here Pete finds the woman he believes to be Melquiades's wife and tells her of his death. The woman claims to have no idea who Melquiades is, despite the fact that Pete presents her with a photograph of Melquiades with the woman and her children. At this moment, the image of Melquiades as an idealized, innocent martyr is shattered. The soft-focus flashbacks depicting Melquiades as a saintly figure bathed in sunshine, we recall, represent Pete's perspective—and Pete's rationality has been called into question. The viewer is left asking if Melquiades has lied to Pete all along, or if perhaps Melquiades too has lost touch with reality and imagined a wife and children who never existed. The most likely explanation is that Melquiades has simply abandoned his wife and children, not fulfilling the promise to send them money from his earnings (which, we are led to assume by Pete's attachment to Melquiades, must have been fair if not bountiful). His wife has been forced, then, to remarry, and in order to maintain good relations with her new husband and perhaps to keep her own feelings of abandonment at bay, has moved forward with her life as though Melquiades never existed. In this light, Melquiades ceases to be the long-suffering innocent and becomes instead a failed provider whose emotional attachment to the wife and children he abandoned is misplaced. Pete, meanwhile, whose loneliness may have led him to believe in a friendship that never really existed, has apparently been manipulated by Melquiades.

What I would like to suggest here is that Pete and Melquiades are both represented in ways that oscillate between emphasizing their perfect moral uprightness and emphasizing their irrationality or untrustworthiness. Moreover, this oscillation puts the social context in which their friendship is forged under critical scrutiny. Pete and Melquiades share what Ahmed would call their attachment to *bad objects* (where "bad objects," of course, are those deemed unworthy of attachment by the dominant society). Melquiades refuses to relinquish his attachment not only to the spouse and children he has left behind, but also to Mexico; this refusal prevents him from integrating himself into the social fabric of the United States, from becoming a viable candidate for citizenship. Pete, meanwhile, remains attached to an undocumented worker, a figure represented in mainstream media images as being unworthy of love, attachment, or political rights. Ahmed writes:

> Membership in an affective community can require not only that you share an orientation toward certain objects as being good, . . . but also that you recognize the same objects as being lost. So if an affective community is produced by sharing objects of loss, which means letting objects go in the right way, then the melancholics would be affect aliens in how they love: their love becomes a failure to get over loss, which keeps them facing the wrong way. (*Promise of Happiness* 141)

Both Pete and Melquiades "face the wrong way," for they refuse to capitulate to a narrative that positions their attachments—to Mexico, to the undocumented—as objects that must be surrendered as a condition of cultural citizenship or national belonging. They resist, in particular, the idea that the humanity of the unauthorized migrant must be sacrificed to protect the national boundaries of the United States.

As "affect aliens," however, Melquiades and Pete also offer a critical perspective from which to reevaluate which objects are deemed to be "good" for emotional attachment and which are deemed to be "bad." Schmidt Camacho asserts: "the narration of migrant sorrows constitutes a political *act* cast against the prerogatives of neoliberal development and the global division of labor—in particular, the erosion of substantive citizenship and communal belonging but also the resurgent forms of racial governance in both countries" (*Migrant Imaginaries* 288, emphasis added). Her account of migrant melancholia, then, presents it as a potential force for change because it generates perspectives and social locations that may potentially foment resistance to the dominant social order. Along similar lines, the act of refusing national melancholia may similarly produce social transformation; the film thus prompts us to reevaluate how nondominant affective states may be tied to political, cultural, and economic factors, and how close attention to the perspectives and circumstances of those experiencing such affective states may generate political solutions to what are perceived as their "individual" problems.

Here it is useful to examine the representation of Melquiades's corpse. In negative reviews of the film, the corpse is frequently cited as evidence indicating the film's poor quality. *The Guardian*'s Bradshaw complains that "the scenes with Melquiades's dead body have a gruesome black comedy that is, frankly, not entirely intentional," while the *Chronicle*'s LaSalle sarcastically wonders if "millions of cinephiles have been waiting for a movie to come along that shows Jones combing a corpse's hair or picking the flesh-eating ants from its dead face." Indeed, the corpse does not appear at all realistic or convincing; it is simply a stiff, blackened doll that Pete and Norton awkwardly tote about. Instead of seeing this as proof of "bad" filmmaking, however, I suggest that we might consider it an invitation to view the dead body of the unauthorized migrant as an unnatural object. We live, certainly, in a world in which the deaths of border crossers are presented as inevitable, as mundane; this occurs in a context in which, as Nevins documents, "the number of crossing-related fatalities has steadily grown, reaching historic highs, averaging more than 350 documented deaths per year between 1995 and 2006, and doubling in terms of national average between 1999 and 2005" (*Operation Gatekeeper* 173). However, there is nothing inevitable about such deaths; we have created the political conditions that give rise to them, and we can create political conditions that will minimize, if not entirely eliminate, them. Seeing migrant deaths as unnatural—and the dead bodies of border crossers as morbid, repugnant, and intolerable—is the first step toward creating these new political conditions.

Along similar lines, the film invites us to look critically at Pete's body. Unlike Melquiades, who inhabits a body for much of the film that is deliberately represented as grotesquely as possible, Pete inhabits a body that viewers identify with a powerful symbol of national ideals. His is the body of the cowboy hero, the Man in Black, the defender of the so-called "American Way." It is the body of Tommy Lee Jones. In *The Three Burials*, however, that body is represented fleeing law enforcement, undertaking a perilous journey through the borderlands of southern Texas and northern Mexico; in other words, that body imbued with national ideals is placed in a context associated in the dominant national imaginary with criminality. As Schmidt Camacho writes, "proponents of anti-immigrant measures commonly represent the undocumented as people with no respect for the rule of law" (*Migrant Imaginaries* 301). As media critics like Leo Chavez and Otto Santa Ana observe, they do this by representing the undocumented in contexts and situations overdetermined by their association with illegality. Placing the body of Pete Perkins into this setting, then, forces audiences to reconsider the social dominance of the white male body. By representing that body in ways that align with otherness, in other words, the film throws into question the very constitution of the affective community that constitutes the United States.

Although the film makes important interventions, however, there is one significant problem with it that must be addressed: Melquiades—for whom the film is named, and who appears as a central figure—is dead for the entirety of the film. (Here I emphasize that the scenes in which Melquiades appears alive are all flashbacks that are explicitly narrated from Pete's perspective.) This is a problem because, as Cheng observes, dominant "white identity in America operates melancholically" (*Melancholy of Race* 11) in both racist and liberal discourses. In particular, Cheng critiques the ways in which, in so-called "liberal" discourses, mourning the racialized subject serves to reify that subject's position outside the national sphere; she argues that "white liberals need to keep burying the racial other in order to memorialize him" (11). Her criticism is, of course, particularly apposite for an analysis of *The Three Burials*, which is explicitly about burying the racialized other; it interrogates the "right" way to bury an undocumented immigrant and concludes with his final burial. Indeed, following this burial, Pete and Norton appear to resolve their differences. The film concludes with Pete giving one of his horses to Norton and telling him that he may return home, prompting Norton to ask Pete if he will be OK. The final words of the film, in other words, are a white man asking another white man about his well-being in the wake of the nation's moral collapse; although the film interrogates national melancholia as a cause of this collapse, it ultimately re-centers white men as the subjects who will be charged with the nation's recovery of its democratic ideals and moral principles.[10] In this way, the film brings to mind the following questions posed by Cheng: "But how does recognizing this melancholic dilemma underlying dominant power *help* those who have been buried and then resuscitated only as serviceable ghosts? . . . In other words, what implications do insights into the melancholic origins of American racial-national identity hold for the study of the racialized subjects?" (original emphasis, 14). To consider these questions, I will now turn to the analysis of *Amigoland*, a novel that focuses on another journey to Mexico, this one a journey undertaken by two elderly Chicanos.

Amigoland: Oscar Casares, Migrant Melancholia, and the Presence of the Past

Oscar Casares's first novel *Amigoland* links the violence that accompanied the establishment of the border to the violence that currently maintains it. As Joseph Nevins points out, "the radical build-up of the boundary and immigration enforcement apparatus that has taken place since the mid-1990s in the U.S.-Mexico borderlands is the outgrowth of long-term processes" (*Operation Gatekeeper* 19)—processes that date back to the 1848 establishment of the boundary line. In order to settle their differences in the present, two elderly brothers must resolve a debate about how their grandfather came to the United States in 1850. Doing so requires confronting the limitations of their aging bodies as they travel to the ranch in Mexico where their grandfather was born. In the course of their journey, they also revisit a historical moment that, as Vicki L. Ruiz argues, "remains shrouded in mystery and misconception" ("Nuestra América" 657): the redrawing of the U.S.-Mexico boundary and its tumultuous aftermath. *Amigoland* thus interrogates what Edward Said calls "the pastness *or not* of the past" (*Culture and Imperialism* 7, original emphasis), revealing how the U.S. conquest of Mexican territory in the nineteenth century continues to shape the identities of ethnic Mexicans living in the United States. As Said observes, conflicts over history involve "not only disagreement about what happened in the past and what the past was, but also uncertainty about whether the past really is past, over and concluded, or whether it continues, albeit in different forms" (3). *Amigoland*, as the story of two brothers born on opposite sides of the U.S.-Mexico border, reveals that the so-called "past" of the U.S. annexation of Texas is not "over and concluded" but persists in the present through political struggles over border enforcement policy and personal struggles over the interpretation of family histories that take place on both sides of the border. Migrant melancholia in this text, then, persists in the characters' lives long after they have secured citizenship in the United States; it functions not only as a means of contesting pervasive disregard for the lives of contemporary Mexican migrants but also as a corrective to what Ruiz calls the "mystery and misconception" surrounding the history of the border.

The relationship between the geopolitical imposition of the present-day U.S.-Mexico boundary and the construction of contemporary Chicana/o identities in the United States is a central concern of Casares's fiction. In addition to *Amigoland*, Casares has also published a collection of short stories, *Brownsville* (2003). Both of his books are (at least partially) set in Brownsville, Texas, and both deal with how the boundary line impacts intimate relationships between family members, lovers, neighbors, and friends nearly two centuries after the signing of the Treaty of Guadalupe Hidalgo. As I have argued elsewhere, these issues coalesce around the representation of disability in the short story "Big Jesse, Little Jesse" (Minich, "Disabling"); this is even more the case in *Amigoland*, where careful attention to the bodily and psychological effects of aging highlight socially constructed divisions of nationality, race, and gender. David G. Gutiérrez argues for the need to rethink "the relationship of Chicano history (that is, the history of ethnic Mexicans in the United States) to the heretofore dominant—and largely separate—national and historical narratives of both Mexico and the United States" ("Migration" 483–84). In Casares's fiction, the representation of vulnerable bodies is central to the process of interrogating and, ultimately, reconceptualizing the relationship between Chicano history and the national histories of Mexico and the United States.

The plot of *Amigoland* is relatively straightforward. Don Fidencio, in his early 90s, is the oldest of twelve siblings, all of whom have passed away except the youngest, Don Celestino. He has recently been placed into a nursing home by his only daughter, Amalia, and struggles with the adjustment from a life in which he lived with full independence to one in which he must depend on nurses and aides. Don Celestino, in his early 70s, is a recent widower in the early stages of a relationship with his Mexican housekeeper, Socorro. Socorro, who is much younger than Don Celestino (in her early 40s), lives in Matamoros and crosses the border daily for work. Don Celestino seeks out Don Fidencio because Socorro wishes to meet his family, even though the two men have not spoken in decades. This causes them to revive an old argument about how their family came to live on the U.S. side of the border: Don Fidencio insists that their grandfather was kidnapped by Native Americans as a child and brought north, while Don Celestino is skeptical of this account. To settle their dispute, the two men travel with Socorro to their grandfather's old ranchito in Mexico. The novel concludes with Don Fidencio deciding to live out his remaining days with distant relatives at the ranchito instead of returning to the nursing home. Meanwhile, Don Celestino becomes increasingly fearful of his own inevitable aging as he witnesses his brother's physical decline, a fear that causes him to retreat emotionally from Socorro; at the end of the novel, she leaves him.

If, as Mary Pat Brady asserts, the U.S.-Mexico border is a "state-sponsored aesthetic project—that is, a project through which the state aestheticizes ideological, nationalist work" (*Extinct Lands* 146), then Casares's fiction might be seen as a counter-hegemonic aesthetic project designed to disrupt this work. In both *Amigoland* and *Brownsville*, the border asserts itself in the text's most quotidian textual details, reflecting how the reality of border enforcement integrates itself into the most minute details of daily life on the border.[11] As a representative example, I would cite a moment when the characters sit down to eat in a café: "A pair of Border Patrol agents sat close to the door, one of them keeping an eye on the kitchen workers, the other more interested in the carne guisada he had on his plate" (183). The point of this scene is not the fact of border policing; rather, it is over conversation in this café that the idea arises for the trip to Mexico. Yet here the border emerges, precisely when it does not seem relevant to the plot, because it remains a social fact that lurks at the edges of the characters' consciousness at all times, present in the most mundane of everyday social interactions. Indeed, these moments are all the more significant because none of the characters experiences a serious incident with border enforcement during the period covered by the novel; the deportations and border-crossing fatalities that Don Fidencio, Don Celestino, and Socorro recall (their own and those of their family members) are all long past. Yet even Casares's U.S. citizen characters continue to live with unrelenting reminders that, as ethnic Mexicans living in the United States, their status within the United States is under constant scrutiny.

One effect of the ubiquity of border enforcement is that its presence becomes manifest in the most intimate of personal relationships. For instance, the border literally divides Don Fidencio from all of his siblings. Unlike the others, Don Fidencio is born on the Mexican side because his parents travel back and forth frequently during the early years of their marriage to earn a living. This accident of birth serves as a continual reminder to him of the arbitrary nature of U.S. border policy. He recalls life before the militarization of the border: "when he was a boy and they would work along one side of the river one year and along the other side the following year, then back again, so much that he sometimes forgot they were two separate countries" (5). After the Great Depression, however, it becomes impossible to forget that the United States and Mexico are separate countries, as he is deported from the country in which he has lived for most of his life and which all of his siblings call home: "And how was he supposed to explain to the agent that because his parents had crossed over to look for work, he was born in Reynosa, just on the other side of the river, but almost all his life he had spent on this side? Another week and he would have been born in the U.S., same as the rest of his family. Yes, even if he had relatives on both sides, really he was American now and had been for many, many years" (14–15).

Although Don Fidencio's birth in Mexico makes him particularly vulnerable in the United States, he is not the only one to question his belonging. Don Celestino, too, recalls that after serving in the U.S. military in World War II, he is not guaranteed the full sociopolitical rights assured by the institution of citizenship:

> And before that, he could remember attending barber school for almost three years because he kept having to leave with his brothers to follow the crops up north to Ohio, to Minnesota, to Iowa, to Michigan, and then by the time he did get his license, the army was ready for him. . . . And when the war ended before he had actually made it overseas, the army shipped him back home, and in Houston he boarded a commercial bus that eventually stopped at a roadside diner near Corpus, and while the rest of the passengers were free to enter the restaurant, because of the times he was forced to sit on the back steps of the kitchen and eat a cheeseburger so greasy it stained his uniform. (85–86)

Both brothers, then, experience traumatic events as young men which cause them to feel that they have, despite being born on opposite sides of the border, each managed to be born on the "wrong" side.

The border that divides the brothers at birth divides them again on the day that Don Celestino attends an Anglo customer at his barbershop before cutting his brother's hair. Here Don Fidencio accusingly tells his younger brother: "You act like one of them" (90), meaning that Don Celestino's U.S. birth has imparted to him a gringo ethic that prevents him from properly honoring family obligations. Following this argument, the brothers do not speak for a decade. Their conflict, then, parallels the ways in which the 1848 redrawing of the U.S.-Mexico boundary affected families at the time, as described by Chicano public intellectual Américo Paredes: "Men were expected to consider their relatives and closest neighbors, the people just across the river, as foreigners in a foreign land" (*With His Pistol* 15). More than a century later, Casares demonstrates, the imposition of the border and the effects of its enforcement have the same consequences, dividing families into categories of "us" and "them."

Furthermore, it is important to note that even as both brothers are excluded from dominant constructions of U.S. citizenship, they are also denied the rights and benefits of national belonging in Mexico. Don Fidencio, in particular, exemplifies Gutiérrez's argument that "Mexican Americans, Mexican immigrants, and Mexican migrants remain deeply ambivalent about their relationship to the nation-state and the national 'community' it supposedly represents—whether that nation-state is the Republic of Mexico or the United States of America" ("Migration" 517). When he is deported to Mexico as a young man, it is "his first time so far beyond the other side of the border" (15). Seventy years later, after he arrives in Mexico to begin the journey back to the family ranchito with his brother and Socorro, he is deeply angered when Socorro reminds him that he needs documentation in order to be there: "And anyway, if I was born on this side, for what do I need papers? . . . So I'm not supposed to be here, but now I can't get back over there? Is that what you want to tell me? Not here and not there?" (236).

Amigoland's representation of the brothers' perception of their own devalued citizenship status is striking, but even more provocative is the way it mediates its representation of these questions of citizenship through the depiction of aging and bodily vulnerability. In this way, it reproduces what Butler has identified as the political consequences of bodily vulnerability:

> In a way, we all live with this . . . a vulnerability to the
> other that is part of bodily life, a vulnerability to a sud-
> den address from elsewhere that we cannot preempt. This

vulnerability, however, becomes highly exacerbated under certain social and political conditions, especially those in which violence is a way of life and the means to secure self-defense are limited. (*Precarious Life* 29)

For Butler, war constitutes the most evident example of social and political conditions under which bodily vulnerability becomes exacerbated; her examples, in fact, are drawn from the so-called U.S. War on Terror. Yet the violent policing of the U.S.-Mexico border serves as an example that is much closer to home. *Amigoland*, indeed, poignantly depicts how the experience of corporeal deterioration intensifies the brothers' experience of second-class citizenship.

The brothers' sense of not belonging politically manifests itself most powerfully in their shared fear of being unable to work. As both border activists and disability scholars have pointed out, migrants and people with disabilities are subjected to constant suspicion about their status as "productive" members of society, put upon to justify their political incorporation into the national body by demonstrating their capacity for work. Indeed, as I discuss in the previous chapter, border enforcement policy discursively relies upon an ideology of ability that conflates the ability to work with worth as a potential citizen. Don Fidencio, angry that the aides at the nursing home have taken away his canes and forced him to use a walker, decides to use instead a dust mop that a member of the cleaning staff has left in the hallway: "He meant to push it only a few steps, maybe clear away some of the specks he could still see on the floor, twinkling like little colored stars, but after a while he turned the dust mop toward the nurses' station" (37). When the nurses and the other residents laugh at him, he brushes off the ridicule: "They thought it was all so curious and funny, an old man cleaning the floors. Never mind that he was doing them a service, something they should be doing themselves. . . . Wait until they saw the work he had done, then we'd see who was laughing" (38). Meanwhile, Don Celestino is horrified when the man who does yard work in his neighborhood offers him the discounted rate he gives to the elderly: "Did he see him walking around with a cane or a walker? Did he have a handicapped tag hanging from his rearview mirror? Had they built a ramp for him to roll his wheelchair up to the front door? If anything, he felt he had more energy to dedicate to his responsibilities around the house" (155–56). This attachment to the ability to work may register for some readers as internalized able-bodied supremacy (which it is, to some extent), but it is also a powerful manifestation of the psychic toll of being reduced in the public eye to a laboring body and little else: the brothers have great difficulty understanding their own societal value as they lose their ability to work.

In addition to worrying about not being able to work, Don Fidencio and Don Celestino worry about losing their memories as they age. Yet it is not the moments of happiness that they struggle to recall; instead, it is the moments when their national belonging is questioned (like being deported or being denied service in a restaurant). Don Fidencio, denied supper for mis-behaving in his nursing home, quells his hunger by recalling his journey back to Texas from Veracruz after the deportation: "He could hear his belly tightening and he was thinking that he might have been hungrier sometime between when the Depression hit and the year he went off to the CCC camps" (12). Don Celes-tino recalls the incident outside the diner as part of an effort to reassure himself that "his mind was sharper than those of much younger men" (85). The brothers are not the only characters who struggle to accept what Said calls "the pastness of the past." Don Fidencio's roommate in the nursing home shouts out loud dur-ing nightmares in which he relives the U.S. invasion of Texas: "I DON'T CARE WHO SENT YOU DOWN HERE—YOU HEAR ME? THIS LAND HAS ALWAYS BELONGED TO MY PEO-PLE!" (125). As Ahmed writes, the dominant narrative about people who refuse to leave the past behind them is that they are perpetuating racism: "if racism is preserved *only* in migrants' memory and consciousness, then racism would 'go away' if only they would let it go away, if only they too would declare it gone"

(*Promise of Happiness* 148, original emphasis). By refusing to declare racism gone, the characters in Casares's novel resist this dominant narrative. Instead, like Ahmed, they remind us of the need to "recognize the impossibility of putting certain histories behind us; these histories persist, and we must persist in declaring our unhappiness with their persistence" (159).

The most contentious history for Don Fidencio and Don Celestino is that of how their family arrived on the U.S. side of the border. Don Fidencio recalls his grandfather's story of being kidnapped by Indians in 1850—just after the signing of the Treaty of Guadalupe Hidalgo—and brought to the United States as a young boy. According to Don Fidencio, their grandfather (also named Fidencio) spends the rest of his life mourning the separation from his family and from Mexico, telling his young grandson: "Tocayo, someday when you are older you should go back and see how things are now, what there is of my ranchito. Tell them I always wanted to go back" (148). Don Celestino, on the other hand, dismisses the story: "The only ones who believed the story were little children" (147). Indeed, the story is an odd one, particularly in the context of Chicana/o literature, where border-crossing narratives tend to privilege families displaced by economic hardship or the Mexican Revolution. Yet, as Nevins reveals, the story reflects the fact that conflicts surrounding Native American land claims also played a role in the U.S. incorporation of Mexican territory; transboundary Native American attacks created conditions of unrest that provided a pretext for U.S. filibusters to claim Mexican lands. In this way, Casares makes visible a history often excluded from both U.S. nationalist narratives and counter-hegemonic Chicana/o accounts of the nineteenth-century border conflict: the violent pacification of the region's Native inhabitants. Don Fidencio recalls the reason for the raid in which their grandfather is taken: "All I know is the army had been trying to kill them off or send them to the north, but over here they were also trying to get rid of them. Nobody wanted them around" (188). Ruiz observes the need for more complex historical narratives exploring how

"Mexican Americans, American Indians, and Euro-Americans could inhabit the same social space and thus complicate U.S. western narratives that privilege a binary relationship between Euro-Americans and a designated 'other'" ("Nuestra América" 655). *Amigoland* reinforces Ruiz's call by recording gaps in the historical memory of these events, represented by the brothers' dispute.

Like the U.S. annexation of Texas, which brought some people into the category of rights-bearing citizens and shut others out of it, the process of aging also entails a loss of rights. Don Fidencio's descriptions of growing old in a nursing home parallel his descriptions of growing up in segregated Texas in the wake of the Depression. Just as he feels uncertain of his political belonging in both the United States and Mexico, Don Fidencio also feels, after arriving at the nursing home, that he is without an "imagined community" (to borrow Benedict Anderson's famous phrase): "He hadn't seen anyone he remembered or who might remember him, which seemed odd given that he had lived and worked in the same town for most of his life. Where the hell is everyone? he kept asking himself. Strangers, all strangers, they had taken everyone he knew and replaced them with strangers. This is where they had sent him to die, with strangers" (16). This feeling of belonging nowhere is accompanied by fears that he will lose more bodily autonomy as his health deteriorates:

> No matter how much he had lost, or they thought he had lost, he was still alert and understood what was happening to him. How long could it be before they moved him over to the U-shaped table where the aides would be feeding him? When would he not be able to dress himself anymore and have to wear his pajamas all day? One of these nights would there really be a need for them to keep the plastic lining on his mattress? (16–17)

Don Fidencio's experience of aging, then, resembles Schmidt Camacho's description of migrant melancholia: a refusal to accept becoming a person without political status, to relinquish the rights he possessed when his body was younger and healthier, to be deprived of the rights he retains as a citizen, as he crosses the boundary between healthy and disabled, between older and elderly.

I have been arguing that Casares depicts the social relations that cause the two brothers to feel politically and socially devalued and exposes the psychic trauma that these relations induce, but I also wish to emphasize the narrative strategies he employs to undermine these social relations. In an earlier essay on Casares, I observed that one of *Brownsville's* most distinctive formal features is its use of a third-person narrator whose style of speaking mirrors that of the collection's working-class, south Texas Chicano protagonists, even as key phrases in the texts occasionally establish a critical distance between the narrator and the character. In *Brownsville*, the effect is to subtly guide the reader toward a critique of the characters' actions and choices while maintaining empathy with the characters as they navigate difficult situations. In *Amigoland*, Casares employs a similar strategy, but to opposite effect. Here, the narrator uses the formal title of "Don" for both protagonists even as (again) the language seems to mimic the characters' speech. Once again, Casares establishes a combination of intimacy and detachment between the narrator and the characters, but instead of promoting a critique of the characters, the text promotes a deferential respect. The title "Don" reminds the reader that these characters are community elders deserving of respect even if they happen to live in a time and place in which their bodies are devalued as they slowly lose function.[12]

Through these formal strategies and thematic elements, *Amigoland* reveals how the experience of aging is informed by race, gender, and social class, as well as by colonial histories. Don Fidencio's experience in the nursing home is not simply that of an unmarked old man, but the experience of an old man who is ethnically marked as Mexican, one who lives in south Texas. For instance, language barriers are a problem in the nursing home, where the staff is largely Anglo and the residents primarily of

Mexican origin: "Not only was he forced to argue with the man about his bib but he had to do this in English, which for him meant stopping to think of the right words before he could open his mouth. A building full of old people who spoke mainly Spanish and no longer had any use for English, if they ever had, and this was the one they had sent to run the place" (18). The novel's depiction of aging thus demonstrates how the racial logic that undergirded the imperial expansion of the United States in the nineteenth century continues to inform even apparently universal experiences like growing old.

Amigoland ends on a note of uncertainty. When Don Fidencio and Don Celestino finally travel back to their grandfather's ranchito and find their long-lost relatives, they discover that the story Don Fidencio has told is true. An elderly woman at the ranchito, Mamá Nene, a distant cousin, mistakes Don Fidencio for his grandfather and welcomes him home, finally convincing him to stay with the family instead of returning. With this ending, Don Fidencio's two central conflicts are resolved: his disidentification with the dominant constructions of belonging in the United States, and his longing to age in a place where he is not deprived of his rights and treated like a lesser person because of the deterioration of his body. Yet Don Celestino is not able to find the same healing: he returns to the United States, and his fears about his age ultimately drive a wedge between him and Socorro. The novel ends with Socorro leaving Don Celestino, who has been unable to accept the certainty that he, like his brother, will soon experience the physical deterioration of old age. That the happy ending takes place in Mexico while the unhappy ending returns to the United States subverts ideas of the so-called "American Dream." Similarly significant is the fact the character whose story is most felicitously resolved at the end of the novel is the one who recognizes and accepts the bodily effects of aging. Unlike the dominant narrative that Ahmed critiques—that the solution to migrant melancholia is for migrants to "get over it" and relinquish their memories of racism and colonialism—*Amigoland* suggests the need for more narratives in which migrants' lives are not seen as disposable and in which the disability that comes with old age is not seen as uselessness.

In both *The Three Burials* and *Amigoland*, the journey from the United States to Mexico is depicted as a reversal of the border-crossing conversion that Saldívar describes in the epigraph to this chapter: border crossers from Mexico are restored to humanity. In *The Three Burials*, it is only in Mexico that Melquiades can be mourned properly; in *Amigoland*, it is only in Mexico that Don Fidencio can age with dignity. In this way, both texts provide a rigorous challenge to the U.S. national image of a free, egalitarian democracy. Ahmed writes that the "happiness duty for migrants means telling a certain story about your arrival as good, or the good of your arrival" (*Promise of Happiness* 158). *The Three Burials* and *Amigoland* both refuse this duty, revealing that "to speak of what is not good" or "to speak from or out of unhappiness" (158) can function as resistance.

At the same time, the representation of aging in these texts marks a significant point of difference between them. In *The Three Burials*, age functions as a means of inscribing visible difference on the dominant body, marking Pete's affective affiliation with those excluded from the national narrative that includes him. In *Amigoland*, the characters already possess bodies that have positioned them outside the national narrative, as racialized subjects, and the social devaluation that comes with age provides an opportunity for them to critically assess that narrative. Don Fidencio rejects it, deciding to finish his life in a place where, even if he does not live as long, his personhood will not be further devalued on the basis of his declining physical capacity. Don Celestino, meanwhile, seeks to disavow his bodily decline. *The Three Burials*, by focusing on Pete's subjectivity, does not allow for a full exploration of how Melquiades experiences the effects of migration, while *Amigoland* establishes as its focus the long-term, intergenerational effects of migrant melancholia. In this way, the work performed by the two texts is ultimately quite different.

At the same time, both texts make possible a critical intervention in my exploration of the body politics of nationalism in Chicana/o and Mexican cultural production. On the surface, *The Three Burials* and *Amigoland* would have little in common with the reformulations of Chicana/o cultural nationalism seen in the works by Arturo Islas, Cherríe Moraga, and Felicia Luna Lemus that I analyzed in the first two chapters of this study. Yet they (like the work of Alex Espinoza discussed in the third chapter) reveal how changing the bodily metaphors we use to conceptualize our nations can force us to reconceptualize the nations themselves. The next—and final—chapter will examine the work of two writers who seek to repudiate nationalism altogether, exploring how bodily images figure in this project as well.

PART THREE

BEYOND CITIZENSHIP

5 /   Overcoming the Nation: Ana Castillo,
Cecile Pineda, and the Stakes
of Disability Identity

This chapter marks a departure from the previous four. Where the others scrutinize forms of political belonging that (more or less) leave intact nationalism and the state—including cultural nationalism and juridical citizenship—this chapter addresses efforts to imagine subjectivities not anchored to a nation. Further, while a guiding principle of the previous sections is that disability constitutes a social location from which to reassess the institutions of *nation* and *citizenship*, here I subject the concept of disability as identity itself to critical scrutiny. Disability theorist Rosemarie Garland Thomson has asserted that "identity is a little bit like nationalism" (quoted in Siebers, *Disability Theory* 73–74); this study treats both identity and nationalism as constructs that can serve both liberatory and normative functions. As previous chapters show, nationalism is simultaneously a state-sponsored, exclusionary discourse buttressed by the ideology of ability (as in the militarization of the U.S.-Mexico border, represented in the work of Alex Espinoza, Tommy Lee Jones, and Guillermo Arriaga) *and* a decolonizing force (as in the ambivalent cultural nationalisms of Arturo Islas, Cherríe Moraga, and Felicia Luna Lemus). Identity, too, can serve emancipatory ends even while homogenizing those it seeks to liberate. In this final chapter, I explore this dual function of identity by examining a genre viewed with particular suspicion by disability scholars and activists: the overcoming narrative. I first review critiques of the overcoming narrative, connecting these to debates about the political efficacy of identity claims, before examining the deployment of the overcoming narrative in two novels by Chicana writers: Ana Castillo's *Peel My Love Like an Onion* (1999) and Cecile Pineda's *Face* (1985). By arguing that Castillo and Pineda appropriate the overcoming narrative in ways that reframe scholarly conversations about identity politics, I elucidate the stakes of disability identity claims. In reading the two novels together, my aim is to help clarify the possibilities that disability identity offers for reconsidering how we conceptualize nationalism and citizenship.

Overcoming Identity Politics?

As disability scholars often note, disability politics differ from those of other minoritized groups because people with disabilities are not underrepresented in dominant cultural texts; instead, images of disability abound in able-bodied culture. Yet these images often do not offer meaningful insights about the lives of people with disabilities. Rather, pervasive disability representations like the overcoming narrative serve as metaphors for problems faced by able-bodied people or to reinforce the marginalization of disabled people.[1] Performance scholar Carrie Sandahl offers a succinct (and delightfully wry) description of a typical overcoming narrative:

> A person in the prime of life suffers a traumatic accident or illness. The newly impaired person then travels through what Elisabeth Kubler-Ross has defined as the five stages of grief: denial, anger, bargaining, depression, and the final stage of acceptance, in which the person accepts his or her limitations and finds renewed joy and purpose in life. The process is usually hastened by a tough-love, able-bodied

lover or assistant who shows the disabled person that his
or her problems boil down to a bad attitude. This narrative
is a favorite version of the American "pull-yourself-up-by-
the-bootstraps" myth, emphasizing individual achievement
over adversity, rather than considering the political and
social aspects of a situation. The very real issues disabled
people face such as discrimination, lack of access, segregation, economic injustice, and so on, are rarely dealt with or
subside once the disabled character adopts a more positive
attitude. ("Black Man, Blind Man" 584)

The popularity of the overcoming narrative stems from its
occlusion of injustice; it assuages nondisabled audiences that
society is equitable, that anyone with the right outlook is capable
of success. Furthermore, as Chris Ewart observes, overcoming
narratives obscure other forms of identity-based oppression. If
their heroes can triumph over adversity, overcoming narratives
imply, surely other groups can "normalize, succeed, and con-
sume" ("Terms of *Dis*appropriation" 148).

For readers of Chicana/o literature, the overcoming narrative
brings to mind the social imperative to assimilate. During political battles over issues like affirmative action, bilingual education, and immigration policy, the popular media overflows with
stories championing racialized minorities and immigrants who
have successfully assimilated; as Paula M.L. Moya points out,
such stories "assume that if there are individuals who do not
'fit in' to American society, those individuals, and not society,
need to change" (*Learning from Experience* 111). Castillo similarly observes that such stories insist "that all peoples residing
in the United States must eventually assimilate into dominant
society and therefore should not be 'pandered' to" (*Massacre of
the Dreamers* 2). In an argument that parallels Sandahl's, Castillo notes that "people of color in the U.S. have not successfully
blended into the infamous melting pot for a number of reasons,"
among them the fact that "historical, institutionalized and leg-
islated racism in the United States does not permit it" (2). Moya,

Castillo, and Sandahl, then, reject narratives placing the responsibility to rise above oppression upon marginalized people, calling instead for the larger political community to accommodate difference. They argue that the exclusion of racialized and disabled minorities must be solved not by overcoming or assimilating but by creating a more just social order.

Given that both the pressure to assimilate and the overcoming narrative rest on the assumption that people should transcend the traits believed to prevent the larger social body from accepting them, it might seem logical to claim identity politics as an antidote. Identity politics, after all, are at least in part about claiming attributes rejected by the dominant society and recasting them as social goods—as beautiful, as rooted in a rich cultural heritage, as deriving from a noble value system, and so on. As Lennard Davis puts it, identity politics allow marginalized identities to be "hypostasized, normalized, turned positive against the negative descriptions used by oppressive regimes" (*Bending Over Backwards* 10). However, while some disability theorists frequently acknowledge the benefits of claiming disability identity, others—including Davis—are skeptical of identity politics. These scholars note that an important theoretical contribution of disability studies stems from the fact that it addresses such a heterogeneous category; because there appears to be so little commonality among people with different kinds of disabilities, disability opens up space to scrutinize *identity* as a concept. As a result, Davis concludes that because "disability is itself an unstable category . . . it would be a major error for disability scholars and advocates to define the category in the by-now very problematic and depleted guise of one among many identities" (23). David T. Mitchell and Sharon L. Snyder advocate the development of theoretical models emphasizing "the productive multiplicity that characterizes movements of disabled people's goals" because "disabled people recognize the intense differences that constitute their bodies . . . as their greatest commonality" ("Disability as Multitude" 182). Robert McRuer, meanwhile, draws from the insight of queer theorists who suggest that "if homosexual identity emerges in the West, we should not automatically expect to find it in other places and times" ("Disability Nationalism" 167); similarly, "we might not find 'disability' or the able-bodied-disabled binary as we think we know them in other places (or time periods)" (171).

These critiques reveal that simply reversing dominant ideas about a marginalized group and claiming as positive its socially maligned characteristics, as some variants of identity politics do, is not sufficient as a means of eliminating institutionalized or systemic forms of oppression. Not only is such an approach based on politically naïve notions of authenticity, it also risks defining a minoritized population according to a limited range of attributes or experiences that cannot prove applicable to everyone in the group. Often, too, the traits most embraced are those least threatening to the dominant society. The normalization of disability identity, as Snyder and Mitchell point out, is disastrous for people with more socially stigmatized disabilities: "Enhanced supercrips are celebrated . . . as symbols of the success of systems that further marginalize their 'less able' disabled kin" ("Introduction: Ablenationalism" 117).

Furthermore, some disability scholars fear that appeals to disability identity can render the disability movement vulnerable to incorporation into what geographer David Harvey calls the neoliberal state. They concur with Harvey, a politically progressive critic of identity politics, who observes that it has proven "extremely difficult within the US left, for example, to forge the collective discipline required for political action to achieve social justice without offending the desire of political actors for individual freedom and for full recognition and expression of particular identities" (*Brief History* 41–42). The potential for identity claims to be folded into neoliberal discourse and state formations is not negligible, leading McRuer to go so far as to conflate "identity and state-based appeals" ("Disability Nationalism" 173). As McRuer observes, disability identity is subjected to "uneven biopolitical incorporation" (171) into the global expansion of neoliberalism; certain assimilable disabled populations are visibly embraced while more marginalized populations (disabled and nondisabled) are targeted for disablement and death.

These critiques of identity resonate in crucial ways with critiques of citizenship as a political goal. Anthropologist Aihwa Ong describes citizenship as "a cultural process of 'subjectification,' in the Foucauldian sense of self-making and being-made by power relations that produce consent through schemes of surveillance, discipline, control, and administration" ("Cultural Citizenship" 737). Certainly, identity is also subjected to "surveillance, discipline, control, and administration," a fact that is particularly salient for people with disabilities, given that disability has a long history of being managed by the state. Snyder and Mitchell, invoking Foucault in a way that parallels Ong's analysis, remind us: "Abnormality has a history, and . . . the appearance of pathological bodies is dependent upon techniques of identification (classification systems of normalcy and deviance)" (*Cultural Locations* 12). Ong echoes the concerns of McRuer, Snyder, and Mitchell when she notes that citizenship obscures hierarchies between minoritized subjects in much the same way that identity can, reinforcing the oppression of those least able to assimilate or overcome. In her comparative study of Chinese businesspeople and Cambodian refugees in the United States, she argues that the two populations constitute "different kinds of minorities" who are "not merely new arrivals passively absorbed into an overarching Asian American identity . . . or united simply on the basis of having been treated 'all alike' as biogenetic others sharing a history of exclusion" ("Cultural Citizenship" 751). To make a claim for the continued efficacy of a politics predicated upon identity, and particularly for an identity politics oriented toward producing an expanded notion of citizenship—as I have done throughout this study—it is therefore essential to take these critiques into account. This is why I have chosen to conclude this study with an extended discussion of disability identity and its relationship to nationalism.

If identity politics—an obvious means of resisting the pressure to overcome and assimilate—colludes with the interests of the neoliberal state, we arrive at a theoretical and political impasse when it comes to formulating legible demands for the accommodation of difference. However, as in earlier chapters delineating how Chicana/o and Mexican cultural producers have given us textual models for theorizing more inclusive understandings of nationalism and citizenship, here I suggest that Castillo and Pineda point us toward models for theorizing disability identity in a more nuanced way. Indeed, it is precisely because I share the concerns of the critics cited above that I believe a reassessment of what sociologist Manuel Castells calls "the power of identity" (*Information Age* 2) to be an urgent theoretical project. This is not only because identity claims continue to hold powerful rhetorical force that is easily marshaled for political activism—as even many critics of identity, particularly proponents of Gayatri Chakravorty Spivak's concept of strategic essentialism, concede[2]—but because I believe that identity politics are just as easily mobilized to contest the neoliberal state as to reinforce it. Furthermore, while it is true that identity claims *can* flatten out the heterogeneous experiences and attributes of the members of an identity group, it does not logically follow that this flattening is necessary or inherent to political projects predicated on identity. Like nationalism, identity can both colonize and decolonize.

Most importantly, rejecting identity politics out of hand does not automatically avoid the theoretical pitfalls of making identity claims. Political movements predicated on identity can certainly be recruited into what Snyder and Mitchell call "neoliberal efforts to normalize the non-normal body" ("Introduction: Ablenationalism" 124), but so too can an anti-identitarian overemphasis on difference and singularity. As Harvey notes, the values of individual freedom and social justice are often incompatible: "Pursuit of social justice presupposes social solidarities and a willingness to submerge individual wants, needs, and desires in the cause of some more general struggle for, say, social equality or environmental justice" (*Brief History* 41). Although Harvey intends to disparage identity claims here, his argument just as easily applies to critiques of identity that privilege singularity and multiplicity—or, as Hiram Pérez puts it, to theoretical models that exchange "too hastily the politics of identity for the politics of difference" ("You Can Have" 187). While some uses of identity are not without problems, then, these problems can only be avoided by serious critical engagement with identity as a concept—not by simply refusing to make identity claims.

In this chapter, I argue that *some* identity claims mobilized by Chicana/o and disability scholars, cultural workers, and activists can, instead of fomenting the formation of constituents to be absorbed into neoliberal state formations, reveal the necessity of imagining forms of political belonging that challenge neoliberalism and the neoliberal state. Castells, who shares Harvey's resistance to neoliberalism, sees identity as one potential challenge to its global dominance, noting that "no identity has, *per se*, progressive or regressive value outside its historical context" (*Information Age* 8). He examines identity-based movements generally viewed as progressive (like feminism and the Zapatista uprising) as well as those seen as regressive (including Christian fundamentalists, and U.S.-based militias) to conclude that while identity *can* be mobilized to affirm the hierarchical regimes governing a given society, it may also lead to "the transformation of the overall social structure" (8). This is particularly true for identities—those Castells labels *project identities*—constructed through progressive political struggle: "In this case, the building of identity is a project of a different life, perhaps on the basis of an oppressed identity, but expanding toward the transformation of society" (10). Along similar lines, Latino queer theorist Ernesto Javier Martínez argues that identities can be "crucial avenues for deep social literacy" (*On Making Sense* 6).

Although Castells has not had a far-reaching impact in disability studies, his concept of project identity aligns with the work of disability scholars who take an identity politics approach. For instance, philosopher Susan Wendell observes that "overlapping patterns of experience among group members . . . , combined with the awareness that many things happened to them because they are identified by *others* as members of the group, can motivate people of diverse experiences to work together for their common welfare, to identify themselves willingly as members of the group, and to redefine for themselves what being one of the group means" (*Rejected Body* 32). In particular, Wendell's emphasis on the process of continual "redefining" as an aspect of identity formation gestures toward a possibility ignored by many of identity's most fervent critics, who tend to view the concept as a fixed, unchanging essence. Where Wendell offers a philosophical argument for the characterization of disability as a socially constructed, non-essentializing but nonetheless material and experiential category, Sandahl offers a practical justification for political projects grounded in identity: "identity politics-based political organizing . . . remains an effective means for social change" ("Black Man, Blind Man" 582). For Sandahl, it is precisely by "galvanizing collective identity"—and not by setting it aside or transcending it—that individuals participating in social movements begin "laying the groundwork for coalition building and social change" (583). Together, by theorizing disability identity as both a diverse range of socially situated bodily experiences that are open to redefinition *and* as a force for social change, Wendell and Sandahl point us toward a notion of disability as project identity.

A robust theoretical defense of identity politics also helps to clarify the importance of scrutinizing narratives that valorize assimilation and overcoming. As Tobin Siebers observes, such narratives function not only to obfuscate oppression and inequality but also to categorize certain classes of people as less than human.[3] Siebers writes: "because human-interest stories usually require their hero to be human, they are obliged, when the focus is disability, to give an account of their protagonist's metamorphosis from nonhuman to human being" (*Disability Theory* 111); in other words, they represent "the able body as normative in the definition of the human" (111). This is important because "if a person does not display rational thinking, healthiness, or technical skills, that person risks being seen as less than human and losing the rights bestowed by membership in the human community" (180). In other words, overcoming narratives reinforce the idea that people earn the right to be seen as human—or, to borrow Hannah Arendt's famous citation of Earl Warren, they earn *the right to have rights*—by demonstrating skills and abilities that justify their inclusion in a social or political body. Furthermore, the question of who "counts" as human remains an urgent concern for scholars in both disability studies and Chicana/o studies. As Moya contends, debates about assimilation are ultimately about "what it means to be fully human" (*Learning from Experience* 107). This is because pressures to assimilate set "collective (racial and, as such, particular) identity in opposition to individual (universal and, as such, raceless) identity," presenting "cultural, racial, or ethnic particularity as supplemental—and occasionally as inimical—to universal humanity" (107). If the overcoming narrative and the story of assimilation bear a certain structural resemblance, then, they also serve a similar ideological purpose: to classify certain people (immigrants and racialized minorities who "refuse" to assimilate and people with disabilities who "refuse" to overcome) as undeserving not only of political rights but also, ultimately, of human status.

The critiques offered by Moya and Siebers resonate with recent work in Latino gay studies. Defending identity against the famously anti-identitarian axiom from Eve Kosofsky Sedgwick that people "are different from each other" (*Epistemology of the Closet* 22), Pérez reminds us: "sometimes, people are not so different from one another" ("You Can Have" 187). In other words, sometimes the similarities between people reflect systemic power imbalances in our society that merit critical attention and are worth naming as identity categories. Pérez notes that the insistence on multiplicity and singularity has, in the context of queer theory, allowed whiteness to function as an invisible norm: "Queer theory, when it privileges difference over sameness absolutely, colludes with institutionalized racism in vanishing, hence retrenching, white privilege. It serves as the magician's assistant to whiteness's disappearing act" (187). Disability studies, if it is serious about accounting for the ways in which disability is informed by and informs the construction of other identity categories, needs to take defenses of identity like that offered by Pérez seriously.

Precisely because a critique of identity politics can inadvertently collude with efforts to neglect the mutual imbrication of different identity categories (as in the "whitening" of queer theory), identity has also seen a recent theoretical resurgence in scholarship dealing with the mutually constitutive nature of categories like race, ethnicity, sexuality, and ability.[4] As Michael Hames-García and Ernesto Javier Martínez argue in the introduction to their groundbreaking anthology *Gay Latino Studies*, "identities are profound epistemic and social realities that structure how we see the world and live in it" (7). Their use of identity is not the uncritically celebratory or oppressively homogenizing use associated with some variants of identity politics. They remind us that even a fraught identity category—in their case, *gay*—"has produced profoundly meaningful and powerful ways of organizing knowledge, belief, and action for many . . . in spite of its descriptive inadequacies" (8). Finally, what is especially helpful in their effort to claim an identity-based theoretical model is their acknowledgment that anti-identitiarian theorizing has many political and ethical valences. As they note, some queer theorists mobilize critiques of identity to buttress the "whitewashing tendencies of queer academic theorizing" (11), thereby reinforcing the "deep suspicion of identity categories that too often serves as a crutch for white academic racism" (11). Nonetheless, they also acknowledge critics working within gay Latino studies who are "ambivalent toward *identity* as a stable or coherent category" but who nonetheless share their "resistance to jettisoning the experience of class, gender, race, and sexuality as lived realities shaping people's lives" (9). The disability theorists whose critiques of identity are cited here (like McRuer and Davis) share this commitment to recognizing the "lived realities" of marginalized people, and I in turn share their concern about uncritically embracing disability as "stable or coherent." Nonetheless, as my readings of Pineda and Castillo will show, identity remains an important category to engage if we are serious about trying to theorize more just and inclusive forms of political belonging.

Peel My Love and *Face* offer a model for thinking about the implications of identity politics in disability scholarship and for imagining what disability as *project identity* might look like. Neither novel offers a simplistic, affirmational version of identity. Instead, *Peel My Love* repudiates identity claims of all kinds, allowing us to test the political efficacy of such disavowals, while *Face*, as Marcial González writes, "exposes the contradictions of identity rather than merely celebrating its formation" (*Chicano Novels* 171). Furthermore, both novels resist what Ong calls "the cultural inscription of state power and other forms of regulation that define the different modalities of belonging" ("Cultural Citizenship" 738). Castillo's text explicitly rejects the impulse of the state to prescribe national identifications, while Pineda's challenges the nation-based formation of the Chicana/o literary canon. In very different ways, both novels point to the continued need for identity-based social movements that are conceptualized in ways that account for the heterogeneity of their constituents, that acknowledge the historical and cultural specificities of identity claims, and that provide grounding for collective political struggle. Rather than seeking identities legible to the neoliberal state—identities that can be tokenized and unevenly assimilated into a global power regime—these novels together point toward the development of identities that can foment alternative political formations.

"One Hundred Percent Anything": Ana Castillo and the Resistance to Ablenationalism

Peel My Love extends a political project Castillo outlines in her 1995 essay collection *Massacre of the Dreamers*. Building upon Adrienne Rich's call for feminists to explore "how a place on the map is also a place in history" (212), Castillo asserts the need for a form of political belonging disarticulated from the nation-state and citizenship. She writes:

> Ours is a world imbued with nationalism, real for some, yet tenuous as paper for others. A world in which from the day of our births, we are either granted citizenship or relegated to the netherstate of serving as mass production drones. . . . As a mestiza, a resident of a declining world power, a countryless woman, I have the same hope as Rich who, on behalf of her country aims to be accountable, flexible, and learn new ways to gather together earnest peoples of the world without the defenses of nationalism. (24)

In *Peel My Love*, Castillo elaborates this hope through a love story in which disabled Chicana flamenco dancer Carmen la Coja (who experiences polio as a child) is torn between two unfaithful lovers (Agustín and Manolo), representing the two unfaithful nation-states that fail to protect her rights (the United States and Mexico). The novel concludes with Carmen accepting that postpolio has ended her dancing career and launching a new career as a singer. At this point, she also refuses monogamy in favor of a polyamorous partnership with both men, suggesting a model for citizenship that does not require allegiance to only one nation (or fidelity to one lover). In this sense, the novel coincides with McRuer's call to challenge the "focus on identity and on incorporation into the liberal state" ("Disability Nationalism" 166) that characterizes some disability scholarship. However, I will argue that the novel's rejection of identity politics undermines its critique of the nation-state, thereby inadvertently revealing the continued importance of identity claims in the effort to reconceptualize political belonging.

In one of the few major critical analyses of *Peel My Love*, Suzanne Bost argues that it depicts a model of subjectivity "free from the rigid racial and sexual classifications instituted by the biological and physical sciences and supported by identity politics" (*Encarnación* 192). As a result, she sees the text privileging the kind of fluidity that critics of identity politics tend to celebrate: "Since individuals contain multiple, different layers of embodiment, and various, sometimes conflicting political desires, identity is an insufficient ground for politics" (188). Yet Bost does not reveal what—if anything—the novel *does* present as sufficient ground for politics. In fact, she also concedes that despite mentioning concerns shared by Chicana/o and disability activists, *Peel My Love* offers "no overt engagement with the political or theoretical content of either of those movements" and contains "no clear political message" (184). While I certainly would not suggest that novels *must* offer political messages, it is curious that Bost critiques identity as "insufficient" for politics but does not consider the absence of a coherent political message in *Peel My Love* worth interrogating. In fact, the novel *is* overtly political, addressing the rights of immigrants, the exploitation of racialized labor, inequities in the U.S. public education system, and the corporatization of health care. As Frederick Luis Aldama notes, "instead of fluidity and ecstasy, Carmen is forced to abide by patriarchal, racist rules" (*Brown on Brown* 105) throughout the text. I would suggest, then, that the disavowal of identity *is* a clear political message emerging from the novel— and therefore, one that merits close critical scrutiny. Indeed, one might ask whether the novel's failure to offer viable political solutions to the issues it raises—all of which relate to identity-based oppression—might result from its rejection of identity. Unlike Bost, who sees *Peel My Love* exemplifying the problems of identity claims, then, I see the text reinforcing their necessity.

To make this claim, I reiterate that although the novel eschews *identity* politics, it does not reject politics altogether. Indeed, one of its most important political critiques emerges from the ways in which it explores exclusionary impulses that so often surface in nationalist movements (both state-sponsored and counter-hegemonic). Even before introducing Carmen's disability, *Peel My Love* reveals her national ambivalence, as she pledges allegiance to her city (Chicago) instead of to the United States or Mexico: "You say your city the way some Americans say their country. You never feel right saying that—my country. For some reason looking Mexican means you can't be American. And my cousins tell me, the ones who've gone to Mexico but were born on this side like me, that over there they're definitely not Mexican" (3). The city of Chicago, then, becomes Carmen's attempt to claim a form of cultural citizenship not tied to the nation-state: "you can say this is my city because Chicago is big and small enough to be your city, to be anybody's city who wants it, anybody at all. Like Nelson Algren said right around the time you were born— *Chicago . . . forever keeps two faces. . . . One for the good boy and one for the bad*" (3, original emphasis). As this reference to "the good boy and the bad" suggests, Carmen's critique of dominant constructions of citizenship is allegorized by her attachment to Manolo (the bad boy from Serbia, Spain, and Mexico) and Agustín (the good boy from Cleveland). Agustín and Manolo appear immediately after Carmen relays the Nelson Algren quote: "And I loved the good boy and the bad one and sometimes they were one and the same" (3). In this way, the novel establishes from the outset both the romantic dilemma that drives its plot and the political concern that drives its cultural intervention.

From a disability studies perspective, a particularly important insight to emerge from the novel results from the way it links Carmen's national ambivalence to what Snyder and Mitchell call *ablenationalism*: "efforts to represent the nation as synonymous with a narrow array of acceptable body types" ("Introduction: Ablenationalism" 115). Carmen describes her childhood in this way:

For a long time things that came in pairs held endless fascination for me. Two things identical and equal to each other

were the essence of symmetry and the sublime. They balanced the universe and were an absolute om. Two sighted
eyes, two ears that heard, a pair of arms or legs that functioned and obeyed one's wishes. One whole brain that kept
it all together. For a long time I was with other children
who could not walk a straight line. (13)

Here *Peel My Love* beautifully captures the consequences of Carmen's segregation in a public school system that isolates her with
"other children who could not walk a straight line" and teaches
her to value balanced, symmetrical bodies above the asym-
metrical, unbalanced bodies that she and her friends possess.
Public education—an institution intended to produce nationalist identification—instructs children with disabilities to accept
their marginal status in ablenationalist discourse. Carmen's fascination with wholeness and symmetry is thus correlated to the
problem introduced in the novel's first chapter of "never feeling
right" when using the words *my country*; read together, these
passages reveal how Carmen is denied full membership in the
body politic as a racialized woman with a disability.

Bringing together the theoretical concerns that occupy the
first two sections of *Accessible Citizenships*, *Peel My Love* critiques both state-sponsored nationalisms and cultural nationalisms. Its critique of cultural nationalism is represented most
explicitly through the character of Agustín, the leader of Carmen's dance troupe and the first of her lovers. Agustín is born
in Cleveland but returns to Spain after college to embrace his
roots: "When he returned to the United States he was no longer
August Ristich, a graduate of the University of Wisconsin, son
of a car salesman, but Agustín el Bailaor, finest flamenco musi-
cian (and sometimes dancer) to ever set foot on North American
shores" (35). Agustín espouses the kind of counter-hegemonic
nationalism that many Chicana/o cultural producers have, since
the 1960s, sought to claim. His cultural nationalism, moreover,
parallels the heteronormative, patriarchal, and ableist tendencies of the versions of Chicano nationalism that queer Chicana/o

writers like Arturo Islas and Cherríe Moraga have forcefully rejected.[5]

However, where Islas and Moraga formulate queer, feminist versions of Chicana/o nationalism that retain its liberatory, decolonizing impulses, Castillo depicts cultural nationalism as a necessarily exclusionary formation. Agustín's cultural nationalism is so rigid that it is even aligned with state-sponsored Spanish nationalism, the very nationalism that has marginalized his own people: "Agustín was not a Spaniard but he had lived in Spain a long time and had picked up the same likes and prejudices of the Andalusions. . . . Agustín thought like a Spaniard down to his core although he wasn't. For a gypsy, I also learned later, an adopted homeland is as good as any" (19). The "likes and prejudices" that Agustín adopts are not only ethnocentric but explicitly ableist: "Calorro is what he called himself. Calorro is what 'the people' are. The rest of the populace consists of gajes, payos. It not only means someone who isn't a gypsy, it is equivalent to idiot. For the calorros there are people: themselves. All the rest are idiots" (30). Agustín's use of the word *idiot* (and its pejorative equivalency between non-calorros and people with cognitive disabilities, both of whom are defined here as "not people") underscores that ablenationalist impulses can be difficult to extricate even from decolonizing, non-state-sanctioned nationalist movements.[6] In this way *Peel My Love* functions as a counterpoint to texts that embrace the reformulation of cultural nationalism, offering a useful depiction of the dangers in such a reclamation.

Despite Agustín's efforts to police the boundaries of calorro identity, his definition of his "people" is so limited that not even he can sustain it. After falling in love with Carmen, he insists that she is also calorra: "I don't know why you keep insisting that you look Indian, he would say, you are one hundred percent calorra, guapa, not an Aztec princess, but a gypsy queen! . . . I never knew what he meant by my being a calorra one hundred percent but the idea of being one hundred percent anything appealed to me so I didn't argue" (33). E.J. Hobsbawm notes that one problem with defining nations through *peoplehood* is that "the criteria used for this purpose—language, ethnicity or whatever—are themselves fuzzy, shifting and ambiguous" (*Nations and Nationalism* 6). For Carmen, these criteria include the "way I dressed, the way I spoke, the way I danced. The way I scooped up the tomato sauce in my plate with a piece of hard bread and drank down my burgundy wine in a single gulp. Not only the way I wore my long hair but the color and texture of it" (33). The combination of traits thought to be culturally inscribed (habits of eating and dress) with those attributed to genetics (hair color and texture) exposes the "fuzzy, shifting and ambiguous" nature of national identity. Indeed, Agustín's view of Carmen as calorra says less about her than it does about him and his need to believe that a calorra is "the only kind of woman who could really get under his skin" (143). Carmen's acquiescence to Agustín's characterization of her, furthermore, connects to her childhood fascination with symmetry, her public school indoctrination into ablenationalism. Like Agustín's belief that "an adopted homeland is as good as any," Carmen's desire to be "one hundred percent anything" demonstrates the emotional, economic, and social consequences of being positioned outside the national body.

Carmen's honorary status as "one hundred percent calorra" is taken away after she falls in love with Agustín's godson Manolo. Her affair with Manolo represents an act of disobedience to Agustín's patriarchal authority: "In the calorro community Agustín was big-big. He wasn't the kind of man you took anything from and furthermore told him you planned on keeping it" (146). Manolo offers not only insubordination but also a new understanding of identity. In contrast to Agustín's cultural nationalism and notions of "adopted homeland," Manolo's sense of national identity is much more undefined: "I've got five passports, he said. Don't ask me how I got them" (84). Carmen describes him as a "Muslim-Christian-Jewish saint of sacrilegious yearnings, Indo-Pakistani with at least one line of maybe Otomí American blood" (84). Through Manolo, Carmen comes to see identity in a way that accommodates more flexibility than Agustín's nationalist framework allows: "Up until then Agustín had represented all his people to me. If he didn't like beer it was because gypsies didn't drink beer. If he kept out of deep water it was a gypsy fear. That's when I learned that with every culture there are two sides. If you believe one thing to be true about a people the very opposite will also be true" (87). This lesson has a larger impact on Carmen's understanding of herself and her place in the world: If there is more than one way to be Rom, she learns, there is also more than one way to be Chicana, to be American, to be Mexican. In this sense, Carmen's status (bestowed upon her by Agustín) as "one hundred percent calorra" is relinquished not only because she disobeys and betrays Agustín, but because she comes to question the value of that one hundred percent. Her fascination with wholeness and symmetry—whole bodies, whole peoples, whole nations, whole *identities*—gives way.

It is Carmen's embrace of a more fluid subjectivity—one unfettered by the homogenizing impulses of both state-sponsored and cultural nationalisms—that leads critics like Bost to conclude that "Castillo's writing . . . resists neat packaging in terms of ethnic, regional, or sexual identities" (*Encarnación* 152). While I agree with this characterization of Castillo's work, I also find it noteworthy that in *Peel My Love* it is precisely at the moment when Carmen begins to "resist the packaging" of identity that she also "overcomes" her disability. When Carmen's lovers abandon her, she is expelled from the calorro community and her symptoms of postpolio increase, leaving her unable to dance. She is then forced to work a series of menial, exploitative jobs before discovering that she has a hidden talent for flamenco singing and embarks upon a new, successful career. At this time, she reunites with her lovers. Up to this point, the novel carefully details the effects of disability oppression in Carmen's life (the pejorative comments from strangers, the workplace discrimination, the difficulties of navigating the health care system), but these problems disappear once she begins singing.

Carmen's final transformation—her move away from the longing for wholeness and symmetry, her transition from dancer to singer—necessitates a new perspective on her disability, one that is consistent with the "positive attitude" that Sandahl sees as a requisite feature of the overcoming narrative. This becomes explicit in an encounter with a fan who tells Carmen not to call herself Carmen la Coja after learning that *coja* means *cripple* in Spanish. Lifting up her dress to expose the leg affected by polio, Carmen explains: "Maybe it's a cultural misunderstanding. . . . In my culture people get called by their most evident characteristic. I really am a *coja!*—so it's okay!" (187–88). Carmen here delights not only in revealing her disability, but also in the fan's confusion at her use of the phrase *my culture*: "She looks bewildered since it isn't clear what culture I'm talking about. We're listed under Latin and International and World and Pop/Reggae" (188). Here the novel equates Carmen's embrace of her disability with her embrace of a cultural identity that is not "one hundred percent anything," as the asymmetry of her body functions as a metaphor for the instability of her national identity.

Although Carmen's embrace of disability might be heartening as a "positive" representation, it is also troubling that precisely as Carmen begins to express more positive feelings about her disability, the novel itself falls into replicating the generic conventions of the overcoming narrative. As Sandahl argues, when disability is used as a metaphor for "the postmodern condition in general" ("Black Man, Blind Man" 583), the result is often that "disabled people themselves disappear" (584). Significantly, the novel here undermines the material effects of Carmen's embodiment. The reason for the end of her dance career is pain resulting from postpolio, but singing is not necessarily less painful: "I wish I could say that the excitement of performing again sent my endorphins off the charts and that I didn't feel anything but the thrill of it all, but after three songs I had to get off stage because of the searing pain going down my spine" (174). Fifteen pages later, however, the significance of this pain is dismissed: "Just having a generally better disposition since my new recording-artist career has eased my aches and pains. I am still living with them but they are not stopping me anymore from living" (199). Carmen's attribution of her diminished pain to her "better disposition" calls to mind Sandahl's description of the "classic" overcoming narrative cited at the beginning of this chapter.

By using disability (and the struggle to overcome it) as a metaphor for Carmen's national ambivalence, the novel reinforces the following argument from Jennifer C. James and Cynthia Wu: "multiple identities can be interrelated, yet . . . when such analogies are made between one form of oppression and another, the comparison often ends up privileging one over the other" ("Editors' Introduction: Race" 8). Here, the comparison of Carmen's national uncertainty and her disability at first seems to privilege the critique of nationalism over the critique of disability oppression. However, the text's use of the overcoming narrative at this point also undermines its resolution of Carmen's national ambivalence. As Snyder and Mitchell point out: "Successful, singular examples of compensation for disability . . . clandestinely operate as an opportunity to critique the inadequacies of those who fail to thrive amid rampant social inequities" ("Introduction: Ablenationalism" 122). By representing its national dilemma through the overcoming narrative, *Peel My Love* reveals national boundaries to be an unsustainable social construct. However, like disability, national boundaries can be socially constructed *and* possess material consequences. The fact that Carmen has ceased to live with these borders in the same way does not mean that they have ceased to exist. The novel, at the end, does not treat nationalism as a damaging institution with inescapable effects (as it does for most of the narrative) but as a fabrication that fails to affect Carmen once she ceases to believe in it. It further implies that citizenship itself is a state of mind, that Carmen's personal embrace of disability might trump ablenationalism, rather than demanding a political struggle to transform an exclusionary national narrative.

This critique returns us to debates in disability studies about the merits (or lack thereof) of identity politics. Although elsewhere in their work they resist using the term *identity*, Snyder and Mitchell theorize a "cultural model" of disability that is useful here: "The cultural model has an understanding that impairment is both human variation encountering environmental obstacles *and* socially mediated difference that lends group identity and phenomenological perspective. . . . An embodied experience can be embraced while also resulting in social discrimination and material effects (such as pain, discomfort, or incapacity)" (*Cultural Locations* 10).[7] A cultural model of disability allows for a more nuanced understanding of identity than what is offered at the end of *Peel My Love*. Carmen's embodied experience would still be seen as culturally mediated, as something interpreted differently in different cultural contexts. However, this embodied experience would also have a material effect; Carmen's aches and pains would play a role in her life, not by "stopping her from living" but by making her experience of embodiment one that requires accommodations from a society that purports to be just. It is this component that is missing from the conclusion to *Peel My Love*; Carmen's personal dilemma is resolved, but the novel does not offer a way to understand the larger problems it depicts beyond their impact on Carmen's unique, singular life. By individualizing Carmen's story, the novel uses disability to critique nationalism, but does not imagine disability as a social force that might have a critical function in the construction of new forms of political belonging.

The problems with the conclusion to *Peel My Love* are not problems of one solitary cultural product. Rather, they are problems that inhere within a larger theoretical impulse to discard identity as a meaningful category of analysis rather than working to critically refine it. The novel points to the need for a form of identity politics that can effectively address identity-based oppression and, in the process, foment social transformation. Indeed, this is a point even many critics of identity agree with; for instance, McRuer describes appeals to identity as "indispensable—necessary but simply and always insufficient" ("Disability Nationalism" 173). Rather than simply tolerating the insufficiencies of a theoretical model that we acknowledge as indispensable, then, I propose that we find ways to mitigate these insufficiencies. I suggest, along with Moya, that it is possible to engage in identity politics without "defending those forms of identity politics that are predicated on the disenfranchisement of others, and with full awareness that all identities are somewhat reductive and potentially co-optable" (*Learning from Experience* 130). Doing so, moreover, allows us to acknowledge that "*some* forms of identity politics that are undertaken by members of marginalized groups in the service of creating economic, social, and political equity between different groups are epistemically and morally justifiable" (130). In the section that follows, I will elaborate how Pineda's novel *Face* uses the overcoming narrative to offer an "epistemic and moral" justification for identity politics.

"A Face Like Anyone Else's": Cecile Pineda's Critical Overcoming Narrative

On the surface, my claim that *Face* helps us reconsider the political importance of identity claims might appear counterintuitive. Pineda herself is not a writer often associated with the Chicana/o literary canon; although she identifies as Chicana, her novels by and large do not feature Chicana/o characters or deal with issues of Chicana/o identity.[8] Furthermore, as González observes, her work is also positioned outside the national parameters of Chicana/o literature: Pineda "does not represent Chicano identity as a cultural formation that originates in Aztlán, in the barrio, or on the U.S.-Mexico border" (*Chicano Novels* 155). The most widely read of Pineda's works, *Face* and *Frieze* (1986), are set respectively in 1950s Brazil and tenth-century Java.[9] If we consider identity politics to be simply about establishing or maintaining the boundaries of a fixed social category and affirming the attributes and experiences considered normative to those occupying it, the fact that Pineda has largely chosen not to represent characters whose identity reflects her own might seem to place her work at odds with identity politics.

Face would also seem to run counter to disability politics, as it is a novel about a man who acquires a disability and then goes to extreme lengths to cure it. However, I argue that Face offers a rare and insightful portrayal of the process by which identities are socially constructed—a process that, as Castells reminds us, "always takes place in a context marked by power relationships" (Information Age 7). The novel's protagonist changes identities upon acquiring his disability, not only because his perception of himself changes but also because his political and social situation changes. The novel thus represents a conceptualization of identity that takes into account both its materiality (the fact that particular identities adhere to people with defined attributes, often ones marked on the body) and its social construction (the fact that these attributes are socially interpreted—and hierarchized—in systemic, non-arbitrary ways). Moreover, because it addresses identity-based oppression and points to the need for social and political change to diminish that oppression, Face engages in identity politics. For this reason I am calling the novel a critical overcoming narrative—a subversive rendering of the overcoming narrative form that reinforces not the imperative to overcome or assimilate but instead the need for society to accommodate marginalized identities.

The plot of Face, even more than that of Peel My Love, appears to follow the classic trajectory of the overcoming narrative as described by Sandahl. The novel tells the story of a working-class, mixed-race Brazilian man, suggestively named Helio Cara,[10] whose face is disfigured beyond recognition after a sudden accident. Unable to afford reconstructive surgery, he is given a rubber mask, which he finds unbearable to wear in the heat, and which he eventually replaces with a handkerchief to cover his face. He is dismissed from his job as a barber because his face is distressing to customers; his girlfriend (Lula) spurns him, saying, "I don't want to look at you" (68). Neighbors throw rocks at his house and set it on fire. Unable to make a living in the Capital and unsafe in his own home, he returns to the rural town where his mother once lived, finds enough work to (almost) subsist, and begins to study the anatomy of the human face. Using needles and thread, plastic from discarded children's toys, and local anesthesia purchased at the town pharmacy, he creates a new face for himself and returns to the Capital. On the surface, then, the text appears to validate Helio's determination, offering what Siebers calls the overcoming narrative's "morality tale" (*Disability Theory* 114). However, the novel also focuses upon the social forces that marginalize and dehumanize Helio after his accident, illustrates how his identity changes as a result of his altered social location, and exposes the injustice of a society that requires Helio to re-injure his own face in order to re-enter humanity.

The account of Helio's dehumanization begins in the novel's prologue, before Helio is introduced. This prologue consists of an address given by a doctor, T.G., at the Twenty-Fifth Annual Meeting of Plastic and Reconstructive Surgery in Rio de Janeiro, describing a man who loses his face in an accident and is rejected by his friends and community. The tone is that of a detached medical observer describing an unusual case: A "terribly mutilated" man taken to a "charity hospital," unable to "afford even meager social security payments on his barber's salary," shunned by neighbors in "the slum district where he had a shack" (3). The doctor describes how the man disappears from the Capital and concludes with a mysterious statement: "You may ask what this man was doing all this time he was in hiding . . . " (3). The doctor's ethnographic tone treats the man as a victim, an object of examination. What is striking, however, is that it is not just the man's medical condition that renders him an object to be studied, but also his social class; it is not only his facial disfigurement put on display but also his slum district, his shack, and his inability to afford even "meager" medical payments. Critics of identity often point out that identities are not coherent since everyone occupies more than one identity category, a point aptly illustrated by this prologue. However, both Castells and Wendell argue that identity can account for the "plurality of identities" (Castells, *Information Age* 6) that an individual may possess. As Wendell points out, nearly all people with disabilities experience some kind of disability-based oppression, "even though the forms this oppression takes, and the ways it is experienced, may vary greatly among societies and according to other factors, such as age, gender, race, class, religion, caste, and sexual identity" (*Rejected Body* 32). *Face,* coinciding with this insight, opens by specifying that the narrative will take place in Rio de Janeiro and that its protagonist will be working-class and disabled; in other words, it alerts readers to the fact that it will *not* offer a universal account of disability identity but will depict a particular disability experience that is related but not identical to the experiences of others who share aspects of Helio's identity.

Given that the prologue poses the suspenseful question of what the man was doing during his disappearance, the reader anticipates that the novel will commence with the reconstruction of Helio's face. However, this is not the case. The novel is divided into two sections ("Capital" and "Hinterland"), the first of which provides an account of Helio's accident and the social marginalization that follows it, and the second of which describes how Helio reconstructs his face. It is the first section that occupies the bulk of the text. It is not until page 107 (in a novel consisting of only 170 pages in total) that we even witness Helio leaving the Capital; more than ten more pages go by before he decides to "make himself a face" (121). The majority of the narrative is focused not on Helio's overcoming of his facial disfigurement but on how his life changes after acquiring a disability. The result is that although the novel is described as being about a man who remakes his face, it is more accurately described as a record of how Helio's society (a society, like that of Pineda and her readers, that is structured by vast inequalities of race, gender, sexuality, class and ability) constructs him as a marginalized subject, as someone less than human, after the accident that disfigures his face.

Helio becomes aware of his new social status while in the hospital. Listening to "the approaching march of the medical students, their footfalls along the terrazzo corridors, their muted remarks, the commanding tone of the chief surgeon bringing them to attention, issuing reports, mapping his strategies" (22), he hears himself described as a medical specimen. The chief surgeon brings the students to each patient, and Helio hears the repeated phrase:

> And here we have . . .
> Always closer. Not yet his turn.
> And here we have . . . (22)

The patients are identified not by their names but by their injured body parts: *"And here we have the knee* (becoming fainter), *the arm . . . the abdomen . . .* (and still fainter) *the scrotum"* (23). Helio recognizes his turn when he hears *the face*: "The patient *(ah, the patient, yes),* the patient is a thirty-six-year-old man of mixed birth *(ah, mixed, yes),* a barber by trade *(ah, by trade, yes),* who happened to descend the harbor stairs once too often. . . . Never, never has the trauma service seen such an injury. A surgical nightmare. The face not simply (ah, yes, 'simply') unrecognizable, Gentlemen . . . " (23). The voice then details the injuries and concludes by answering not Helio's questions but those of the medical students, who want to know when they will be able to examine the patient again: "How much time, you ask? Oh, perhaps six weeks, perhaps two months, it depends on the healing (and parting), we expect a major address by the trauma team, next month perhaps" (23). The people who matter are the medical students who want to know how the case will be treated, to gain medical expertise from an anonymous body, not the working-class, racialized person who inhabits that body. The function of this scene, then, is to reveal Helio's new social status as an object to be studied by others. It prepares the reader and Helio for later confrontations with Helio's boss (denying him a job), girlfriend (ending their relationship), and neighbors (refusing him food and throwing rocks at his home).

"Capital," which depicts Helio navigating a new life with a disability, also shows him becoming a different person, someone with an altered identity:

> He could imagine taking his life—the old one, before—
> taking it off like a coat and leaving it, on this step perhaps,
> high overlooking the bay, and quite calmly walking away,
> leaving it there, still warm. Would someone find it, try it on
> perhaps, enter it seamlessly, wear it like a sleeve—Lula, the
> barber shop—without thinking about it? . . . What if it had
> been that way? No pain. Removing it, peeling it from him
> like a layer of being, leaving it sprawled on a bench. And
> what was left of his old life before the fall? The barber shop,
> the boss, Mario, they had all vanished. They were carrying
> on without him, had been now for nearly a season. (9–10)

It is not that the accident alters his body, but that he takes off his old life (or identity) "like a coat" and acquires a completely new one. Bost, in her analysis of *Peel My Love*, argues that the "radical otherness" of disabled bodies reveals "the insufficiency of our normative identity categories" and demands "that we think about bodies beyond what we normally think of as identity" (192).[11] What the above passage suggests, however, is that a society that treats people with certain bodily variations as less than equal will correlate corporeal difference to the formation of minoritized identities. Instead of going "beyond" identity categories, *Face* reveals how nonnormative bodily markers are linked to structural inequalities. Helio is not "radically other" because his facial injuries make him essentially so, as Bost might observe, but he is nonetheless radically *marginalized* in a society that treats his new face—combined with the marks of race, gender, and class that he already possesses—as a sign of inherent inferiority. It is not the concept of identity that proves "insufficient" for describing his new situation but a theoretical apparatus that cannot simultaneously account for the materiality of his new embodiment and the construction of his new social identity.

Part of the injustice that Helio experiences stems from others' refusal to acknowledge how his new face exposes him to new forms of identity-based oppression. As Helio is discharged from the hospital, he is subjected to another address from the chief surgeon. As in the passage previously analyzed, Helio learns about his circumstances not because his doctor explains them to him but because his doctor explains them to students in his presence: "Our record of public assistance is a generous one, sometimes too generous, in my opinion. But aesthetics go unsubsidized, at least for the moment. There are no funds for reconstruction, Gentlemen. Because the face, the face, Gentlemen, is a cosmetic matter, cosmetic at best" (34). Moya observes that pressure for racialized minorities to assimilate emanates from the assumption that "that which is 'human' transcends what are merely racial, ethnic, or gender trappings" (*Learning from Experience* 108)—in other words, the assumption that such "trappings" cannot constitute meaningful identities. Here, too, the doctor assumes that Helio is the same person he has always been, that his face his merely a "cosmetic" anomaly unrelated to his interactions with the world around him. To use Moya's language, the doctor fails to acknowledge Helio as "an embodied human being whose identity has been, and continues to be, constituted in and through social interaction" (122). In this way, the doctor asserts that because Helio's altered embodiment will have no major impact on his ability to perform work, its effects will be negligible. The possibility that Helio's face might prove disabling because of entrenched discrimination is not acknowledged. This refusal to recognize how Helio's new embodiment results in a new identity, then, constitutes another (more covert) layer of oppression, beyond the overt discrimination he experiences at work and in his neighborhood.

"Capital" lays the groundwork for a subversion of the overcoming narrative by establishing the social salience of disability identity but also inscribes its critique of overcoming in its very structure. Although *Face* is largely a linear narrative, the first five chapters proceed out of order. The first two describe Helio in the aftermath of his accident, in the Capital, wandering the streets, struggling to remember what has happened to him. The next two chapters describe the accident and depict Helio awakening in an unfamiliar hospital bed. Finally, the fifth chapter describes the events preceding the accident: Helio in bed with Lula, a knock at the door delivering a telegram about his ailing mother, his hurried rush to the post office. By beginning a linear narrative in such a disjointed way, the novel accomplishes several things. First, it brings the reader into the confused and frightened state of its protagonist, who seeks not only to piece together his fragmented memories but to understand how his new embodiment is related to his new social circumstances. More importantly, it subverts the reader's expectations for narrative progress, which the overcoming narrative relies upon. Instead of offering a chain of events from trauma to healing, culminating in heroic triumph over adversity, *Face* offers a portrait of a character in the process of acquiring a new identity. In this way, the novel's form itself marks a stark deviation from the traditional overcoming narrative.

"Hinterland" offers an even more seditious rendering of the overcoming narrative by depicting Helio engaged in the act of at-home, do-it-yourself facial reconstruction. When Helio decides to create a new face, his sheer determination might appear lifted directly from a human-interest story in a popular magazine: "He would make himself a face. He did not have to wait. He would make it here, where he knew no one anymore, where no one could tell him how he had to look, what he had to be—now that he had fallen—now he no longer belonged, even to himself. There was no one here to say it, to say it could not be done. Or that he might not do it, that he had no right. No one at all" (121). Although Helio perceives himself free of constraint, his ability to rebuild his own face is subject to rigid social controls. First, there is the issue of purchasing supplies. Although he finds seasonal work watering coffee bushes for fifty cruzeiros per night, the procaine he needs to numb his face for each tiny incision costs thirty cruzeiros (ten for each centiliter), leaving him little money to purchase food and necessities. Second, there are the graphic descriptions of Helio performing surgery on himself, sterilizing old scissors and a razor blade, injecting the procaine, cutting his face open, and sewing it closed: "Carefully bending the blade with the constant pressure of thumb and forefinger he lifts off the scar tissue. With his fingers he applies pressure to stem the bleeding. . . . He stitches the incision closed as best he can with the needle and very fine thread" (133). Finally, he performs difficult physical labor while recovering from surgery, once even while still bleeding. To make matters worse, he is dismissed from his job after being attacked in the fields. Despite Helio's perception of himself as free to remake his identity, then, the novel shows him working within and against extraordinary social and physical limitations. This provides a marked contrast to the overcoming narrative's emphasis on "positive attitudes" and demonstrates how the construction of identity is regulated by systemic inequalities.

Here I wish to pause and note that these barriers that Helio confronts as he remakes his face might appear to position the novel as simply an extreme overcoming narrative—one in which the protagonist confronts extraordinary difficulties in order to triumph. However, I would also note here that these obstacles that Helio overcomes prompt the novel's readers to consider what alternatives there might be to his actions. Helio even asks himself: "What pain would he have to accept to remake it? Was his pain enough to make that pain left? Everywhere he went, he had been searched out, found out, smoked out like vermin in rotting wood" (140). Clearly, his actions are necessary in a society that does not permit him to earn a living and treats him like "vermin in rotting wood." However, given the fact that Helio's oppression is socially constructed, the text prompts its readers to consider whether Helio's effort to overcome his disability should be the solution to the discrimination he faces. González, who offers a Marxist analysis of the novel, makes a similar point about its treatment of class conflict. He observes that even though "Helio does not seek to attain a critical consciousness of his situation" (162), nonetheless the reader "stands to learn more from the object lesson of the novel than does the protagonist himself" (171). By demonstrating how arduous Helio's act of individual overcoming is and prompting consideration of how the society in which Helio lives might better accommodate him, *Face* reveals the necessity of identity-based political solutions.

The scant critical bibliography on *Face* describes it as an existential novel dealing with questions about the meaning of human existence. Juan Bruce-Novoa describes the novel in his introduction to the 2003 edition as an "allegory of the human condition" ("Face to Face" xx). What is striking about this characterization is how closely it aligns "the human condition" with a discourse of overcoming: "A man suddenly slips off his life-path, losing his identity, and must struggle against great odds and menacing forces to reinvent himself before being allowed to return" (xxvii). The novel's investigation of existential themes about the nature of human existence is evident, and references to writers like Jean-Paul Sartre and Samuel Beckett explicitly connect it to the existentialist literary tradition. In one early scene, Helio attempts to apply for government assistance for facial reconstruction. He loses his way in the halls of a government building, but when he finds a door that should lead outdoors, he encounters a wall of bricks and a sign in red letters: "NO EXIT" (44). The reference here is, of course, to Sartre's 1945 *No Exit*, in which a group of dead characters conclude that "Hell is—other people" (45). What differentiates Pineda's novel from Sartre's more canonized text, however, is its insistence that there is no universal human condition: human existence is marked by hierarchies of race, class, gender, sexuality and ability, and any philosophical investigation of "the" human condition must take human beings' differential identities into account.

The novel's insistence on the particularity of human experience is even more explicit in its reference to Beckett's play *Waiting for Godot* (1949). The reference to Beckett surfaces in the character of Teofilho Godoy, the T.G. of the novel's prologue, a doctor who agrees to help Helio, partly out of pity and partly to further his own research agenda. (Helio is unable to benefit from the doctor's offer, however, because his neighbors' violent threats force him to leave the Capital.) As González observes, "both *Godot* and *Face* are ultimately balanced on similar questions: Will the future for these characters . . . be determined by an external force, or will it be shaped by the deliberate actions of socially conscious individuals?" (*Chicano Novels* 172). He notes that, like Godot in Beckett's play, Godoy figures in *Face* as a deity of sorts. Godoy "represents religion, science, the state, and bourgeois culture," apparatuses that, in "modern capitalism, . . . have come to assume a godlike character" (177). To González's analysis, I would add that all of the institutions represented by Godoy (religion, science, the state, and bourgeois culture) have been recruited, at various historical moments, in the social management of disability and disabled people. The reference to Beckett's play in *Face,* then, highlights how identity-based political movements must figure in answers to this question.

The element of the novel that most distinguishes *Face* from other overcoming narratives, however, is its ending. As a *critical* overcoming narrative, *Face* has a very different conclusion from that of the traditional overcoming narrative. Throughout the novel, Helio's goal is the same as that of most protagonists of overcoming narratives, to "be just like everyone else once more" (140). Yet Pineda reveals that Helio has never been "just like anyone." He recalls strolling though the Capital, "appraising the women in their tangas, their breasts bobbling, their bodies glistening with salt water, their looks inviting, appraising his dark body and his face alive with wanting, and the knowledge he could have them. Like anyone" (140). The description of Helio's "dark body," however, reveals that he has always been marked, not like anyone. The novel returns to this point upon the completion of Helio's facial reconstruction, which he deems a success:

> It is a face; it is not particularly striking, certainly not attractive or handsome. It evokes neither origins nor class.

It is unremarkable—like anyone else's. But no. Not like
anyone. It is his, his alone. He has built it, alone, sewn it
stitch by stitch, with the very thin needle and the thread of
gossamer. It has not been given casually by birth, but made
by him, by the wearer of it. (168)

Despite Helio's satisfaction with his handiwork, this new face is
not—and will not be—like that of "anyone." Even as his new face
betrays neither "origins nor class," it remains marked by Helio's
experience. As a result, *Face* denies its reader a happy ending in
which Helio's facial reconstruction magically changes his interactions with the social world. The novel ends with Helio back in
Rio, running into a woman he believes to be Lula, accompanied
by a new man: "Then they both look up at him" (170). Where a
traditional overcoming narrative would end with unequivocal
proof of the success of Helio's facial reconstruction, *Face* does
not reveal what happens next. This is the uncertainty of identity
politics predicated not on the uncritical affirmation of identity
but on an unrealized future in which identity oppression no
longer exists. We do not know how identity will change in the
absence of oppression that targets marked bodies, and we cannot know without eliminating that oppression.

Pineda's critical overcoming narrative, then, is not simply
a record of how a heroic protagonist triumphs over the forces
impeding him, but rather an interrogation of the socially-
constructed forces that rob him of his status as a human being.
Furthermore, by depicting its protagonist engaged in gruesome acts of self-mutilation that do not, in the end, guarantee
his readmittance to the human, the novel prompts its readers
to seek identity-based, political, collective solutions to Helio's
dilemma. In this sense, *Face* reinforces Moya's claim that "we
live in a troubled society. . . . For this reason, if people do not fit
into our society, we should consider the possibility that we need
to change society instead of people" (*Learning from Experience*
127). Therefore, although the novel does not clearly prescribe the
precise content of the social change it demands, it demonstrates

that identity-based oppression requires not an individual solution but a politics predicated upon identity.

To conclude, I cite Wendell's argument that the future meaning of the category of "people with disabilities" will be determined by "what meanings people with disabilities give it through their cultural interpretations and their political actions" (*Rejected Body* 32). I pair this argument with Ong's critique of citizenship as an institution that has failed to account for the uneven racialization of different categories of citizens—even those, like Asian immigrants, assumed to possess the same racial identity—and that must, therefore, be subjected to critical scrutiny as a worthy political goal. In different ways, both Wendell and Ong point to a future in which politicized identity categories—*people with disabilities, immigrants,* and *citizens*—will not retain the same meaning they currently possess. If that future is to be a more just and democratic one, moreover, these categories cannot retain the hierarchies that exist within them (what Snyder and Mitchell call the "'less-able disabled" versus the "non-impaired impaired"; the assimilated immigrant versus the unassimilable migrant; the normative citizen versus what Mae Ngai calls the "alien citizen"). In such a future, even Wendell imagines the possibility that the category *people with disabilities* "would . . . disappear" (33). Nonetheless, we do not yet occupy such a future. While I share, then, certain critiques of both identity and citizenship as they are normatively constructed, I also share Sandahl's belief in "the continued relevance and efficacy of identity-based theory, politics, and performance" and her concern that setting aside either identity or citizenship as critical categories may be "troubling and premature" ("Black Man, Blind Man" 582). Instead of theorizing for a post-identity or post-national future, we need to theorize for the present we currently occupy, one in which nationalisms and identity categories—however normalizing and co-optable they may be—structure our social world in profound ways and impact people's life chances.

Published fifteen years apart, *Face* and *Peel My Love* emerge from slightly different intellectual currents and historical moments. *Face* was published as neoliberal doctrine ascended to global dominance, aided by the policies of political leaders like Ronald Reagan and Margaret Thatcher[12] but at a moment when identity politics still resonated in some sectors of academia, which had recently benefited from increased intellectual diversification resulting from the civil rights movements of the 1960s and 1970s and from the particular form of identity politics practiced by feminists of color (exemplified by publications like Cherríe Moraga's and Gloria Anzaldúa's 1981 anthology *This Bridge Called My Back*). *Peel My Love,* on the other hand, emerges at a time when neoliberalism has been firmly established as a world-system and theoretical models rejecting identity politics have become entrenched in the academy. While both novels offer cogent critiques of the neoliberal state, *Peel My Love* demonstrates that too fervent a rejection of identity politics may leave us without the theoretical tools to effectively contest this state. *Face,* meanwhile, reveals that while identity politics may seem theoretically dated in the present intellectual climate, there are models of identity that allow for more nuanced—and therefore less normative and more inclusive—ways of theorizing the concept. A comparative analysis of the two novels reinforces Siebers's claim that "human-rights discourse will never break free from the ideology of ability until it includes disability as a defining characteristic of human beings" (*Disability Theory* 178). However, it takes this claim one step further by revealing that human-rights discourse must account for identity in all its forms.

Epilogue

From March to May of 2006, millions of people across the United States took to the streets to advocate for the rights of immigrants. These protests became the largest and most geographically dispersed mobilization of people for immigration reform in the history of the United States, with demonstrations organized in more than one hundred cities around the country and, at the largest gathering in Los Angeles, drawing a crowd estimated at more than 500,000 people. The impact of these protests continues to be felt in the U.S. political landscape, as the demonstrations and resulting media coverage galvanized people on both sides of what is now delicately called *the immigration debate*. Because they provided a forum for the unprecedented visibility of undocumented immigrants fearlessly claiming their rights in the public sphere, these protests set the stage for the courageous public interventions undertaken, as I write these words, by DREAMers and UndocuQueer youth.[1] The original impetus for these protests was the Border Protection, Anti-Terrorism, and Illegal Immigration Control Act of 2005 (H.R. 4437), a bill that (among its other provisions) would have classified undocumented immigrants and citizens who provide any form of assistance to them as felons.[2] However, the protests soon evolved to exceed this goal, so that many of the participants began to see their objective as nothing less than the radical transformation of the U.S. immigration system.

As the objectives of protesters evolved, so too did the symbols they used, the most obvious example being a concerted effort to feature the United States flag in the demonstrations. At the early March gatherings, some participants carried Mexican and Central American flags to show pride in their nations of origin— a fact that received extensive attention from anti-immigrant groups. As conservative pundit Charles Krauthammer snidely scolded: "If you are appealing to Americans to give you the rights and privileges of citizenship, it is not a good idea to hail Mexico, and it's an even worse idea to hold up signs such as 'This is our continent, not yours!'" By the time the April demonstrations (in which the largest number of people participated) took place, protest organizers had begun asking participants to wave only the U.S. flag (and, furthermore, to wear white tee-shirts to augment the visibility of the red, white, and blue flags). For instance, immigration reform advocate Cardinal Roger Mahony, Archbishop of Los Angeles, urged supporters to leave non-U.S. flags at home: "Do not use them because they do not help us get the legislation we need."[3] The use of American flags in the protests resulted in news photographs that were visually quite striking: not only did the prominent use of the American flag appeal to U.S. citizens who wanted to see their country as a just, democratic, welcoming, and appealing destination for immigrants, but they also gave the protests a uniform look so that marches taking place in cities as disparate as Nashville, Tennessee, and Mountain View, California (where I participated), projected the image of a mass movement united around a singular goal and political message. To this day, photographs from these protests are easily recognizable to anyone who followed the story. We still remember seeing images on the news from around the country and believing, truly, that (as we chanted at the rallies) "*el pueblo unido jamás será vencido*."[4] Indeed, one of these photographs, taken by the talented photojournalist Nhat V. Meyer of the *San*

Jose Mercury News and featuring a man named Rubén Velasco of San Jose, California, appears on the cover of this book.

Yet even at the time, this use of the U.S. flag was not uncritically embraced by all who participated. When I marched, I dutifully wore an old white tee-shirt (no small accomplishment for one who adopted the dour, mostly black wardrobe of the humanities graduate student as readily as I), but I did not wave a flag of any kind. Like many, I was uncomfortable with the idea that people should be obliged to prove their fidelity to a nation-state that refused to guarantee their rights. Signs of dissent were visible, although occasionally quite subtle, as evidenced by this report on a Chicago protest from Oscar Avila and Antonio Olivo of the *Chicago Tribune:* "American flags bobbed overhead while also decorating shawls, placards and the scarf on a baby's head. That dominant motif was set off by the colors of Ecuador, Colombia, Guatemala and, of course, Mexico." And it soon became clear that the use of the U.S. flag was not enough to appease critics of the movement. Krauthammer, for instance, interpreted the use of the U.S. flag as a cynical political ploy while condescendingly insinuating that few of those carrying U.S. flags could even speak the country's dominant language: "Many of the hundreds of thousands of Hispanic demonstrators who poured out into the streets on Monday may not know much English, but they've learned the language of American politics: Flags. Tons of flags. And make them American." (Krauthammer also conveniently ignored the substantial ethnic diversity of the protests, emphasized in other reports. For instance, Avila and Olivo noted contingents of Chinese, Polish, and Irish immigrants at the Chicago demonstration.) For me—at the time just beginning the research that ultimately led me to write this book—the act of critically scrutinizing the political symbols that were used by the protest organizers, and subsequently making choices about how to engage with these symbols as I participated in local demonstrations, provided long-term lessons about the continued power of nationalist symbols and rhetoric.

Accessible Citizenships responds to the enduring power of the idea of national belonging. Nationalism may have been deemed passé by cultural critics, and the nation itself may have been declared obsolete by transnational corporations. Yet, as the 2006 immigration protests powerfully revealed and as ongoing efforts to secure U.S. citizenship for undocumented immigrants emphasize, those excluded from the protective sphere of citizenship continue to feel the force of the nation. The problem identified by Hannah Arendt in 1951 remains more urgent than ever: *How can we begin to respect human rights—above and beyond the rights of the citizen—when we have not, as a species, found ourselves capable of creating an entity other than the nation that is capable of guaranteeing these rights?* Arendt's still-unanswered question helps us to understand not only why the use of the U.S. flag in the 2006 demonstrations was so rhetorically persuasive. Her question also helps us to understand the counter-hegemonic force of Chicana/o cultural nationalism and the revolutionary power of an idea like Aztlán.

Still, I find it important to reiterate that my interest in nationalism is not ultimately about reaffirming its power, even as I have sought to understand why some of the writers whose work I hold most dear—Arturo Islas, Cherríe Moraga, Felicia Luna Lemus—reveal a latent (or, in the case of Moraga, not so latent) investment in forms of cultural nationalism that some critics have so hastily dismissed as retrograde, exclusionary, and oppressive. I have argued that the work of these writers reminds us of nationalism's power to make ethical claims. But I have also demonstrated that their work is ambivalently nationalist, always reminding us of the flaws inherent in any nationalist project. Precisely because of this ambivalence, I have asserted that nationalism continues to merit serious critical interrogation. As the work of Alex Espinoza, Tommy Lee Jones, Guillermo Arriaga, and Oscar Casares further demonstrates, the consequences of being left outside the protective fold of the nation remain all too clear. Finally, I have chosen to conclude this book with readings of novels by Ana Castillo and Cecile Pineda because their work reveals how even our attempts to think and imagine beyond the nation form often end up revealing the profound difficulty of escaping its influence.

Given that nations and nationalisms retain their powerful presence in our social landscape, I have argued here that rigorous analysis of the metaphors and images that we employ to imagine our national communities remains an important critical endeavor for scholars concerned with theorizing toward a more just world. My focus in *Accessible Citizenships* has been the bodily metaphors and images that activist cultural workers employ when they envision nationhood. By emphasizing these bodily metaphors, I have sought to demonstrate the kinds of critical insights that can emerge when crafting a theoretical framework from the tools of both Chicana/o and disability studies.

Until now, critics have tended to assume that nations are imagined through images of the socially dominant body—which, in the white supremacist, ableist, and heteropatriarchal world we live in, is a white, male, able-bodied, and heterosexual one. The prevailing critical assumption has further been that on those rare occasions when images of disability are used to represent the national collective, they signal national failure or decay. The alignment of the nation with this socially dominant body (and its corollary, the alignment of deviation from this norm with social or political crisis) has had deleterious consequences for those whose embodiment differs from this norm, limiting their access to the rights and benefits of citizenship.

[handwritten margin note: disabled as limited]

This paradigm has proven remarkably useful for interpreting many mainstream texts. Yet, as I argue in this book, it is less helpful for understanding counter-hegemonic efforts to engage with the concept of nationalism, which employ different kinds of bodily metaphors. Nationalism does not have to be conceptualized through this singular, hegemonic bodily ideal. The cultural workers I have discussed throughout this study have chosen images of disability to represent their engagements with nationalism, and in doing so have sought to transform our very conceptualization of the nation itself. They have attempted to make the nation more open, more just, more democratic. It remains my hope that following their lead can ultimately help us to conceptualize new forms of political collectivity, even if our starting point is ultimately as imperfect as the nation form.

Here I think again of my choice not to wave a U.S. flag at the 2006 demonstrations, and I think also of the different choice made by Velasco, a man I do not know personally but whose image graces the cover of my book. While I could not see an emancipatory use for the U.S. flag in 2006, Velasco made a different choice, opting instead to use the U.S. flag to declare himself part of its national narrative. Waving that flag in the San Jose protest march, he claimed a place for his brown, disabled body within the larger U.S. national body. And in doing so, he offered the United States an opportunity to become just a little more inclusive, a little more free, and a little more fair. Velasco's political intervention at that protest was, in fact, made in the same spirit as those made by the writers whose work I have discussed in this book, all of whom have chosen to work within the limits of the nation form even as they reveal its problems and exclusions.

At the same time, none of the cultural workers discussed in this book unequivocally embraces the nation form. Indeed, the fundamental ambivalence of citizenship as a means of claiming rights is captured in photographer Meyer's image of Velasco, for at the moment that the picture was taken, the U.S. flag was flying backwards, signaling (if ever so subtly) that nationalism is not, in fact, the best way forward. Indeed, while my effort in this book has been to look seriously at the nation form by closely examining its representation in activist cultural production, my hope is that this close examination will, ultimately, lead us to imagine new forms of political collectivity that are not bound by the nation.

Notes

Introduction

1. In a recent Salon.com report drawing from data derived from the University of Michigan's Social Science Data Analysis Network, Daniel Denvir notes that Los Angeles was the tenth most segregated urban area in the United States in 2011; it is the only city west of the Great Lakes to appear in the top ten. According to the U.S. Census, income inequality in the city remains extremely high, with half of all income earned in Los Angeles County going to the highest-paid 20 percent of its residents while the lowest-earning 20 percent receive only 3.1 percent of the city's total earned income; the city of Los Angeles also has the largest uninsured population of any U.S. city besides New York. The history of the city is marked by a number of high-profile events that emphasize its long history of racial inequality. Los Angeles was the site of the Zoot Suit Riots of 1943, in which large numbers of white sailors and marines brutally attacked local Mexican American, Filipina/o, and African American youth. Police brutality against men of color in the city—particularly African American men—spurred two racialized uprisings in the second half of the twentieth century (the Watts Riots of 1965 and the 1992 Los Angeles Civil Unrest, also called the Rodney King Uprising). Finally, two key features of the Los Angeles cityscape—Dodger Stadium and the freeway system for which the city is so widely known—are built on land initially occupied by working-class residents of color displaced from their homes through eminent domain abuse.

2. The foundation of Chicana/o cultural nationalism, Aztlán is the original homeland of the Mexica people (also called the Aztecs) and is located in

the present-day U.S. Southwest; the Mexica migrated south to Tenochtitlán (now Mexico City) before the Conquest.

3. Ngai convincingly demonstrates that the particular process by which Mexicans have been incorporated into the United States is an "expression of the legacies of slavery and conquest" (*Impossible Subjects* 138). She bases this argument on the Bracero Program, a contract labor program that brought hundreds of thousands of Mexicans to work temporarily in the United States between 1942 and 1964, despite the fact that since "the end of the Civil War, Americans had believed that contract labor, like slavery, was the antithesis of free labor, upon which democracy depended" (137). Further support for her argument lies in the fact that part of the impetus for the U.S.-Mexican War, through which the United States illegally seized half of Mexico's territory, was the desire to incorporate Texas as a slave state.

4. In the context of queer theory, Eve Kosofsky Sedgwick, a cultural critic widely believed to reject identity politics as essentialist, makes a similar (if less optimistic) point:

> To the degree—and it is significantly large—that the gay essentialist/ constructivist debate takes its form and premises from, and insistently refers to, a whole history of other nature/nurture or nature/ culture debates, it partakes of a tradition of viewing culture as malleable relative to nature: that is, culture, unlike nature, is assumed to be the thing that can be changed. . . . I remember the buoyant enthusiasm with which feminist scholars used to greet the finding that one or another brutal form of oppression was not biological but "only" cultural! I have often wondered what the basis was for our optimism about the malleability of culture by any one group or program. (*Epistemology of the Closet* 41)

Although Sedgwick and Moya diverge on the question of identity's usefulness as a ground for political action, then, they nonetheless concur that its status as a social construct does not in any way detract from its impact on people's lives and life chances.

5. Another critique of the mural project is that the OOC sponsored the murals but made no provision for their upkeep; in the years since the murals were painted, a number of them have been tagged so much that they have essentially become unrecognizable. Indeed, for a long time, *Hitting the Wall* contained so many tags that the image of the runner in the wheelchair was invisible. As a result, several of the Olympic murals (those for which the artists or advocates were unable to remove the graffiti and restore the murals) have been whitewashed. For more on this point, see Jones.

6. The RCAF was originally formed in 1969 as the Rebel Chicano Art Front but changed its name as a playful response to the fact that the acronym RCAF was frequently confused with the acronym for the Royal Canadian Air Force.

7. Rodríguez has documented an extensive corpus of nationalist "family portraits" featuring many of the same formal elements as *La Familia*: the father/husband is physically much larger than the mother/wife; the mother/wife's gaze is averted or turned downward; and there is a male child.

8. In this, I concur with Davidson, who observes in the wake of NAFTA a "literary community formed through shared economic interdependencies" that complicates " the idea of 'imagined communities' produced within the nation-state" ("On the Outskirts" 736).

9. See, for instance, the work of Rosa Linda Fregoso, Alicia Schmidt Camacho, José David Saldívar, José E. Limón, and Héctor Calderón.

10. It is noteworthy, however, that the majority of the texts examined in this study deal with physical, rather than cognitive or psychiatric, disabilities; one reason for the difficulty in finding texts that deal with cognitive and psychiatric disabilities may indeed be precisely the desire that Mitchell and Snyder describe to "unmoor" racialized identities from "debilitating" cognitive associations.

1 / Enabling Aztlán

An earlier version of this chapter was previously published in the journal *Modern Fiction Studies*.

1. Although I note in passing certain biographical details shared by Islas and his character, I do not wish to overstate their significance; as John Alba Cutler has noted, a critical tendency to conflate Islas himself with his most famous character "imbues [*The Rain God*] with a degree of immediacy that seems untenable for so highly refined and self-consciously fictive a text" ("Prosthesis" 19).

2. In particular, the work of Frederick Luis Aldama is notable for this emphasis. Aldama is the leading scholar of Islas's work, having published a critical biography of Islas (*Dancing With Ghosts*), an edited anthology of critical essays about Islas's work (*Critical Mappings of Arturo Islas's Fictions*), and an edited collection of Islas's unpublished writings (*The Uncollected Works*).

3. These include the groundbreaking anthology *This Bridge Called My Back: Writings by Radical Women of Color*, co-edited by Cherríe Moraga and Gloria Anzaldúa, as well as their first solo-authored books (Moraga's *Loving in the War Years: lo que nunca pasó por sus labios* and Anzaldúa's *Borderlands/La Frontera: The New Mestiza*).

4. I use "Chicano" as a masculine adjective, "Chicana" as a feminine adjective, and "Chicana/o" as a gender-inclusive adjective. I use "Chicano nationalism" when referring specifically to masculinist formulations of cultural nationalism.

5. As of this writing, two profound threats to Chicanas/os in the United States are visible in the form of two pieces of legislation recently signed into law in the State of Arizona and being promoted in other states as well. The

first, Arizona Senate Bill 1070, implicitly endorses racial profiling by allowing police officers to demand proof of immigration status from any person who appears to be an undocumented resident of the United States; those who cannot produce such documentation, regardless of their status, are subject to punishment. Even as parts of this law have been declared unconstitutional by the Supreme Court, aspects of it remain in effect, and the law has inspired the passage of similarly draconian legislation in states like Georgia and Alabama. The second, Arizona House Bill 2281, bans ethnic studies programs in public K–12 schools and specifically targets the Tucson Unified School District's Mexican American Studies program.

6. In an earlier published essay on Islas, I wrote that Miguel Chico here rids himself of this monster, but I am persuaded by Cutler's observation that Miguel Chico's struggle with the monster is described with great compassion: "It is the embrace in this passage that I find significant, a moment of physical contact spurred by sudden and surprising 'tenderness,' which Miguel Chico sees only after he faces the monster" (27).

7. Aldama's archival research on earlier drafts of *The Rain God* indicates that Islas edited out references to Miguel Chico's preference for sexual practices involving bondage and discipline; these practices do appear briefly in *Migrant Souls*, where Miguel Chico jokes about them. As a result, it is striking that this passage reveals the young Miguel Chico attracted to literary images of anti-normative bodies as well as of anti-normative sexual practices. Although Miguel Chico's love of a torture scene is *The Rain God*'s only direct reference to BDSM in the novel, it is not a subtle one, despite some critics' claims that the novel reads as closeted.

2 / "My Country Was Note Like That"

1. In her latest book, *A Xicana Codex of Changing Consciousness*, Moraga writes of her political practice: "Some days I've called that practice lesbian feminism, on other days Indigenism; some years it was Chicano nation, other years, radical women-of-color activism" (70). Here Moraga does not entirely abandon nationalism but sets it alongside other activist modes that surface in her writing without giving it privileged status, suggesting that she does not see nationalism as a political end in and of itself. A more prominent example of her move away from nationalism is, of course, her play *The Hungry Woman*, which I examine in detail in this chapter.

2. Although the verb "to crip" is often used in disability studies as an analogue to the verb "to queer," with this usage I am specifically relying upon Carrie Sandahl's definition: cripping involves "the act of coming out as a crip queer, the public display of sexualized bodily difference, and the process of bearing witness to past and present injustice" ("Queering the Crip" 28).

3. Because this reader has not revealed her/hir/himself to me, I cannot thank her/hir/him by name, but the comment struck me as insightful and fair, and I am grateful for it.

4. A second edition of *Loving* was published in 2000 with seven new pieces written during the 1990s (essays and poems) and some changes to the original text (notably the replacement of the word "cunt" with the Mexican Spanish word "chocha").

5. See Yarbro-Bejarano, Sharpe, Rueda Esquibel, and my own 2011 essay on Moraga for different takes on her nationalism.

6. Accounts of Coyolxauhqui's motivations vary. In some (more masculinist) versions, she is embarrassed by her aging mother's pregnancy; in *The Hungry Woman*, she feels betrayed by it: "traición is what she smells entre los cuatro vientos" (55).

7. The mural was painted in 1994 by the Maestrapeace Collective (Juana Alicia, Miranda Bergman, Edythe Boone, Susan Kelk Cervantes, Meera Desai, Yvonne Littleton, and Irene Pérez).

8. I discuss the ideology of ability in greater detail in the following chapter.

9. See Yarbro-Bejarano, Sharpe, and Soto for different takes on the stakes of this movement in Moraga's work.

10. I discuss interracial desire in Islas's work in chapter one of this study. Terri de la Peña's most widely read novel *Margins* tells the story of Roni, a young Chicana lesbian grieving the death of her lover Joanna; during the course of the novel, Roni experiences a failed romance with her Italian American neighbor Siena before finding love with fellow Chicana lesbian Rene Talamantes.

11. The descriptions of Frank and his father changing the colostomy bags bring to mind similar descriptions in the work of Arturo Islas, discussed in chapter one.

12. Whenever I teach this novel, my students are unfailingly outraged by the idea that Frank would return to Nathalie. Indeed, many profess to "hate" her.

13. I discuss *El Plan Espiritual de Aztlán* in more detail in chapter one.

3 / So Much Life in the Still Waters

1. See Graham, Schlikerman, and Uribe.

2. See Graham.

3. See Novoa.

4. According to legal scholars, involuntary medical repatriations violate domestic and international laws. Kendra Stead notes that deportation "is the province not of hospitals, but of the federal government" ("Critical Condition" 332), while Vishal Agraharkar argues that such repatriations violate international human rights laws that prohibit "subjecting individuals to cruel, inhuman or degrading treatment" ("Deporting the Sick" 581) in the process of deportation. Agarharkar further observes that the U.S. Constitution guarantees the rights of all *persons* (not just all citizens) in the United States, and that "the right to due process is not limited to aliens who are lawfully within United States territory" (589).

5. See Graham, Schlikerman, and Uribe. These comments were visible on the article on the date of my last access.

6. See Graham, Schlikerman, and Uribe.

7. The work of Otto Santa Ana is a representative example. Santa Ana is a highly regarded scholar of immigration whose work I admire very much and cite in this chapter because of his brilliant analyses of the negative metaphors used to represent immigrants in the mainstream media. However, when Santa Ana proposes to replace these negative metaphors with what he calls "insurgent metaphors," he proposes metaphors predicated on the able body capable of performing physical labor: "Immigrants are the strong working **arms** of California's economy" (*Brown Tide Rising* 300, original emphasis). In other words, Santa Ana's insurgent metaphors consistently challenge the racism of anti-immigrant public rhetoric but not (in all instances) its ableism.

8. A botánica, as defined by Alfredo Gomez-Beloz and Noel Chavez, is a store (often located in a Latina/o community) that "offers medicinal herbs, religious amulets, and other products used by Latinos for remedies" ("The Botánica" 538). Gomez-Beloz and Chavez note, furthermore, that the proprietors of botánicas are often curanderas/os or folk healers, and that some botánicas emphasize the "magico-spiritual aspect of healing" (538) and predominantly stock religious items while others, which are focused on the "naturo-spiritual aspect of healing" (538), stock herbs, vitamins, and homeopathic products. The botánica in *Still Water Saints* offers both types of healing.

9. Chavez defines the Latino Threat Narrative as one that presents Latina/o immigrants as "unwilling or incapable of integrating, of becoming part of the national community" (*Latino Threat* 2).

10. Althusser writes: "I might add: what thus seems to take place outside ideology (to be precise, in the street), in reality takes place in ideology. What really takes place in ideology seems therefore to take place outside it. That is why those who are in ideology believe themselves by definition outside ideology: . . . ideology never says, 'I am ideological'" (*On Ideology* 49).

11. The novel is set in a suburb of Los Angeles, which I define as part of the borderlands, following Nevins's description of a "thickened" U.S.-Mexico boundary: "Increasingly, for example, U.S. authorities, in the name of national security, are employing Border Patrol checkpoints far in the interior of the United States—ranging from locales across Arizona to White River Junction, Vermont (more than 100 miles from Canada). This has the effect of 'thickening' the territorial boundaries of the United States in terms of its agents and practices of surveillance and control" (*Operation Gatekeeper* 184). In defining greater Los Angeles as part of the borderlands, I also draw upon a history of Chicana/o cultural production, ranging from the Cheech Marin film *Born in East L.A.* (1987) to the short story "INS and Outs" by Harry Gamboa Jr. (1983), depicting Los Angeles as a site in which

people of Mexican or Latin American origin are constantly subjected to the scrutiny and abuse of immigration authorities.

12. Careful readers will note that Rosa does return to Perla for help with weight loss later, after she has married, had a child, and become a hair stylist; some might argue that this undermines my argument. In response, I would point out that the story does not conform to the traditional "triumph over obesity" narrative supported by the ideology of ability for two reasons: first, Rosa's accomplishments all take place before her (potential) weight loss and are therefore not attributable to it, as is often the case with discourses treating obesity as something to conquer, and second, her decision to lose weight does not occur within the space of her narrative, meaning that her story on its own still functions as a repudiation of bodily normativity. I will, however, admit to some personal ambivalence about Rosa's later return to Perla. On the one hand, when I teach this novel, my students routinely point out to me that lower-income and Latina/o communities have high rates of obesity, that obesity is linked to other health problems, and that uncritically valorizing obesity could be read as socially irresponsible. On the other hand, the solution to the high rates of obesity in lower-income communities is social, not individual, and requires addressing larger questions of food distribution instead of privileging individual weight loss. My own view is that the enforcement of narrow beauty norms and the social stigmatizing of obesity are just as harmful, if not more so, and my personal wish for Rosa as a character is that she love her body unconditionally throughout her life. With that said, I also believe that Rosa's complicated relationship to the ideology of ability—occasionally rejecting it, occasionally submitting to it—functions as a realistic representation of the ways in which most of us live with this ideology. Furthermore, I stand by my statement that Rosa's story subjects narrow beauty standards to *critical scrutiny* even if it does not take a defined position. I am grateful to the students who have taken my Latina/o literary survey course at Miami University for debating this question so thoroughly with me.

13. At the same time, because the novel also critiques death caused by injustice, state neglect, and oppression, the acceptance of death in old age in Juan's story is not a passive acquiescence to the devaluing of the lives of marginalized people.

14. One exception is the story of Azúcar, a transgender dancer who finds an abandoned baby and decides to use the money she has been saving for gender reassignment surgery to raise the baby. The fact that her story shares with Rodrigo's a lack of resolution is linked to the fact that both are stories that cannot be accounted for within the legal framework of the society in which they are set. As much as the reader might root for Azúcar to raise the baby and become its mother, there are clear legal obstacles to a happy ending here.

15. See Schlikerman.

4 / No Nation for Old Men?

1. Butler's analysis specifically examines the effects of civilian deaths from the U.S. wars in Iraq and Afghanistan, but as John "Rio" Riofrio notes, her analysis also beautifully applies to the U.S.-Mexico border. Riofrio also cites Butler's *Precarious Life* in his analysis of *The Three Burials,* although his emphasis is not melancholia.

2. Almost simultaneously, and without citing one another, Alicia Schmidt Camacho developed the concept of *migrant melancholia* as Sara Ahmed developed that of the *melancholic migrant.* Their work has significant overlaps but also differs in some crucial respects: Schmidt Camacho's migrant melancholia refers to the migrant's refusal to relinquish her personhood as she migrates to a national context that refuses to recognize it; Ahmed's melancholic migrant refuses to relinquish her memories of the racism she experiences in her new homeland.

3. He previously directed a made-for-TV movie called *The Good Old Boys* (1995).

4. These films also contain noteworthy disability representations.

5. Jones later provided the narration for the 2007 documentary film *The Ballad of Esequiel Hernández,* directed by Kieran Fitzgerald.

6. As a representative example, *In the Valley of Elah* includes a sequence early in the film that depicts Jones's character, Hank Deerfield, a patriotic veteran whose son has gone to war in Iraq, engaged in the daily ritual of polishing his shoes. The sequence includes a somewhat overdetermined shot of Jones's bare feet, aged and wrinkled, positioned next to new-looking, shiny, freshly polished, perfectly preserved shoes. The visual contrast between the pristine shoes and Jones's withered feet highlights the film's overarching message about the gap between the image of functional democracy that the United States presents globally and the conflict lurking under its veneer.

7. The film did win a Western Heritage Award from the National Cowboy and Western Heritage Museum in Oklahoma City.

8. "Una de las personalidades de la literatura y cinematografía más significativa del México contemporáneo." My translation.

9. Here I am quoting from Riofrio's forthcoming book; this particular chapter was circulated as a work in progress to Stanford University's Trans-American Studies Working Group and is quoted with permission.

10. John "Rio" Riofrio, whose insightful take on the film has been quite influential to my own thinking on it, has a somewhat different interpretation of the ending than I do; despite this one point of disagreement, I highly recommend his analysis.

11. In my 2010 essay on the short story "Big Jesse, Little Jesse," I describe how the protagonist of that story cannot even sit down to a meal at a local café without noticing a pair of Border Patrol agents sitting nearby; their walkie-talkies are described as "standing guard next to the salt and pepper

shakers" (Casares, *Brownsville* 104), reinforcing the point that border policing is as much a mundane part of the characters' lives as table salt.

12. I am grateful to the students who took my Latina/o literature survey
course at Miami University in Fall 2011 for helping me think through the
implications of this particular stylistic choice. I had not noticed it until one
of my students asked me why both brothers were named Don; this somewhat
humorous moment prompted a delightful discussion of literary technique.

5 / Overcoming the Nation

1. See Mitchell and Snyder (*Narrative Prosthesis* 52) and James and Wu
("Editors' Introduction" 5).

2. Strategic essentialism is a concept that both Spivak and I avoid using. I
avoid the term because I see it as a way to avoid making a theoretically rigorous claim for the use of identity politics, while Spivak herself has repudiated
her own term because she believes it has been used to smuggle identity politics back into critical discourse: "The strategic use of essentialism . . . just
simply became the union ticket for essentialism. As to what is meant by
strategy, no one wondered about that" (Danius and Jonsson 35).

3. Siebers does not explicitly identify the stories he critiques as overcoming narratives, using instead the term "human interest stories"; however,
the description he offers corresponds precisely to the overcoming narrative:
"Human-interest stories display voyeuristically the physical or mental disability of their heroes, making the defect emphatically present, often exag-
gerating it, then wiping it away by reporting how it has been overcome, how
the heroes are 'normal,' despite the powerful odds against them" (*Disability
Theory* 111).

4. Examples include Alcoff (especially *Visible Identities*), Alcoff et. al.,
Hames-García (especially *Identity Complex*), Mohanty, Moya and Hames-
García, Moya, and Siebers (especially *Disability Theory*).

5. For a discussion of Islas and Moraga and their relationships to cultural
nationalism, see chapters one and two.

6. This is not the only instance in the novel in which Agustín demonstrates a pejorative attitude toward people with cognitive disabilities. During his first meeting with Carmen, which is arranged by her high school
teacher, he asks Carmen's teacher: "And who am I to criticize what God
in His Heaven has created? . . . Is this the student from the school for the
retarded that you've always told me about?" (*Peel My Love* 20–21).

7. In *Cultural Locations of Disability*, Snyder and Mitchell acknowledge
that they are not the first disability scholars to use the term *cultural model*.
However, because I am referring here specifically to their development of
the concept, I attribute it to them.

8. One exception might be her 2001 memoir *Fishlight: A Dream of Childhood*, which describes growing up in New York City with a Mexican father
and Swiss mother, although this text is certainly not set in a Chicana/o or

Latina/o neighborhood and its events in many cases do not conform to what many readers expect of a "typical" Chicana/o experience.

9. The exact date of the novel is not clearly specified, although the novel's prologue takes place during the 1970s; however, the city in which the majority of the novel takes place is referred to in the text as both "the Capital" and as "Rio." Since Brasília replaced Rio de Janeiro as Brazil's capital city in 1960, I assume the novel to be set in the 1950s.

10. *Cara* is Portuguese (and Spanish) for the words *face* and *expensive*.

11. I quote Bost at length here because I want to be careful to differentiate not only her ideas from mine but also her language. In particular, I would resist aligning disability unconditionally with "radical otherness" since, as disability activists often point out, everyone lucky enough to live long enough will become disabled at some point.

12. Harvey offers a thorough documentation of this process.

Epilogue

1. DREAMers is the current colloquial term for undocumented students advocating passage of the DREAM (Development, Relief, and Education for Alien Minors) Act, which as of this writing has not become federal law, although twelve states have passed versions of it (California, Illinois, Kansas, Maryland, Massachusetts, Nebraska, New Mexico, New York, Texas, Utah, Washington, and Wisconsin). The UndocuQueer movement emerged among queer youth working within the movement to pass the DREAM Act, and gained visibility as a result of artist Julio Salgado's "I Am UndocuQueer!" art project.

2. Although H.R. 4437 was passed by the U.S. House of Representatives in late 2005, it was (fortunately) never approved by the U.S. Senate.

3. Mahony is quoted in Peter Prengaman's report on the protests. It should be noted that although Mahony was known for his support of immigrant rights (although his injunction to use only American flags indicates a more conservative approach taken than that of many immigrant rights leaders), he also is remembered for his protection of priests in the Catholic Church's sex abuse scandal.

4. "The people united will never be defeated."

WORKS CITED

Agraharkar, Vishal. "Deporting the Sick: Regulating International Patient Dumping by U.S. Hospitals." *Columbia Human Rights Law Review* 41, no. 2 (Winter 2010): 569–600.

Aguilar Grimaldo, Roberto. "Recibe Guillermo Arriaga homenaje en Tamaulipas." *El Universal*. Monday, September 12, 2005. Web. February 28, 2012. <http://www.eluniversal.com.mx/espectacu-los/64468.html>

Ahmed, Sara. *The Promise of Happiness*. Durham, NC: Duke University Press, 2010.

Alcoff, Linda Martín. "The Problem of Speaking for Others." *Cultural Critique* 20 (Winter 1991–1992): 5–32.

———. *Visible Identities: Race, Gender, and the Self*. Oxford: Oxford University Press, 2006.

Alcoff, Linda Martín, Michael Hames-García, Paula M.L. Moya, and Satya P. Mohanty, eds. *Identity Politics Reconsidered*. New York: Palgrave MacMillan, 2006.

Aldama, Frederick Luis. *Brown on Brown: Chicano/a Representations of Gender, Sexuality, and Ethnicity*. Austin: University of Texas Press, 2005.

———. *Dancing with Ghosts: A Critical Biography of Arturo Islas*. Berkeley: University of California Press, 2005.

Almaguer, Tomás. "Chicano Men: A Cartography of Homosexual Identity and Behavior." *The Lesbian and Gay Studies Reader*, ed.

Henry Abelove, Michèle Aina Barale, and David Halperin, 255–73. New York: Routledge: 1993.

Althusser, Louis. *On Ideology*. 1971. London: Verso, 2008.

Americans With Disabilities Act. U.S. Department of Justice ADA Home Page. Web. Accessed March 14, 2011. <http://www.ada.gov/pubs/ada.htm>

Amores perros. Dir. Alejandro González Iñárritu. Perf. Emilio Echevarria, Gael García Bernal, and Goya Toledo. Filmax, 2000.

Anderson, Benedict. *Imagined Communities: Reflections on the Origin and Spread of Nationalism*. Rev. ed. New York: Verso, 1991.

Anzaldúa, Gloria. *Borderlands/La Frontera: The New Mestiza*. San Francisco: Aunt Lute Books, 1987.

Anzaldúa, Gloria, and Cherríe Moraga, eds. *This Bridge Called My Back: Writings by Radical Women of Color*. London: Persephone Press, 1981.

Arendt, Hannah. *The Origins of Totalitarianism*. 1948. New York: Harcourt, 1994.

Arriaga, Guillermo. *Un dulce olor a muerte*. 1994. New York: Atria Books, 2007.

———. *La noche del búfalo*. 1999. New York: Atria Books, 2002.

Avila, Oscar, and Antonio Olivo. "A show of strength." *The Chicago Tribune*. March 11, 2006. Web. Accessed January 11, 2013. <http://articles.chicagotribune.com/2006-03-11/news/0603110130_1_immigration-debate-pro-immigrant-illegal-immigrants>

Babel. Dir. Alejandro González Iñárritu. Perf. Brad Pitt and Cate Blanchett. Paramount Vantage, 2006.

The Ballad of Esequiel Hernández. Dir. Kieran Fitzgerald. Documentary Educational Resources, 2007.

Bebout, Lee. *Mythohistorical Interventions: The Chicano Movement and Its Legacies*. Minneapolis: University of Minnesota Press, 2011.

Bérubé, Michael. "Citizenship and Disability." *Dissent* 50, no 2 (Spring 2003): 52–57.

Born in East L.A. Dir. Cheech Marin. Perf. Cheech Marin, Paul Rodriguez, and Daniel Stern. Universal Studios, 1987.

Bost, Suzanne. *Encarnación: Illness and Body Politics in Chicana Feminist Literature*. New York: Fordham University Press, 2010.

Bradshaw, Peter. "Three Burials." *The Guardian*. March 30, 2005. Web. Accessed September 30, 2011. <http://www.guardian.co.uk/culture/2006/mar/31/12>

Brady, Mary Pat. *Extinct Lands, Temporal Geographies: Chicana Literature and the Urgency of Space*. Durham, NC: Duke University Press, 2002.

Bruce-Novoa, Juan. "Face to Face: An Introduction." In *Face*, by Cecile Pineda, xvii–xxi. San Antonio: Wings Press, 2003. xvii–xxi.

Butler, Judith. *Precarious Life: The Powers of Mourning and Violence*. London: Verso, 2006.

———. *Undoing Gender*. New York: Routledge, 2004.

Calderón, Héctor. *Narratives of Greater Mexico: Essays on Chicano Literary History, Genre, and Borders*. Austin: University of Texas Press, 2004.

Casares, Oscar. *Amigoland*. New York: Little, Brown, and Company, 2009.

———. *Brownsville: Stories*. Boston: Back Bay Books, 2003.

Castells, Manuel. *The Information Age, Volume Two: The Power of Identity*. 2nd ed. Oxford: Blackwell Publishing, 2004.

Castillo, Ana. *Massacre of the Dreamers: Essays on Xicanisma*. New York: Plume (Penguin), 1995.

———. *Peel My Love Like an Onion*. New York: Anchor Books, 1999.

Chavez, Leo R. *The Latino Threat: Constructing Immigrants, Citizens, and the Nation*. Stanford, CA: Stanford University Press, 2008.

Cheng, Anne Anlin. *The Melancholy of Race: Psychoanalysis, Assimilation, and Hidden Grief*. Oxford: Oxford University Press, 2000.

Cutler, John Alba. "Prosthesis, Surrogation, and Relation in Arturo Islas's *The Rain God*." *Aztlán: A Journal of Chicano Studies* 33 (Spring 2008): 7–32.

Danius, Sara, and Stefan Jonsson. "An Interview with Gayatri Chakravorty Spivak." *Boundary 2* 20, no. 2 (1993): 24–50.

Davidson, Michael. "On the Outskirts of Form: Cosmopoetics in the Shadows of NAFTA." *Textual Practice* 22, no. 44 (2008): 733–56.

Davies, Telory W. "Race, Gender, and Disability: Cherríe Moraga's Bodiless Head." *Journal of Dramatic Theory and Criticism* 21, no. 1 (Fall 2006): 29–44.

Davis, Lennard. *Bending Over Backwards: Disability, Dismodernism and Other Difficult Positions*. New York: New York University Press, 2002.

De la Peña, Terri. *Margins*. Seattle: Seal Press, 1992.

Denvir, Daniel. "The 10 Most Segregated Urban Areas in America." Salon.com, March 29, 2011. Web. Accessed April 1, 2011. <http://www.salon.com/2011/03/29/most_segregated_cities/>

Dunning, Stefanie K. *Queer in Black and White: Interraciality, Same Sex Desire, and Contemporary African American Culture.* Bloomington: Indiana University Press, 2009.

Durand, Jorge, Douglas S. Massey, and Emilio A. Parrado. "The New Era of Mexican Migration to the United States." *The Journal of American History* 86, no. 2 (September 1999): 518–36.

Edelman, Lee. *No Future: Queer Theory and the Death Drive.* Durham, NC: Duke University Press, 2004.

Espinoza, Alex. *Still Water Saints.* New York: Random House, 2007.

Esquibel, Catriona Rueda. *With Her Machete in Her Hand: Reading Chicana Lesbians.* Austin: University of Texas Press, 2006.

Ewart, Chris. "Terms of *Dis*appropriation: Disability, Diaspora and Dionne Brand's *What We All Long For.*" *Journal of Literary and Cultural Disability Studies* 4, no. 22 (2010): 147–61.

Fanon, Frantz. *The Wretched of the Earth.* 1963. New York: Grove Weidenfeld, 1991.

Fitzpatrick, Robert. "The Olympic Arts Festival." *Olympic Review* 198 (April 1984): 247–49. Web. Accessed February 16, 2011. <http://www.la84foundation.org/OlympicInformationCenter/OlympicReview/1984/ore198/ORE198o.pdf>

Flores, William V. "New Citizens, New Rights: Undocumented Immigrants and Latino Cultural Citizenship." *Latin American Perspectives* 30, no 2 (March 2003): 87–100.

Flores, William V., and Rina Benmayor. "Introduction: Constructing Cultural Citizenship." In *Latino Cultural Citizenship*, ed. William V. Flores and Rina Benmayor, 1–23. Boston: Beacon Press, 1997.

Fregoso, Rosa Linda. *MeXicana Encounters: The Making of Social Identities on the Borderlands.* Berkeley: University of California Press, 2003.

———. "We Want Them Alive! The Politics and Culture of Human Rights." *Social Identities* 12, no. 2 (March 2006): 109–38.

Fuentes, Carlos. *La frontera de cristal.* Mexico City: Alfaguara, 1995.

Gamboa, Harry Jr. *Urban Exile: Collected Writings of Harry Gamboa Jr.* Minneapolis: University of Minnesota Press, 1998.

Garland Thomson, Rosemarie. *Extraordinary Bodies: Figuring Disability in American Culture and Literature.* New York: Columbia University Press, 1997.

Goldman, Shifra M. "How, Why, Where, and When It All Happened: Chicano Murals of California." In *Signs from the Heart: California Chicano Murals*, ed. Eva Sperling Cockcroft and Holly

Barnet-Sánchez. Albuquerque: University of New Mexico Press, 1990.

Gomez-Beloz, Alfredo, and Noel Chavez. "The Botánica as a Culturally Appropriate Health Care Option for Latinos." *The Journal of Alternative and Complementary Medicine* 7, no. 5 (2001): 537–46.

González, Marcial. *Chicano Novels and the Politics of Form: Race, Class, and Reification.* Ann Arbor: University of Michigan Press, 2009.

The Good Old Boys. Dir. Tommy Lee Jones. Perf. Tommy Lee Jones, Terry Kinney, and Frances McDormand. Warner Archive, 1995.

Graham, Judith. "Why we wrote about a paralyzed undocumented immigrant sent back to Mexico." *Chicago Tribune*, February 7, 2011. Web. Accessed March 16, 2011. <http://newsblogs.chicagotribune.com/tribnation/2011/02/why-we-wrote-about-a-paralyzed-undocumented-immigrant-sent-back-to-mexico.html>

Graham, Judith, Becky Schlikerman, and Abel Uribe. "Undocumented worker who became quadriplegic is moved to Mexico against his will." *Chicago Tribune*, February 6, 2011. Web. Accessed March 16, 2011. <http://articles.chicagotribune.com/2011-02-06/news/ct-met-quadriplegic-immigrant-deporte20110206_1_advocate-health-care-ojeda-mexican-hospital>

Gutiérrez, David G. "Migration, Emergent Ethnicity, and the 'Third Space': The Shifting Politics of Nationalism in Greater Mexico." *The Journal of American History* 86 (September 1999): 481–517.

Halberstam, Judith. *The Queer Art of Failure.* Durham, NC: Duke University Press, 2011.

Hames-García, Michael. *Fugitive Thought: Prison Movements, Race, and the Meaning of Justice.* Minneapolis: University of Minnesota Press, 2004.

———. *Identity Complex: Making the Case for Multiplicity.* Minneapolis: University of Minnesota Press, 2011.

Hames-García, Michael, and Ernesto Javier Martínez. "Introduction: Re-Membering Gay Latino Studies." In *Gay Latino Studies: A Critical Reader*, ed. Michael Hames-García and Ernesto Javier Martínez, 1–18. Durham, NC: Duke University Press, 2011.

Harvey, David. *A Brief History of Neoliberalism.* Oxford: Oxford University Press, 2005.

Hobsbawm, E.J. *Nations and Nationalism since 1780: Programme, myth, reality.* 2nd ed. Cambridge: Cambridge University Press, 1992.

Inda, Jonathan Xavier. "Foreign Bodies: Migrants, Parasites, and the Pathological Nation." *Discourse* 22, no. 3 (Fall 2000): 46–62.

In the Electric Mist. Dir. Bertrand Tavernier. Perf. Tommy Lee Jones, John Goodman, and Peter Sarsgaard. TFM Distribution, 2009.

In the Valley of Elah. Dir. Paul Haggis. Perf. Tommy Lee Jones, Jason Patric, and Charlize Theron. Warner Bros., 2007.

———. "The Value of Immigrant Life." In *Women and Migration in the U.S.-Mexico Borderlands*, ed. Denise A. Segura and Patricia Zavella, 134–57. Durham, NC: Duke University Press, 2007.

Islas, Arturo. "Afterword: Can There Be Chicano Fiction? Or Writer's Block." *Miquiztli* 3, no. 1 (Winter–Spring 1975): 22–24.

———. *Migrant Souls.* New York: William Morrow, 1990.

———. "On the Bridge, At the Border: Migrants and Immigrants." Fifth Annual Ernesto Galarza Commemorative Lecture. Stanford University, Stanford, CA. 1990. Web. Accessed October 21, 2010. <http://chs.stanford.edu/pdfs/5th_Annual_Lecture_1990.pdf>

———. *The Rain God: A Desert Tale.* 1984. New York: HarperCollins/Perennial, 1991.

———. *The Uncollected Works*, ed. Frederick Luis Aldama. Houston: Arte Público Press, 2003.

———. "Writing From a Dual Perspective." *Miquiztli* 2, no. 1 (Winter 1974): 1–2.

James, Jennifer C., and Cynthia Wu. "Editors' Introduction: Race, Ethnicity, Disability, and Literature: Intersections and Interventions." *MELUS* 31, no. 3 (Fall 2006): 3–13.

Jones, Robert A. "A Long Goodbye for the Olympic Murals." *Los Angeles Times*, September 27, 1998. Web. Accessed April 1, 2011. <http://articles.latimes.com/1998/sep/27/local/me-26951>

Krauthammer, Charles. "Immigrants must choose." *The Washington Post*, April 14, 2006. Web. Accessed January 10, 2012. <http://www.washingtonpost.com/wp-dyn/content/article/2006/04/13/AR2006041301663.html>

LaSalle, Mike. "Tommy Lee Jones abuses a corpse in poky Western." *The San Francisco Chronicle*, February 3, 2006. Web. Accessed September 30, 2011. <http://www.sfgate.com/movies/article/Tommy-Lee-Jones-abuses-a-corpse-in-poky-Western-2542079.php>

Limón, José E. *American Encounters: Greater Mexico, the United States, and the Erotics of Culture.* Boston: Beacon Press, 1999.

Lemus, Felicia Luna. *Like Son.* New York: Akashic Books, 2007.

————. *Trace Elements of Random Tea Parties*. New York: Farrar, Straus and Giroux, 2003.

Lonesome Dove. Dir. Simon Wincer. Perf. Robert Duvall, Danny Glover, and Tommy Lee Jones. Motown Productions, 1989.

Love, Heather. *Feeling Backward: Loss and the Politics of Queer History*. Cambridge, MA: Harvard University Press, 2007.

Lowe, Lisa. *Immigrant Acts: On Asian American Cultural Politics*. Durham, NC: Duke University Press, 1996.

Lubhéid, Eithne. "Introduction: Queering Migration and Citizenship." In *Queer Migrations: Sexuality, U.S. Citizenship, and Border Crossings*, ed. Eithne Lubhéid and Lionel Cantú Jr., ix–xlvi. Minneapolis: University of Minnesota Press, 2005.

Marcotić, Nicole, and Robert McRuer. "Leading With Your Head: On the Borders of Disability, Sexuality, and the Nation." In *Sex and Disability*, ed. Robert McRuer and Anna Mollow, 165–82. Durham, NC: Duke University Press, 2012.

Martínez, Ernesto Javier. *On Making Sense: Queer Race Narratives of Intelligibility*. Stanford, CA: Stanford University Press, 2013.

McRuer, Robert. *Crip Theory: Cultural Signs of Queerness and Disability*. New York: New York University Press, 2006.

————. "Disability Nationalism in Crip Times." *Journal of Literary and Cultural Disability Studies* 4, no. 2 (2010): 163–78.

Minich, Julie Avril. "Disabling La Frontera: Disability, Border Subjectivity and Masculinity in 'Big Jesse, Little Jesse' by Oscar Casares." *MELUS: Multi-Ethnic Literatures of the United States* 35, no. 1 (Spring 2010): 35–52.

————. "Enabling Aztlán: Arturo Islas, Disability and Chicana/o Cultural Nationalism." *Modern Fiction Studies* 57, no. 4 (December 2011): 694–714.

————. "'You Gotta Make Aztlán Any Way You Can.'" Disability in Cherríe Moraga's *Heroes and Saints*." In *Disability and Mothering: Liminal Spaces of Embodied Knowledge*, ed. Cynthia Lewiecki-Wilson and Jennifer Cellio, 260–74. Syracuse, NY: Syracuse University Press, 2011.

Mitchell, David T., and Sharon L. Snyder. "Disability as Multitude: Re-working Non-Productive Labor Power." *Journal of Literary and Cultural Disability Studies* 4, no. 2 (2010): 179–94.

————. *Narrative Prosthesis: Disability and the Dependencies of Discourse*. Ann Arbor: The University of Michigan Press, 2000.

Mohanty, Satya P. *Literary Theory and the Claims of History: Postmodernism, Objectivity, Multicultural Politics.* Ithaca, NY: Cornell University Press, 1997.

Moraga, Cherríe L. *Heroes and Saints and Other Plays.* Albuquerque, NM: West End Press, 1994.

———. *The Hungry Woman.* Albuquerque, NM: West End Press, 2001.

———. *The Last Generation: Prose & Poetry.* Boston: South End Press, 1993.

———. *Loving in the War Years: lo que nunca pasó por sus labios.* 2nd ed. Cambridge, MA: South End Press, 2001.

———. *Waiting in the Wings: Portrait of a Queer Motherhood.* Ithaca, NY: Firebrand Books, 1997.

———. *A XicanaCodex of Changing Consciousness: Writings, 2000–2010.* Durham, NC: Duke University Press, 2011.

Moya, Paula M.L. "Another Way to Be: Women of Color, Literature, and Myth." In *Doing Race: 21 Essays for the 21st Century,* ed. Hazel Rose Markus and Paula M.L. Moya, 483–508. New York: W.W. Norton and Company, 2010.

———. *Learning from Experience: Minority Identities, Multicultural Struggles.* Berkeley: University of California Press, 2002.

Moya, Paula M. L., and Michael Hames-García, eds. *Reclaiming Identity: Realist Theory and the Predicament of Postmodernism.* Berkeley: University of California Press, 2000.

Moya, Paula M.L., and Ramón Saldívar. "Fictions of the Trans-American Imaginary." *Modern Fiction Studies* 49, no. 1 (Spring 2003): 1–18.

Muñoz, José Esteban. *Cruising Utopia: The Then and There of Queer Futurity.* New York: New York University Press, 2009.

My Family. Dir. Gregory Nava. Perf. Rafael Cortes, Esai Morales, Edward James Olmos, and Jimmy Smits. New Line Features, 1995.

Nava, Michael. *Howtown.* Boston: Alyson Books, 2003.

Nevins, Joseph. *Operation Gatekeeper and Beyond: The War on "Illegals" and the Remaking of the U.S.-Mexico Boundary.* New York: Routledge, 2010.

Ngai, Mae M. *Impossible Subjects: Illegal Aliens and the Making of Modern America.* Princeton, NJ: Princeton University Press, 2004.

No Country for Old Men. Dir. Ethan Coen and Joel Coen. Perf. Javier Bardem, Josh Brolin, and Tommy Lee Jones. Miramax, 2007.

Novoa, Mónica. "Chicago Hospital Deports Quadriplegic Man, Hate Speech Cheers." *Colorlines,* February 14, 2011. Web. Accessed

March 16, 2011. <http://colorlines.com/archives/2011/02/chicago_
hospital_deports_quadriplegic_man_hate_speech_cheers.html>

Oboler, Suzanne. "Redefining Citizenship as a Lived Experience." In
Latinos and Citizenship: The Dilemma of Belonging, ed. Suzanne
Oboler. New York: Palgrave Macmillan, 2006.

O'Hehir, Andrew. "Beyond the Multiplex." Salon.com., December 15, 2005. Web. Accessed August 5, 2011. <http://www.salon.
com/2005/12/15/btm_41/>

Ong, Aihwa. "Cultural Citizenship as Subject-Making." *Current
Anthropology* 37 (December 1996): 737–62.

———. *Flexible Citizenship: The Cultural Logics of Transnationality.*
Durham, NC: Duke University Press, 1999.

Padilla, Yolanda. "Felix beyond the Closet: Sexuality, Masculinity, and
Relations of Power in Arturo Islas's *The Rain God*." *Aztlán: A Journal of Chicano Studies* 34, no. 2 (Fall 2009): 11–34.

Paredes, Américo. *With His Pistol in His Hand: A Border Ballad and
Its Hero*. 1958. Austin: University of Texas Press, 2003.

Paz, Octavio. *El laberinto de la soledad*. 1950. Mexico City: Fondo de
Cultura Económica México, 1997.

Pérez, Hiram. "You Can Have My Brown Body and Eat It, Too!" *Social
Text* 84, no. 3 and 85, no. 4 (2005): 172–91.

Pineda, Cecile. *Face*. 1985. San Antonio: Wings Press, 2003.

———. *Fishlight: a dream of childhood*. San Antonio: Wings Press,
2001.

———. *Frieze*. 1986. San Antonio: Wings Press, 2007.

El Plan Espiritual de Aztlán. In *Aztlán: Essays on the Chicano Homeland*. ed. Rudolfo A. Anaya and Francisco Lomelí, 1–5. Albuquerque: University of New Mexico Press, 1989.

Prengaman, Peter. "Across California, Thousands March." *Orange
County Register*, April 11, 2006. Web. Accessed January 10, 2013.
<http://www.ocregister.com/news/san-188907-people-country.
html>

Puga, Ana Elena. "Melodrama and the Performance of Migration: A
Central American Cinderella." *Migration & Reterritorialization*,
October 12, 2008. Web. Accessed September 7, 2011. <http://performance-migration.wikidot.com/ana-elena-puga>

Ramírez, Pablo A. "Toward a Borderlands Ethics: The Undocumented
Migrant and Haunted Communities in Contemporary Chicana/o
Fiction." *Aztlán: A Journal of Chicano Studies* 35, no. 1 (Spring
2010): 49–67.

Rich, Adrienne. *Blood, Bread and Poetry: Selected Prose, 1979–1985.* New York: W.W. Norton & Company, 1986.

Riofrio, John "Rio." "Latinos in a Post 9/11 Moment: The Public Latino Body in *The Three Burials of Melquiades Estrada* and *Americanos.*" Unpublished paper. February 29, 2012.

Rodríguez, Luis J. *Always Running: La Vida Loca: Gang Days in L.A.* 1993. New York: Touchstone, 2005.

Rodríguez, Richard T. "Carnal Knowledge: Chicano Gay Men and the Dialectics of Being." In *Gay Latino Studies: A Critical Reader*, ed. Michael Hames-García and Ernesto Javier Martínez, 113–40. Durham, NC: Duke University Press, 2011.

———. *Next of Kin: The Family in Chicano/a Cultural Politics.* Durham, NC: Duke University Press, 2009.

Rosaldo, Renato. "Cultural Citizenship, Inequality, and Multiculturalism." In *Latino Cultural Citizenship*, ed. William V. Flores and Rina Benmayor, 27–38. Boston: Beacon Press, 1997.

———. "Race and the Borderlands in Arturo Islas's *Migrant Souls*." In *Critical Mappings of Arturo Islas's Fictions*, ed. Frederick Luis Aldama, 243–50. Tempe, AZ: Bilingual Press/Editorial Bilingüe, 2008.

Ruiz, Vicki L. "Nuestra América: Latino History as United States History." *The Journal of American History* 93, no. 3 (December 2006): 655–72.

Said, Edward W. *Culture and Imperialism.* New York: Alfred A. Knopf, 1993.

Saldaña-Portillo, María Josefina. *The Revolutionary Imagination in the Americas and the Age of Development.* Durham, NC: Duke University Press, 2003.

Saldívar, José David. *Border Matters: Remapping American Cultural Studies.* Berkeley: University of California Press, 1997.

———. *The Dialectics of Our America: Geneology, Cultural Critique, and Literary History.* Durham, NC: Duke University Press, 1991.

———. "The Hybridity of Culture in Arturo Islas's *The Rain God*." In *Cohesion and Dissent in America*, ed. Carol Colatrella and Joseph Alkana, 159–73. Albany: State University of New York Press, 1994.

———. *Trans-Americanity: Subaltern Modernities, Global Coloniality, and the Cultures of Greater Mexico.* Durham, NC: Duke University Press, 2012.

Saldívar, Ramón. *The Borderlands of Culture: Américo Paredes and the Transnational Imaginary.* Durham, NC: Duke University Press, 2006.

———. *Chicano Narrative: The Dialectics of Difference.* Madison: University of Wisconsin Press, 1990.

———. "Historical Fantasy, Speculative Realism, and Postrace Aesthetics in Contemporary American Fiction." *American Literary History* 23, no. 3 (2011): 574–99.

Sánchez, Rosaura. "Ideological Discourses in Arturo Islas's *The Rain God.*" In *Criticism in the Borderlands: Studies in Chicano Literature, Culture, and Ideology,* ed. Héctor Calderón and José David Saldívar, 114–26. Durham, NC: Duke University Press, 1991.

Sandahl, Carrie. "Black Man, Blind Man: Disability Identity Politics and Performance." *Theatre Journal* 56, no. 4 (December 2004): 579–602.

———. "Queering the Crip or Cripping the Queer?: Intersections of Queer and Crip Identities in Solo Autobiographical Performance." *GLQ: A Journal of Lesbian and Gay Studies* 9, no. 1 (December 2002): 25–56.

Santa Ana, Otto. *Brown Tide Rising: Metaphors of Latinos in Contemporary American Public Discourse.* Austin: University of Texas Press, 2002.

Sartre, Jean-Paul. *No Exit and Three Other Plays.* 1946. New York: Vintage, 1989.

Schlikerman, Becky. "Quadriplegic immigrant dies after Chicago-area hospital returned him to Mexico." *Chicago Tribune,* January 4, 2012. Web. Accessed October 22, 2012. <http://articles.chicagotribune.com/2012-01-04/health/ct-met-quelino-death-20120104_1_quelino-ojeda-jimenez-mexican-family-mexican-hospital>

Schmidt Camacho, Alicia. "Ciudadana X: Gender Violence and the Denationalization of Women's Rights in Ciudad Juarez, Mexico." *CR: The New Centennial Review* 5, no. 1 (May 2005): 255–92.

———. *Migrant Imaginaries: Latino Cultural Politics in the U.S.-Mexico Borderlands.* New York: New York University Press, 2008.

Schweik, Susan M. *The Ugly Laws: Disability in Public.* New York: New York University Press, 2009.

Sedgwick, Eve Kosofsky. *Epistemology of the Closet.* 1990. Berkeley: University of California Press, 2008.

Sharpe, Christina. "Learning to Live without Black Familia: Cherríe Moraga's Nationalist Articulations." In *Tortilleras: Hispanic and U.S. Latina Lesbian Expression,* ed. Inmaculada Perpetusa-Seva and Lourdes Torres, 240–57. Philadelphia: Temple University Press, 2003.

Siebers, Tobin. *Disability Aesthetics*. Ann Arbor: University of Michigan Press, 2010.

———. *Disability Theory*. Ann Arbor: University of Michigan Press, 2008.

Snyder, Sharon L., and David T. Mitchell. *Cultural Locations of Disability*. Chicago: The University of Chicago Press, 2006.

———. "Introduction: Ablenationalism and the Geo-Politics of Disability." *Journal of Literary and Cultural Disability Studies* 4 (2) (2010): 113–26.

Soto, Sandra K. "Cherríe Moraga's Going Brown: Reading Like a Queer." *GLQ* 11, no. 2 (2005): 237–63.

Stead, Kendra. "Critical Condition: Using Asylum Law to Contest Forced Medical Repatriation of Undocumented Immigrants." *Northwestern University Law Review* 104, no. 1 (Winter 2010): 307–33.

Tatonetti, Lisa. "'A Kind of Queer Balance': Cherríe Moraga's Aztlán." *MELUS: Multiethnic Literatures of the United States* 29, no. 2 (Summer 2004): 227–47.

The Three Burials of Melquiades Estrada. Dir. Tommy Lee Jones. Perf. Tommy Lee Jones, Barry Pepper, Dwight Yoakam. Sony Classics, 2005.

Tongson, Karen. *Relocations: Queer Suburban Imaginaries*. New York: New York University Press, 2011.

21 Grams. Dir. Alejandro González Iñárritu. Perf. Benicio del Toro, Sean Penn, and Naomi Watts. Focus Features, 2003.

Viego, Antonio. "The Place of Gay Male Chicano Literature in Queer Chicana/o Cultural Work." In *Gay Latino Studies: A Critical Reader*, ed. Michael Hames-García and Ernesto Javier Martínez, 86–104. Durham, NC: Duke University Press, 2011.

Volk, Steven S., and Marian E. Schlotterbeck. "Gender, Order and Femicide: Reading the Popular Culture of Murder in Ciudad Juárez." *Aztlán: A Journal of Chicano Studies* 32, no. 1 (Spring 2007): 53–86.

Warner, Michael. *The Trouble With Normal: Sex, Politics, and the Ethics of Queer Life*. Cambridge, MA: Harvard University Press, 2000.

Wendell, Susan. *The Rejected Body: Feminist Philosophical Reflections on Disability*. New York: Routledge, 1996.

Wu, Cynthia. *Chang and Eng Reconnected: The Original Siamese Twins in American Culture*. Philadelphia: Temple University Press, 2012.

Yarbro-Bejarano, Yvonne. "Laying it Bare: The Queer/Colored Body in Photography by Laura Aguilar." In *Living Chicana Theory*, ed. Carla Trujillo, 277–305. Berkeley, CA: Third Woman Press, 1998.

———. "Queer Storytelling and Temporality in *Trace Elements of Random Tea Parties* by Felicia Luna Lemus." *Aztlán: A Journal of Chicano Studies* 38, no. 1 (Spring 2013): 73–93.

———. *The Wounded Heart: Writing on Cherríe Moraga*. Austin: University of Texas Press, 2001.

Ybarra, Patricia. "The Revolution Fails Here: Cherríe Moraga's *The Hungry Woman* as a Mexican Medea." *Aztlán: A Journal of Chicano Studies* 33, no. 1 (Spring 2008): 63–88.

Index

About the Author

Julie Avril Minich is Assistant Professor of English, Mexican American Studies, and Women and Gender Studies at the University of Texas at Austin.